The Complete
GREEK
COOKBOOK

Η ΠΛΗΡΗΣ

ΕΛΛΗΝΙΚΗ ΜΑΓΕΙΡΙΚΗ

Η ΠΛΗΡΗΣ ΕΛΛΗΝΙΚΗ ΜΑΓΕΙΡΙΚΗ

Η ΚΑΛΥΤΕΡΕΣ ΣΥΝΤΑΓΕΣ ΑΠΟ 3000 ΧΡΟΝΙΑ ΕΛΛΗΝΙΚΗΣ ΜΑΓΕΙΡΙΚΗΣ

The Complete
GREEK
COOKBOOK

THE BEST FROM THREE
THOUSAND YEARS OF
GREEK COOKING BY
THERESA KARAS YIANILOS

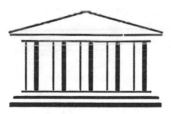

AVENEL BOOKS · NEW YORK

TO MY FATHER AND MOTHER
CONSTANTINOS KARADIMOS AND KEREAKULLA ZAKAS
KARADIMOS, WHO EMIGRATED TO AMERICA
AND BROUGHT WITH THEM THEIR STRENGTH,
LOVE FOR FREEDOM
AND PRIDE IN THEIR HERITAGE.

This edition is published by Avenel Books
a division of Crown Publishers, Inc.
by arrangement with Funk & Wagnalls
i j k l m n o
Manufactured in the United States Of America

CONTENTS

Preface: Greek Food and Hospitality

COOKING AND DINING IN ANCIENT GREECE

COOKING IN MODERN GREECE

PREFACE

GREEK FOOD AND HOSPITALITY

ΕΛΛΗΝΙΚΑ ΦΑΓΤΤΑ ΚΑΙ ΦΙΛΟΞΕΝΙΑ
(ellenika fayeta kai filoxksenia)

The ancient Greeks began the art of cookery one thousand years before Christ, and Greek recipes have influenced many cuisines. You may discover that Greek recipes in this book have a ring of familiarity or you may even know some of them under different names. Menus from Homer and Plato, nine hundred years old, are as similar as the list of foods your doctor gives out when he tells you to diet.

Most Greek food is simple to prepare. A meal can be made from a bit of cheese, a few olives, some fresh bread, and a piece of roasted meat or fried fish. Often, a complete meal will consist of fresh vegetables, quickly boiled, sprinkled with olive oil and lemon juice, or perhaps be only a casserole of vegetables and meats. Desserts and cakes are usually drenched with syrup.

Yet the love for sumptuous feasts and elegant presentation of food is part of the Greek heritage. Legends about the fabulous meals and menus that the *maigeires* or chefs of ancient times prepared have endured through centuries. A Greek cook has always been considered a prize: whether a respected slave cooking for lords of the Roman Empire, or today's professional creating savory meals for patrons of restaurants, hotels, ships, and airlines.

The concept that preparing and cooking food is an art is still very much a part of the Greek psyche. Greek hospitality extends to friends and strangers alike and always includes a ritual of eating and drinking. To allow a visitor to leave without serving him something would be barbaric. For a guest to refuse to partake, even a token nibble, would be equally intolerable. You may have heard the old saying: "When Greek meets Greek, they start a restaurant." At any rate, it is true that when a Greek meets a friend, they sit down and eat.

The kind of Greek cooking found today in the United States has evolved primarily from peasant cookery. Many of the Greeks who emigrated to the United States in the first decades of this century were poor unsophisticated people from small agrarian villages. With them came certain attitudes, customs, and traditions regarding food which could be traced back into ancient pagan Greek history, and more recently to Christian and Moslem influences.

The plenitude of America's larder, however, and the great variety and availability of even unseasonal foods encouraged certain refinements. New cooking methods replaced the painstaking procedures required for some of the ancient recipes, and many special dishes formerly made only on great occasions or holidays can now be made frequently. Modern daughters urged mothers, aunts, and grandmothers to explain every step of their recipes; they then adapted them using new ingredients and convenience foods, and devised short cuts with modern methods and appliances.

Attitudes about food have also changed, even including those which originated from religious practices. In Greece, on many fast days throughout the year, the eating of meats and animal products such as milk, fats, and butter was prohibited. Since the fasts coincided with the scarcity of these products, adhering to the Orthodox fast for a full forty days before Christmas, Easter, and other religious holidays was easier to follow in Greece than in the United States. It is my personal observation that very few modern men and women maintain the full traditional forty days' fast in bountiful America. Many devout Greek Orthodox Christians have recognized the body's need for protein foods and no longer consider it a sin (*amartia*) to eat meat, butter or milk. A token fast from certain animal products is usually two days or a week at the most.

Regional differences in recipes, still existing in isolated parts of Greece, have disappeared in the United States where recipes are readily exchanged from cook to cook and ingredients easily purchased.

Importers of Greek foods have made many of the exotic foods available at specialty shops. Even that American institution, the supermarket, carries gourmet foods, so many unusual recipes can be served at almost any time.

The recipes in this book reflect the simplified, modern approach to Greek cooking: step-by-step instructions; modified proportions of sugars, fats, and oil; the use of instant foods and spices; tested short-cut methods and the recommended use of appliances.

ΚΑΛΗ ΟΡΕΞΗ (kali orexi) Good Appetite!

ACKNOWLEDGMENTS

To all those friends whose enthusiasm and advice helped to make this book complete:

Edwin and Gloria Self
Mrs. J. Edwin Lee (Alice)
Steve Aposperis
Verna Cook Shipway
Warren Shipway
Tom Dammann
Harry Antoniades Anthony

A special thank you to my family—my daughters, Becky and Karen, who cooked and tested recipes, my son, James, for all his help, and most of all my husband, Spero, for his untiring patience, understanding, and constructive assistance in every phase.

COOKING
AND
DINING
IN
ANCIENT
GREECE

Η ΜΛΓΕΙΡΙΚΗ ΚΑΙ ΤΑ ΓΕΥΜΑΤΑ
ΤΗΣ
ΑΡΧΑΙΑΣ ΕΛΛΑΔΟΣ

(e maiyereky keh
ta yevmata tis
arhayas Elleados)

HISTORY OF
GREEK COOKING

ΙΣΤΟΡΙΑ ΤΗΣ ΕΛΛΗΝΙΚΗΣ ΜΑΓΕΙΡΙΚΗΣ
(istoria tis Ellenikis maiyerikis)

The poets and philosophers of Sophocles' time, four hundred years before Christ, not only discussed the merits of the Parthenon, they held long discourses on the art of cookery. Traditionally, cooks and priests were one and the same. They alone knew how to butcher meats for all sacrificial rites.

For centuries the preparation of food was considered the prerogative of men. Furthermore, recipes were exchanged between men rather than between women. Dining was considered another one of the arts. Sophisticated men's clubs where gourmets gathered to discuss the merits of different foods, native and foreign, were numerous, and virtually all the foods familiar to the world today were known and used by the ancient Greeks.

From 900 B.C. to 158 B.C., a span of seven hundred years, Greece was a powerful military force in the Mediterranean, with bases or colonies on the coast of Asia Minor, Cyprus, Egypt, Gaza, Italy, France, Spain, Sardinia, Persia, and India. Greek colonists brought with them beautiful pottery, sculpture, and crafts. Typical Greek foods such as olives, cheese, figs, oil, wheat, barley, wine, and honey were introduced along with Greek cuisine. Even today similar recipes, many with the same names, are found in all of these countries. The aesthetics in shopping for food were considered important. The market place was no crowded bazaar but an attractive shopping plaza called the *agora,* consisting of individual shops, statues, fountains, and altars.

By the fifth century B.C., Greeks knew how to bake over twenty kinds of breads, from pancakes to sourdough, and many kinds of sweet cakes. Some of these cakes were decorated and given as prizes to Olympic athletes or carried in festivals, just as cakes are decorated today for birthdays, holidays, weddings, and anniversaries.

Rome became the power in the Mediterranean after 158 B.C. The Romans' undisguised respect and admiration for Hellenic culture fostered their national pride although their status under Rome was that of a subjugated people. From their Greek teachers the Romans learned how to appreciate the arts including the art of dining.

Combined forces of Christian Romans and Greeks overpowered the Romans in 312 A.D. and moved the seat of culture away from Rome, choosing the site of the ancient city of Byzantium rather than Athens to build the great Christian city of Constantinople which remained for 1000 years as the largest city in the world. These Byzantines retained the best of their two heritages, Greek art, language and literature plus Roman laws and government and called themselves *Rhomaioi* (*Romans*), a name still used by Greeks today, to distinguish themselves from the pagan connotation of the word Hellenism. They added to the Greek way a love for the ornate that outdid both the Romans and Greeks.

Today, the manner of cooking of northern Greece and the mountainous areas differs from that of the southern and coastal regions. The historical reasons are many. While the sophisticated and genteel Byzantines ruled with religious zeal throughout Greece, including the outlying islands of Crete, Rhodos and Zakynthos, there were periodic invasions of Goths and Visigoths well into the thirteenth century. In A.D. 500 the barbaric Huns reached Corinth. The Huns disgusted the Greeks. They used knives to cut their food at the table and preferred a fat called butter, which the Greeks considered a body salve, not a substitute for olive oil.

The Slavs and Avars came to Greece in the seventh century; the Slavs remained and settled. To this day, rabbit, in the Greek stew called *stifatho,* is known by the Slavic word, *kounelli.*

Crete, off the southern tip of Greece, became a Moslem territory in the ninth century, and the people of Crete, the Kritiki, had to abstain from their favorite meat: pork.

In northern Greece, the Bulgars crossed over the border and taught Greek mountaineers the secret of making yogurt. No sooner had the Byzantines chased them out when the Vlachs, a nomadic people from Roumania, invaded Thessaly in the eleventh century and called it Great Walachia. They brought their own recipe for a hot spiced preserved beef called *pastourma* and one for noodles known as *trahana,* but the Greeks never cared much for it or them . . . and when someone is called a *vlachos* today, he is being told he is gauche, a country bumpkin, a nomad who does not know the refinements of civilized living.

By the 1200s Venetians sailed over the Ionian Sea and settled in the coastal regions of Greece. They built beautiful castles in the islands and left a heritage of cookie recipes, made with semolina, farina. To this day the women of the Ionian Islands are famous for their honey cookies called *fenekia,* meaning Venetian.

The Crusaders also marched through into Thessaly, Thessaloniki, the central and southern parts of Greece, staying long enough in the thirteenth century to teach the Cypriots a new way of making wine. They may have dropped some lemon seeds from the lemon trees they discovered in Palestine, thereby introducing that most versatile fruit of all to Greece.

Serbs, Italians, and Franks came to Greece during the 1300s and 1400s. The Italians shared their pasta secrets, which Marco Polo had brought back from the Far East, and taught the Greeks how to make macaroni and spaghetti, while the Franks or French built splendid châteaux in Peloponnesus and gathered more than just a few recipes. The great Byzantine era came to an end in 1453 when Constantinople fell to the Moslem Ottoman Turks who had already established themselves in other parts of Greece. They changed the name of the Byzantine Christian city to Istanbul and ordered that the Turkish language be spoken. The teaching of the Greek language and the freedom of the church were tolerated, but Turkish influences crept into everyday life, and recipes as old as Mount Olympus were now called by Turkish names. The Greek cooks learned to add great amounts of garlic to meat and vegetables to please the Turkish palate. The famous Greek dish of *Moussaka* was born when the Arabs introduced the vegetable, eggplant. Greeks shared the same delight as the Turks over the hot beverage made from coffee beans some Arab discovered growing in Ethiopia. The ancient Greek custom of men's clubs was revived with the *cafenion*—the coffee house which sprang up in every village. The Greeks always had a sweet tooth but the Turkish habit of nibbling sweetmeats at all hours was contagious. The Turkish candy called *lokoum* and *halvah* remain favorite confections today. When the Turks were finally driven out of Greece in 1821, three hundred seventy-one years later, they left behind a new flavor in Greek cooking.

Following the Turks, the British arrived and watched over Greece until 1940. They introduced potatoes, tea, beef, margarine, and a drink called *tsintsibira,* gingerbeer. The French now returned some of the Greek recipes they had borrowed centuries before, laden with sauces and tomatoes, a South American fruit. Among the upper class Greeks and in restaurants it became *très chic* to give every recipe a French name. The French term *à la,* meaning "in the style of," was added to everything. The French had discovered the secret of making chocolates, cakes, and marzipans, and the Greeks were delighted to add new words to their vocabulary: *tortes* for the many-layered cake with frosting between layers; *keik* for the cake with the frosting on top. They copied the French custom of molding chocolate into rabbits, baskets, chickens, eggs, and other symbols at Easter, and Greek confectioners spread this custom to the United States.

The Americans went to war-torn Greece in 1943 to help the Greeks fight the invading Nazis. They stayed to reconstruct, bringing large sums of money with the Marshall Plan, plus definite food preferences and individualistic ideas. They taught the Greeks new methods of agriculture. Once barren lands began to produce with abundance. American tourists came in great numbers and the Greeks learned to like ham and eggs, bacon, hamburgs, hot dogs, fried potatoes, sodas and milk shakes, as well as an old American Indian food, corn on the cob, which is now sold on the streets of Athens cooked on charcoal braziers alongside a three thousand year old recipe of *kokkoretsi* sausage.

The Greeks' fierce pride in their heritage has kept the basic culture intact. Whether a slave under Roman rule, a captive under Turkish domination, or a newly arrived immigrant, the Greek is always aware that he is the direct descendant of men like Plato, Homer, Aristotle, Demosthenes, Aristophanes. The Greek who begins life in a new land on the bottom step of society as a dishwasher needs only to remember how Aesop left a legacy of poetry while cooking as a slave. If some of the recipes seem long and time consuming, it is only because the Greek does not consider cooking a chore . . . IT IS ART!

THE KITCHEN IN ANCIENT GREECE

Η ΑΡΧΑΙΑ ΕΛΛΗΝΙΚΗ ΚΟΥΖΙΝΑ (e arhaya ellehniki kouzina)

The Greek pottery you see in a museum is likely to be an ancient Greek's prized dinnerware, or kitchen ware, or perhaps, cooking utensil. Just as a hostess today takes pride in her bone china and doesn't mind when guests turn over the cups to see the mark, so did the ancient Greek cherish the fine pottery of Corinth. It was unnecessary to turn one's *kylix* (cup) over, however; the potters were artists who signed their work on the face of it. They favored designs of mythological characters, animals, gods, flowers, and leaves. The Greek fret or key appeared over and over again with many variations.

Styles and colors changed slowly. The black slim figures and thin-line designs on red pottery originated in Corinth in the sixth century B.C. One hundred to two hundred years later, in the fourth and fifth centuries B.C., the finest pottery had a white background with red, yellow, and purple designs. Reproductions of these ancient pots are manufactured in Greece today, but only as art objects, whereas the originals were functional. The amphorae used for storing wines were lined with resin pitch from pine trees to prevent the jars from sweating and souring the wine. The Greeks grew to like the taste of resin in their wine, and so the famous *retsina* wine was born. The wines of ancient Greece were very strong, and water was often mixed with them before drinking. The wine *krater,* a mixing bowl, was always very ornate, often personalized with mottoes and names of owners. In warm weather, wine was put into a *psykter*—a piece of pottery that resembled an upside down vase—and then set into a wide mouth *lekane* into which cold water had been poured. A slender ladle was used to reach into the cool depths of the *psykter.* Wine was always drunk out of a *kylix,* with both hands resting on the handles on each side, a custom seen today in the drinking of brandy from a large snifter. These kylix drinking bowls were beautifully decorated, both inside and out, made of fine pottery or wrought out of gold or silver with exquisite design. A line was drawn one inch up, inside the cup to indicate how deep the wine should be poured. Since these cups were large that was not a niggardly quantity. The water was added to the wine, the amount determined by the drinker.

Little is known about kitchens in ancient Greece. They had to be large, if only to accommodate all the slaves.

The floors were two feet deep, made of broken brick, ground charcoal, lime and sand then polished smooth with pumice. Oils and water would disappear into the porous stone and drain off, keeping the floor dry. Large bee-hive shaped ovens were outdoors. Smaller loaves of bread and cakes were baked in portable clay ovens set on top of charcoal braziers or under cooking bells which were heated first and then piled around with coals. A most important piece of household equipment was the mortar made of a shallow, thick walled clay pottery or a hollowed out tree trunk in which grain was pounded. For grinding the flour, a millstone was set in the middle of a broad basin on three legs that stood waist high.

The cooking utensils, ΜΑΓΕΙΡΙΚΑ (maiyerika), and many pots and pans which the Greeks used are the same today. Readily identifiable are the tools of the chef of ancient times: the soup ladle, skewers, meat hook, mortar, cheese scraper, skillet, stirring stick, bowls, skinning knife, cleavers, axe, small kettles, frying pans, boiling pots, casseroles and lamps. The frying pan, *teganon* or *tegani* is still an indispensable item in the Greek kitchen, not only for frying but also for stews and stuffed grape leaves. The kettles and cauldrons used then are available today, made of copper instead of bronze or iron and known by the Arabic word, *kazani,* instead of the Greek word, *lebes.* The three-legged pot called a *kakkave* is still known by that name, and many stews and soups are cooked in *kakkaves,* just as they were thousands of years ago. A woman cooking a mid-day stew in a casserole (*lopas, lopida*) or a *chytra* (kettle) which is resting on a tripod or cooking stand over the fire in the hearth can still be seen in some small Greek villages today.

A dinner service would consist of two-handled drinking cups

(*poterion*) usually glazed black, not as delicate as the kylix which was reserved for wines. Mugs and pitchers (*chous*) or porringers, *one-handlers* as they were called, had generous sized handles for fingers to clutch and to hang on the wall when not in use. The stemmed dishes (*trivlyion*) came in various sizes, the large ones for fruit and olives, and the smaller ones for salt, vinegar and silphium . . . the mustard seed the ancient Greeks loved for its sharp peppery flavor. Large amounts of food were served in two handled serving platters called the *kane* or *pazopsis*. Serving platters embellished with fish designs were called *ichthuai,* meaning fish.

The finger bowl remained an integral part of the dinnerware until the seventeenth century. The Greeks did not use tableware of any kind; fowl was torn apart and eaten with the hands or carvers prepared meats before they were served or skewered them before broiling. Pieces of bread were used as napkins to wipe hands and face after each course, then thrown to the dogs.

The wealthier Greeks began to use silver plates in about the fifth century, and the demand for decorated pottery declined until the art disappeared completely.

For thousands of years, water has been carried in a jar called a *hydria.* The design is still the same. It has three handles—two for lifting and one for carrying. To this day women are seen in the villages balancing these jars gracefully on their shoulders as they return from the well.

The oil flask, *lekythos,* a delicate vase with a long slender neck designed for pouring oil slowly, also came in various sizes, depending on whether it was to be used at the table, kitchen, bath or in the burial rites.

Some amphorae are large enough to accommodate a person. They were made with handles on each side of the neck, and a flat base or pointed bottom so they could be set firmly in the ground. Amphorae were used to store liquids and foods such as honey and wheat, and came in many sizes, the large ones holding a standard measurement of nine gallons. All had wide openings large enough for a ladle and were fitted with tight covers.

FEASTING IN
ANCIENT GREECE

ΑΡΧΑΙΑ ΕΛΛΗΝΙΚΑ ΣΥΜΠΟΣΙΑ
(arhaya ellehnike symposia)

The pattern of eating four times a day, quite common in the Western world, seems to have originated with the ancient Greeks. Homer, 900 B.C., describes the four meals as breakfast ἀκράτισμα (akratisma); luncheon αριστον, (ariston); evening meal ἑσπέρισμα (hesperisma), a small meal or cocktail hour; dinner δεῖπνον (deipnon).

Plato advised eating the following to reach a ripe old age: salt, olives, cheese, bulbs, green vegetables, figs, chickpeas, beans, myrtleberries, and beechnuts. This ancient advice sounds very contemporary.

The kind of extravagant feast usually associated with Greeks and Romans is found in a description (by Athenaeus) of a wedding banquet given in A.D. 200 by a wealthy Macedonian named Caranus. His guest list numbered twenty men (no women were allowed). As each guest entered the room he was crowned with a gold tiara, his to keep, and escorted to his couch on which he reclined during the dinner that was to continue throughout the day and night. A table was placed next to the couch and slaves were stationed behind him. His silver cup or kylix, into which various wines would be poured throughout the meal, would also be his to keep.

The first course consisted of an assortment of roasted chickens, ducks, ring doves, geese, and a huge loaf of bread, all piled high on enormous bronze platters. The second course was served on large silver platters, with more fowl, geese, hares, goats, pigeons, turtle doves, partridges, and cakes. This was followed by an interlude of dancing girls, gifts of perfume, more gold crowns. Then, a third course: more silver platters, each one with a huge roasted pig, cut open, belly up, stuffed with roasted thrushes, ducks, birds, eggs, oysters, and scallops.

Fourth and fifth courses consisted of even more silver platters with roasted kid or young goat and crystal platters with all kinds of baked fish; different kinds of breads were on more silver platters. As entertainment, naked female jugglers blew fire from their mouths, and dancers and clowns performed. Hot wine was served in gold cups, while tremendous roasted boars on pure gold serving dishes were paraded into the room as the sixth course.

Second tables, as the tripod dessert tables were called, were brought in, and the seventh and last course, different kinds of oakes in boxes, was served.

A trumpet sounded to signal the end of the banquet. Each departing guest took with him the crowns, perfumes, food, bronze, silver, gold platters and cups he had received. He could sell these gifts at the marketplace and realize enough money from them to buy more slaves, land, houses, or whatever he desired. Gluttonous as this feast may seem, the custom of a rich man sharing his wealth by giving sumptuous dinners has not been confined only to the ancient Greeks.

RECIPES FROM ANCIENT GREECE

ΣΥΝΤΑΓΕΣ ΑΠΟ ΤΗΝ ΑΡΧΑΙΑ ΕΛΛΑΔΑ
(syntages apo tin arhaya ellada)

The opulence and sophistication of how the ancient Greeks cooked and dined can only be suggested in the few recipes in this chapter. In researching this chapter, one fact becomes clear: people have been trading recipes for thousands of years.

SPICED WINE HIPPOCRATES

ΚΡΑΣΙ ΙΠΠΟΚΡΑΤΟΥΣ   (krasi IPPOKRATOUS)

This is a delicious prescription concocted by the great physician Hippocrates who lived in the fifth century B.C. He even invented a bag in which to filter this wine. How delighted the patient must have been to be told he had to take this medicine. Chilled, it is a flavorful punch; hot, a relaxing grog.

SERVES 6
1 quart wine, red or white
1 cup honey
3 cloves
1 teaspoon cinnamon
½ teaspoon allspice
1 teaspoon orange peel

SERVES 1
1 cup wine
2 tablespoons honey
¼ teaspoon, each: orange peel, cinnamon, allspice

Mix all ingredients and heat slowly over low heat. Strain into decanter or cup.

CICADA APPETIZERS ARISTOPHANES

ΑΚΡΙΔΑ ΜΕΖΕΣ   (akritha mezes)

Next time you see chocolate-covered grasshoppers in your gro-
cer's gourmet section and feel like laughing, just remember that
they are an ancient Greek appetizer. Fried grasshoppers or
cicadas are described by Aristophanes and other ancient Greek
writers who thought them delicious and said they were crunchy
and nut-like in flavor.

Catch grasshoppers—large ones, preferably. Allow 4 grasshoppers per person. Fry in 2 tablespoons olive oil. Keep pan
covered while cooking so you don't lose them.

SPARTAN STEW

ΜΕΛΑΣ ΖΩΜΟΣ   (melas zomos)

According to Plutarch, this stew tasted terrible. Everyone knows
about the Spartans, who believed in austerity, self-discipline, and
temperance as a way of life.

The Spartans ate their meals communally, seated at tables,
not reclining on couches, and everyone in Sparta ate the same
dish, a mixture of pork fat, chopped meat, vinegar, and salt,
called *melas zomos*—black broth. The fame of this dish spread
far and wide so Dionysius, a king in Sicily, imported a Spartan
cook to make this dish for him. When Dionysius tasted it, he
spat it out. The cook explained that the main seasonings were
missing. It was hunger and thirst which made this Spartan dish
taste good.

Athenaeus recorded later in his *Deipnosophists* that the Spartans soon gave up black broth. They also gave up austerity and
temperance shortly thereafter.

ROASTED BIRDS APPETIZERS HOMER

ΠΕΡΙΣΤΕΡΙΑ ΟΡΕΚΤΙΚΑ   (peristeria orektika)

When you sing the 16th century English rhyme of "Four and
twenty blackbirds baked in a pie" and "Wasn't that a dainty dish

to set before the king?" you are praising a very old Greek recipe. Roasted blackbirds and other small birds like thrushes, pigeons, sparrows, squabs and warblers were considered a great delicacy for thousands of years. These birds are eaten in Greece today as they were in the time of Homer who was given a present of thrushes when he sang his epic poem about them, titled *EPIKICHLIDES.*

Allow 2 birds per person: pigeons,
  squabs, quails or partridges
¼ pound butter
½ pound Feta cheese
½ teaspoon thyme

½ teaspoon oregano
salt and pepper to taste
⅛ teaspoon garlic powder
  (optional)
2 slices toasted bread, cut into cubes.

Heat butter in a large frying pan. Roll birds in hot butter. Butter a shallow baking dish with some of the hot butter and spread bread cubes. Stuff birds with cheese and place on top of bread. Sprinkle with herbs, seasonings and garlic, and baste with remaining butter. Bake in a pre-heated oven at 375 degrees for 40 minutes.

ARCHAIC BREAD

ΑΡΧΑΪΚΟΣ ΑΡΤΟΣ　　　　　　　　　　　　　　　(arhayekos artos)

The earliest kind of Greek bread was a simple, flat, hard-crusted hearth bread, coarse and heavy because the barley flour used in it had a low gluten content. Barley in its original form is still grown in the regions around the Red and Caspian seas. This ancient recipe, described by Athenaeus in a third century book on cookery, is still followed throughout the Near East.

2 cups warm water or scalded milk
  cooled to lukewarm
2 teaspoons salt
1 tablespoon honey

2 tablespoons olive oil
2 tablespoons barley meal
6 cups flour, barley or stone ground
  whole wheat

Mix all ingredients except flour into a 2-quart jar. Place jar in a pan of hot water and let stand in a warm place free of drafts until fermentation begins—approximately twelve hours or more. Replace hot water every 4 hours. Mix in 2 cups of the flour. Set aside once again in a warm place. Replace hot water in pan. A sponge should be formed in 4 to 6 hours.

Put 4 cups flour in a bowl, make a well, and add sponge. Knead well, lightly dusting your hands with flour until dough is smooth.

Shape and put into oiled loaf pan. Cover with damp towel and place in a warm draft-free place to rise for 4 to 6 hours. It will not rise as high as modern breads.

Bake in preheated oven at 375° F. for 10 minutes. Reduce to 350° F., bake 50 minutes.

WILD BULB AND LENTIL CONCH

ΒΟΛΒΟΙ ΜΕ ΦΑΚΗ   (volvoi meh faki)

Some ancient Greeks didn't agree that this dish known as conch was suitable only for poor people and slaves. It is an ancient recipe still popular today. Obviously the poor people became so used to it they grew to like it.

½ pound bulbs of the wild grape hyacinth (Volvoi)

1 cup lentils, including pods
Twelfth part of a coriander seed

Peel bulbs. Boil all ingredients together in a potful of water until tender. Serve as the main and only dish of the day.

COMIC POETS STUFFED FIG LEAVES

ΘΡΙΩΝ   (thryon)

Greek poets would sometimes use lists of foods or inventories in their plays for comic effect. This recipe for dolmathes was so popular that the audience would be certain to laugh every time they were mentioned.

1 dozen or more fig leaves
FILLING:
1½ cups flour
¼ teaspoon salt
4 tablespoons shortening

2 eggs
¼ cup milk
1 tablespoon honey
½ cup cheese: feta, cottage, or parmesan

Mix flour and salt with shortening until blended. Add remaining ingredients and mix into a dough.

Blanch fig leaves by pouring hot water over them. Drain.

Place a tablespoon of dough at the stem end and roll, tucking in the sides. Place in a casserole dish, side by side. Add a cup of hot water. Cover. Simmer 35 minutes.

SHRIMP ANANIUS

ΓΑΡΙΔΕΣ ΑΝΑΝΙΑΣ   (garides Ananius)

The satiric poet Ananius, 550 B.C., considered luscious fat shrimps to be worth all the trouble of marketing, and gave the following curt advice:

Find the fattest shrimp in the market. Do not bother to haggle with the fishmongers. They are too independent and will ignore you. Order your *maiygeires* to boil the shrimp with salt, leaves of bay tree, and marjoram. Serve hot on a fig leaf.

1 cup water	½ teaspoon marjoram
1 cup white wine or beer	½ teaspoon salt
1 bay leaf	1 pound raw shrimp

Bring water, wine or beer and spices to a full rolling boil. Plunge in shrimp. Allow water to come to a boil again and boil shrimp for 2 minutes. Remove from liquid and serve.

BONED OYSTERS

ΣΤΡΕΙΔΙ ΜΕ ΜΑΡΓΑΡΙΤΑΡΙ   (estridi meh margaritari)

This recipe, which I'm sure you would enjoy following, comes from Chares of Mytilene, Lesbos, an historian of the third century:

Use only the large Asiatic oysters caught in the Indian Ocean, Black Sea, or the Persian and Arabian gulfs.
    Use the delicious white meat only. Discard the round white bone sometimes discovered inside the shell—or give it to some Persian. They seem to prefer these bones to gold; they call them "pearls."

1 dozen oysters, fresh or frozen	½ cup oil
1 cup flour	salt and pepper to taste

Drain liquid from jar. Roll in flour. Heat oil until hot in a large frying pan. Fry oysters on medium-high heat for 5 minutes turning over once. Sprinkle with seasonings and serve.

BAKED FISH ARCHESTRATUS

ΨΑΡΙ ΨΗΤΟ ΑΡΧΙΣΤΡΑΤΟΣ   (psari psito Arhestratus)

Archestratus was a Greek from Syracuse (or Gela) who wrote one of the earliest known cookbooks, about 330 B.C. His recipe for baked fish gives this following advice:

Buy the best fish you can find, preferably from Byzantium. Sprinkle with marjoram. Wrap fish in fig leaves. Bake.
Have slaves serve it on silver platters.

1 pound white fish
½ teaspoon marjoram
salt and pepper
Juice of 1 lemon

4 chopped scallions
12 fig leaves or 1 small jar grape
   leaves
1 cup water or wine

Cut fish into 1 inch pieces. Sprinkle with herb, seasonings, salt, pepper, and lemon juice. Pour hot water over fresh fig leaves or grape leaves to soften. If canned, rinse brine off with cold water.
Spread leaves out one by one. Place a piece of fish and a bit of scallion near the stem. Roll beginning at the stem, tuck in the sides and finish rolling. Place rolls side by side in an oiled baking pan with wine. Bake in pre-heated oven at 350° F. for 20 minutes.

ROAST PEACOCK WITH PLUMAGE

ΠΑΓΩΝΙ ΨΗΤΟ ΜΕ ΟΛΑ ΤΑ ΠΤΕΡΑ   (pahgoni psito meh ola ta ptera)

Three thousand years ago peacocks, peahens, and their eggs were considered to be a great delicacy. There were special dishes for cooking the eggs. Today peacock is no longer eaten in Greece. Originally bred on the island of Samos, the peacock became so important to the economy of the island it was used as a symbol on the coins of Samos. The peacock became so outrageously expensive that one ancient Greek art lover, named Anaxandrided, said,
"Isn't it crazy to keep peacocks in the house when for all that money you can buy two statues?"

1 large peacock, pheasant, or wild
   fowl

BASTING SAUCE:
½ cup oil or melted butter
1 cup wine
1 teaspoon each: thyme, savory,
   marjoram
Chopped parsley or flowers
1 teaspoon salt
pepper to taste

STUFFING:
chopped liver (from fowl)
1 cup currants or raisins
1 cup chopped nuts

When you buy or order the fowl, give instructions to poultry man to prepare and dress bird, to skin bird carefully and not chop off head or feet, and to truss legs to breast.

When preparing to bake the fowl, spread tail feathers in a fan and set aside to use as decoration later. Oil a large baking pan and place fowl in it. Wrap head with damp cloth to protect it while baking.

Mix stuffing and fill cavity. Mix basting sauce and baste fowl. Continue to baste while baking. Roast 2 hours in preheated oven at 350° F.

Allow to cool 30 minutes and decorate for presentation. Gild feet and beak with gold nail polish. Put tail feathers in place. Place a piece of cotton soaked in whisky in beak. Light it as bird is being served. Place peacock on a bed of parsley. Arrange flowers, leaves, and jewelry around it.

ROAST CAMEL ARISTOTLE

ΚΑΜΗΛΑ ΨΗΤΗ   (kamela psiti)

Today the camel is a gastronomical curiosity to the Western world. Greeks no longer consider it edible, but in ancient Greece camel meat was served to royalty. Aristophanes mentions camel meat in his writings, and Aristotle praises it as being tasty.

Allow 1 pound meat per person:
   hump, stomach, or feet
MARINADE:
1 cup olive oil

Juice of 2 lemons
2 garlic cloves
1 tablespoon oregano
cumin and coriander

Mix marinade in a bowl. Marinade camel for 4 hours turning meat over if skewered. Spoon sauce over meat if left whole. Bake for 2 to 3 hours at 325° F., or allow 30 minutes per pound.

PUDDING OF BARLEY GROATS NICANDER

ΠΙΛΑΦΙ ΜΕ ΚΡΙΘΑΡΙ   (pilafi meh krithari)

The poets of Greece wrote of love, tragedy, life, and good food. Nicander of Colophon, didactic poet of the second century B.C., recorded this recipe for a fragrant pudding. In addition, he mentions the use of the spoon for the first time in history. The archaic directions are as follows:

Boil some kid or capon. Pound 2 or 3 handfuls of barley groats in a mortar until like fine meal. Mix in a little olive oil. Pour meal into boiling broth after first having removed the meat. Cover pot to allow groats to swell. When pudding has cooled, eat it using hollow pieces of bread as μυστρον (mystron) spoons.

1 quart water   1 cup barley groats
2 teaspoons salt   2 tablespoons olive oil
2 pounds kid or capon

Boil kid or capon, at low heat for 2 hours. Remove meat to a dish. Bring broth to a rolling boil and add groats. Cover pot and reduce heat to simmer for 25 minutes, or until groats are soft.

COOKING
IN
MODERN
GREECE

Η ΜΑΓΕΙΡΙΚΗ ΤΗΣ ΣΥΓΧΡΟΝΟΥ ΕΛΛΑΔΟΣ
(e maiyereke tis syhronou Ellados)

CONCERNING
THE RECIPES

INTRODUCTION

In planning a Greek menu, you will discover many recipes in this book are interchangeable. A vegetable recipe when served hot may be used as the vegetable course; the very same recipe, served cold, may be considered a salad. Certain desserts are appropriate for an elegant dinner or buffet; others are best suited for the family meal. Some soups are hearty enough to be a main course in themselves.

All recipes, unless otherwise stated, will serve 4.

The names of the recipes in this book are direct translations of the Greek. In cases where specific names have become associated with certain recipes—such as *dolmathes* or *dolmas, baklava, moussaka, filo*—the word has been included as part of the title. The phonetic pronunciation of the Greek name for each recipe is in parenthesis.

WHERE TO BUY GREEK FOODS

A list of addresses where you can buy typical Greek foods would be outdated in no time, because the little Greek grocery store with its wholesale-retail sign is disappearing from the American scene. Only in large cities like Los Angeles, Chicago, and New York do they promise to exist for awhile.

I suggest you make inquiries at the gourmet counter of any large supermarket or department store for things you need.

One excellent way to discover the source of typical Greek foods in your community is to call the Greek Orthodox Church. There is one in practically every city across the United States and in many countries, including Japan. Because the Greek Orthodox Church is the hub of Greek ethnic social life, there is usually someone at the church who can direct you to the nearest grocery store that caters to the Greek community.

APPETIZERS AND MEZETHES

THE LITTLE SNACK

ΜΕΖΕΔΕΣ   (mehzehthes)   ΟΡΕΚΤΙΚΑ   (orektika)

The Greek *meze* is a snack that is eaten at any time of the day, usually accompanied by a beverage. If you have visited Greece, you will remember the many delightful sidewalk cafes called *tavernas* where you sat in the sun, ordered cool beer which all the native Greeks seemed to be drinking, and nibbled on many of the typical *mezethes* listed here. *Mezethes* may be part of a buffet meal or may be served during the cocktail hour, which often extends to 10 P.M. in Greece. Dinner is served at 11 P.M. or later. Sometimes these foods are served as appetizers, *orektika,* but it is not the traditional Greek custom to serve an elaborate array of tidbits at the beginning of dinner, although many Greek families in the United States and Greece do, having adopted the French tradition of serving hors d'oeuvres.

FISH AND SEAFOOD

ΨΑΡΙΑ ΚΑΙ ΘΑΛΑΣΣΙΝΑ
(psaria kai thalassina)

ANCHOVIES (canned)
ΧΑΜΣΙ (hamsi)

Drain oil. Arrange anchovies on dish with lemon slices as garnish; or place individually on crackers or toast.

CAVIAR DIP TARAMA
ΤΑΡΑΜΑ (tarama)

1 small jar of tarama or other red roe
juice of ½ lemon
1 cup mayonnaise
1 teaspoon onion powder
1 slice fresh bread
1 tablespoon cold water
Mix ingredients in blender until smooth. Serve chilled with crackers. If you prefer to make canapés, butter crackers or toast before spreading dip to avoid sogginess. (For traditional recipe, see page 103.)

CLAMS (MUSSELS)
(fresh or frozen)
ΜΗΔΙΑ (midia)

Little mussels are called sea quinces, or *kydonia* in Greece, and are sold in many little villages along the edge of the sea.

Use any kind of small clams or oysters. Steam 3 minutes in covered pot in 1 cup water and ½ teaspoon salt. Split shells open, sprinkle with lemon juice, and serve in shells.

SKEWERED FISH
ΨΑΡΙΑ ΣΟΤΒΛΑΚΙΑ
(psaria souvlakia)

Cut 1 pound boneless white fish into small chunks. Dip into lemon juice and skewer 4 or 5 pieces on individual skewer. Sprinkle with thyme, rosemary or tarragon, and salt. Broil 5 minutes, turning on all sides.

SKEWERED SHRIMP
ΓΑΡΙΔΕΣ
ΣΟΤΒΛΑΚΙΑ

Cut raw shrimp in half after peeling. If small, leave whole. Dip in lemon juice and olive oil. Roll in grated cheese.

(garides souvlakia)	Skewer 3 or 4 on each skewer. Broil 3 minutes turning on all sides.
SHRIMP IN MUSTARD SAUCE (canned) ΓΑΡΙΔΕΣ ΜΕ ΜΟΤΣΤΑΡΔΑ (garides meh moustarda)	Place shrimp in bowl with sauce in which they were canned. Serve with crackers.
MARINATED BABY OCTOPUS (canned) ΧΤΑΠΟΔΙ ΤΗΣ ΤΕΝΕΚΕΔΕΣ (oktapodi tis tenekedes)	Add a touch of garlic powder and rosemary to marinade in which octopus was canned. Serve in marinade with forks; or garnish canapés with pieces of octopus.
SMOKED OYSTERS (canned) ΣΤΡΕΙΔΙΑ (streidia)	Drain oil. Serve in dish or place individually on crackers.
FRIED SMELTS ΜΑΡΙΔΕΣ ΤΗΓΑΝΙΤΕΣ (marides tiganites)	(See page 106).
SKINLESS SARDINES ΣΑΡΔΕΛΛΕΣ (sardelles)	If unable to purchase those canned in Greece, look for the ones canned in Portugal or Spain, prepared in olive oil. Drain oil. Serve with slices of lemon and toasted bread.
SNAILS (bottled, including shells) ΣΑΛΙΓΚΑΡΙΑ (saligaria)	Blend ¼ cup soft butter with ⅛ teaspoon garlic powder. Stuff shells with snail meat, add a little of the butter mixture. Dip in bread crumbs flavored with grated cheese. Bake for 10 minutes at 400° F.
SMOKED SNAILS (canned) ΣΑΛΙΓΚΑΡΙΑ ΜΕ ΛΑΔΙ (saligaria meh ladi)	Drain oil. Arrange in dish or place individually on crackers or toast.

STUFFED SQUID   (See page 108).
ΚΑΛΑΜΑΡΑΚΙΑ
  ΠΑΡΑΓΕΜΙΣΤΑ
  (kalamarakia
  parayemista)

TUNNY FISH   This famous fish from the waters near
  LAKERDA (bottled)   Istanbul can be served directly from the
ΛΑΚΕΡΔΑ (lakerda)   jar, with slices of lemon.

CHEESE AND EGGS

ΤΥΡΙΑ ΚΑΙ ΑΥΓΑ
(tyrya kai avgha)

FETA CHEESE   Drain brine. Slice cheese into 1″ cubes.
  (canned, bottled, or   Serve with soft rolls.
  fresh)
ΦΕΤΑ (feta)

FETA CHEESE BUNS   Use any biscuit dough recipe or pre-
ΚΟΤΛΟΥΡΑΚΙΑ ΜΕ   pared packaged refrigerated dough.
  ΦΕΤΑ   Place a small amount of crumbled
  (koulourakia meh   cheese in center of biscuit and bake for
  feta)   10 minutes. Serve hot.

KOPANISTI (canned,   Serve this soft cheese with cheese
  bottled)   knife and crackers.
ΚΟΠΑΝΙΣΤΗ
  (kopanisti)

PEASANT'S FRIED   Use any hard cheese that doesn't melt
  CHEESE   when heated, such as Kaseri, Kefaloteri,
ΣΑΓΑΝΑΚΙ   or Haloumi. Parmesan may be sub-
  (saganaki)   stituted. Slice 1½″ thick. Fry in hot but-
                         ter for 3 minutes on each side. Serve im-
                         mediately with toast or crackers.

YOGURT   Serve chilled in small bowls.
ΓΙΑΟΥΡΤΗ (yaourti)

YOGURT MEZE   Mix 2 cups yogurt, 1 teaspoon onion
ΓΙΑΟΥΡΤΗ ΜΕΖΕ   powder, 1 tablespoon vinegar, ½ tea-
  (yaourti meze)   spoon dill. Serve with crackers, chips, or

strips of vegetables such as green pepper, celery, carrots, or cauliflower.

ARCADIAN EGGS
ΑΥΓΑ
ΛΑΔΟΛΕΜΟΝΟ
(avgha latholemono)

Boil eggs 15 minutes. Plunge in cold water. Peel. When cool, cut in quarters and place in a marinade of ¼ cup olive oil and juice of 1 lemon. Salt to taste.

BYZANTINE EGGS
ΑΥΓΑ ΒΡΑΣΤΑ
(avgha vrasta)

Simmer eggs slowly for 3 hours in strong coffee, ¼ cup olive oil and the skins of 1 onion. Keep covered with coffee at all times during cooking. Plunge into cold water. Peel. Chill before serving. Serve whole, preferably on a white dish, with a dab of mayonnaise.

GREEK SAUSAGES AND SPICED MEATS

ΛΟΥΚΑΝΙΚΑ
(loukanika)

BEEF OR LAMB SOUVLAKIA
ΣΟΥΒΛΑΚΙΑ
(souvlakia)

Cut beef or lamb meat into small cubes. Place 4 or 5 on individual skewers. Sprinkle with lemon juice, salt, garlic powder, and oregano. Broil in shallow pan 5 minutes, turning over once.

SPICED BEEF PASTOURMAS
ΠΑΣΤΟΥΡΜΑΣ
(pastourmas)

This is a delicious spiced meat which looks like half a slab of bacon covered with red pepper, and is flavored with garlic. Slice thinly. May be eaten without cooking, or fried for 3 minutes on lightly oiled pan.

FILET OF HAM LOUTSA
ΛΟΥΤΣΑ
(loutsa)

The Cypriots of Cyprus make this delicious filet of ham, which is sometimes available in the United States. Rub a roll of boned pork loin with garlic, salt, cracked pepper, lemon juice, coriander,

and cumin. Bake slowly 3 hours at 325°
F. Slice thinly; serve hot or cold.

JELLIED PORK
(bottled)
ΠΗΚΤΗ (pikti)

Serve chilled. (For traditional recipe, see
page 142.)

KOKKORETSI,
BARBECUED
ΚΟΚΚΟΡΕΤΣΙ
(kokkoretsi)

(For traditional recipe, see page 141.)

LIVER MEZE
ΣΥΚΟΤΙ ΜΕΖΕ
(sykoti meze)

Use beef, calves', or chicken livers. Cut
into bite-size pieces. Fry in 2 tablespoons butter. Season with salt, pepper,
and onion powder while frying. Serve
hot, skewered or on toast rounds.

MEAT BALLS
KEFTEDES
ΚΕΦΤΕΔΕΣ
(keftedes)

1 pound ground lean beef, veal, or lamb.
1 teaspoon each: parsley flakes, garlic
powder, onion powder, spearmint flakes.
1 egg. Mix all ingredients. Make small
balls. Roll in flour and fry in 2 tablespoons hot oil until brown on all sides.
Serve hot or cold. (For traditional recipe,
see page 132.)

WINE SAUSAGES
ΛΟΥΚΑΝΙΚΑ ΜΕ
ΡΕΤΣΙΝΑ
(loukanika meh
retsina)

Follow recipe for Messinia Sausages,
below, with the following additions:
Marinate pork in 1 cup retsina wine for
4 hours before forming sausages. Add 1
teaspoon cumin to spices.

MESSINIA
SAUSAGES
ΛΟΥΚΑΝΙΚΑ
(loukanika)

1 pound coarse-ground sausage meat,
1 teaspoon grated fresh orange rind,
1 teaspoon thyme
1 teaspoon savory
⅛ teaspoon cracked pepper

Mix ingredients and form into sausages.
Add a few tablespoons water to frying
pan and cover for a few minutes. Continue frying until brown. Serve hot. (For
traditional recipe, see page 142.)

SPICY SAUSAGES
SOUTZOUKAKIA
ΣΟΤΤΖΟΤΚΑΚΙΑ
(soutzoukakia)

1 pound coarse-ground sausage or beef. ½ teaspoon each: parsley flakes, cumin, coriander seed, garlic powder, onion powder. Mix ingredients. Shape into small sausages the size of a fat finger and roll in flour. Fry in 2 tablespoons hot oil until brown. Serve hot or cold. (For traditional recipe, see page 134.)

VEGETABLES

ΧΟΡΤΑΡΙΚΑ
(hortarika)

FRIED ARTICHOKES
ΑΓΚΙΝΑΡΕΣ
ΤΗΓΑΝΙΤΕΣ
(aginares tiganites)

(See page 79.)

PICKLED
ARTICHOKES
(bottled)
ΑΓΚΙΝΑΡΕΣ
ΛΑΔΟΞΕΙΔΟ
(aginares
ladoxksido)

Serve at room temperature in the marinade in which they were canned.

BABY BEETS MEZE
(canned)
ΠΑΝΤΖΑΡΙΑ
ΛΑΔΟΞΕΙΔΟ
(pantzaria
ladoxksido)

Buy the tiniest whole, canned beets you can find. Drain liquid. Marinate beets in ¼ cup olive oil, 2 tablespoons vinegar. Serve whole.

BEAN PURÉE
ΦΑΣΟΛΑΔΑ
ΠΟΤΡΕΣ
(fasolada poores)

Use any kind of canned or boiled beans. Include 1 or more cups of liquid in which beans were cooked or canned. Mix in blender until smooth. Mix in ¼ cup olive oil, 2 tablespoons vinegar, 1 teaspoon onion powder or chopped green onions, and a sprinkle of cayenne pepper and salt to taste. Serve chilled with crackers.

BEAN PURÉE WITH
   YOGURT
ΠΟΤΡΕΣ ΜΕ
   ΓΙΑΟΤΡΤΗ
(poores meh yaourti)

Substitute olive oil with 1 cup yogurt or sour cream in above recipe. Omit pepper.

BEAN SALADS
ΦΑΣΟΛΟΣΑΛΑΤΑ
(fasolosalata)

Drain liquid from boiled or canned chickpeas, fava beans, or garbanzo beans. Add ¼ cup olive oil and 2 tablespoons vinegar, and toss well. Sprinkle with 1 teaspoon oregano and salt to taste. Serve in bowls. (For traditional recipe, see page 81.)

EGGPLANT DIP
ΜΕΛΙΤΖΑΝΑ ΠΟΤΡΕ
(melitzana pooreh)

Bake whole eggplant in hot oven at 375° F. for 30 to 45 minutes, depending on size. Rinse with cold running water to loosen skin. Chop eggplant meat and mix in blender with ½ teaspoon each: garlic powder, onion powder, sugar, lemon juice, and ¼ cup mayonnaise. Serve chilled with sesame seed crackers.

STUFFED
   EGGPLANTS
   (bottled)
ΜΕΛΙΤΖΑΝΕΣ
   ΠΑΡΑΓΕΜΙΣΤΕΣ
(melitzanes
   parayemistes)

These are tiny eggplants stuffed with pine nuts. Serve at room temperature.

GARBANZO NUTS
   STRAGALIA
ΣΤΡΑΓΑΛΙΑ
(stragalia)

Dried garbanzo beans or chickpeas, that are salted and eaten like nuts and can be bought bottled or in bags.

GRAPE LEAVES
   DOLMAS (canned)
ΝΤΟΛΜΑΔΕΣ
(dolmathes)

Prepared grape leaves stuffed with rice or meat filling may be served directly from the can without any further cooking. (For traditional recipe, see page 89.)

GREEK OLIVES
  (bottled)
ΕΛΑΙΕΣ (elyies)

Strain olives. Serve with rolls, slices of bread, and feta cheese.

MARINATED
  MUSHROOMS
ΜΑΝΙΤΑΡΙΑ
  ΛΑΔΟΛΕΜΟΝΟ
  (manitaria
  ladolemono)

Wash mushrooms and simmer, either whole or sliced, in 2 tablespoons salted water for 4 minutes. Cool. Add ¼ cup olive oil and juice of ½ lemon, and allow to stand 1 hour. Serve chilled or at room temperature.

PICKLED
  VEGETABLES
  TOURSI (bottled)
ΤΟΥΡΣΙ (toursi)

Serve directly from jar into salad bowls for individual servings, or into one large bowl for buffet service. (For traditional recipe, see page 74.)

PISTACHIO NUTS
ΦΙΣΤΙΚΙΑ (fistikia)

These nuts are to the Greek what peanuts are to the American. Serve in bowls in shells (it is not necessary to peel them beforehand).

SALONIKA PEPPERS
  (bottled)
ΠΙΠΕΡΙΕΣ (piperyes)

Drain and arrange on plate. Serve with cheeses and various kinds of bread. They are slightly hot.

SALTED SEEDS
  PASATEMPO
ΠΑΣΑΤΕΜΠΟ
  (pasatempo)

Spread squash or pumpkin seeds on baking pan. Salt lightly. Bake 325° F. for 30 minutes.

TAHINI SALAD
ΤΑΧΗΝΙ

Tahini is a delicious paste made of sesame seeds and oil, with the consistency of peanut butter. The flavor is more subtle than peanut butter. Add 1 cup Tahini to recipe for Bean Purée; mix in well. Serve chilled or at room temperature.

TAVERNA GARLIC
  DIP SKORDALIA
ΣΚΟΡΔΑΛΙΑ
  (skordalya)

1 teaspoon garlic powder or 5 fresh cloves garlic
½ cup mayonnaise
1 teaspoon vinegar
2 cups mashed potatoes

Mix in blender until smooth in order listed. Serve chilled with chips for dipping. Serve warm when used as a sauce over fish.

PASTRIES

ΠΗΤΕΣ   (pittes)

The most delicious appetizers in Greek cookery are pies and tarts made of *filo* pastry. They are called *trigona* or *bourekakia* (bourek).
To fill ½ pound filo, cut in strips of approximately 1″ × 12″

CHEESE TARTS TRIGONA ΤΥΡΟΠΗΤΕΣ ΤΡΙΓΩΝΑ (teropittes trigona)	1 cup Feta, cottage, or hoop cheese, crumbled 2 eggs, beaten 1 tablespoon cornstarch 1 teaspoon salt, if using cottage or hoop cheese
SPINACH TARTS ΣΠΑΝΑΚΟΠΗΤΑ ΜΠΟΥΡΕΚΙΑ (spanakopitta bourekia)	1 package frozen chopped spinach, defrosted 2 eggs, beaten 1 cup Feta, cottage, or hoop cheese, crumbled 1 teaspoon salt if using cottage or hoop cheese
SEAFOOD TARTS ΘΑΛΑΣΣΙΝΑ ΜΠΟΥΡΕΚΙΑ (thalassina bourekakia)	1 can any kind of shellfish: clam, scallops, shrimp, lobster, or crab, chopped and drained well 1 egg, beaten 4 green onions, chopped 1 tablespoon cornstarch
MEAT TARTS ΚΡΕΑΤΟΠΗΤΕΣ (kreatopittes)	2 cups slivered or chopped cooked meat of any kind: ham, chicken, beef, lamb, or pork 4 green onions, chopped salt and pepper to taste

1 egg, beaten
¼ cup chopped nuts

Mix filling desired, using a fork or spoon. Place a teaspoon of filling at one end of filo strip and roll into a tart (see pages 148 and 153 for directions). Bake 45 minutes in 350° F. oven. Serve hot.

NUT TARTS
ΣΚΑΛΤΣΟΥΝΑΚΙΑ
(skaltsounakia)

2 cups chopped walnuts, pecans, or almonds
½ cup orange or apricot marmalade
½ teaspoon cinnamon

Mix filling. Follow directions for rolling and baking tarts as above. Allow to cool before serving.

THE LEGEND OF
ATHENA AND
THE OLIVE TREE

Ο ΜΥΘΟΣ ΤΟΥ ΕΛΑΙΟΔΕΝΔΡΟΥ
(o mythos tou elayolendrou)

A charming Greek legend tells how the olive tree was introduced to Greece, and how Athens got its name. Two powerful Greek gods on Mount Olympus, the sea god Poseidon and the goddess of wisdom, Athena, vied to become the patron deity of the great city at the foot of their mountain. To settle the dispute, a contest was held, and the people gathered to judge whose gift would be the greater. Handsome bearded Poseidon threw his huge trident into the dry earth and produced a spring instantaneously. The people were impressed and awed. Then Athena quietly bent down and from the barren earth coaxed a rather unpretentious bush to life. It certainly didn't look like much. She explained how this tree —an olive—would produce black fruit to be the poor man's food, and how its oil would light lamps, feed, cleanse, and perfume the body, and make the city grow rich with trade. So the city was named for her, and Athena became its patron deity forever. In her honor, the citizens erected a thirty-foot ivory and gold statue of Athena and built a shrine to house it—the Parthenon.

OLIVE OIL

ΕΛΑΙΟΛΑΔΟΝ   (eleyoladon)

Olive oil is used as a flavoring over boiled vegetables, or even to spread over a slice of bread for a snack. Like butter, it can turn rancid if kept uncovered, therefore I advise storing it in a dark bottle with a cap in the refrigerator.

Olive oil is one of the ubiquitous products of Greece and some regions are particularly known for the fine quality of their oil. Kalamata in the Messinia region and Sifnos, in the Cyclades, produce exceptional oil. Mytilene also has a fine grade.

The first pressing of the olives produces an oil that is strong in flavor and deep green in color. Many people prefer the deep golden amber aromatic oil which results from the second pressing, but even then it is common to cut and dilute this oil with a flavorless oil such as soy or corn oil. I suggest doing this in cooking recipes.

GREEK OLIVES

ΕΛΑΙΕΣ   (elyes)

If you have ever been in a small Greek or Italian grocery store, you will remember the pungent odors coming from the ripe olives in huge barrels. These olives, sold by the pound, are ready to be eaten as is, but a marinade adds to their flavor.

BLACK OLIVES are ripe when picked, have wrinkled skins, and are usually small and round, and slightly bitter and salty.

AMPHISSA OLIVES come from Amphissa in the Parnassus region and are black and juicy.

KALAMATA OLIVES come from the city of Kalamata, Messinia. They are large, oblong, with soft flesh and smooth purple skin and are considered the most delicious.

GREEN OLIVES are picked unripe, have an oblong shape, firm flesh, smooth skin, and tart flavor.

OLIVE MARINADE

ΛΑΔΟΞΤΑΟ   (ladoxksitho)

1 cup olive oil   **1 clove garlic**
½ cup vinegar   **1 teaspoon oregano**
1 bay leaf

Cut a slit in each olive. Fill a jar with olives. Cover with marinade. Olives will keep many months and improve with marinating.

CURING OF HOME-GROWN OLIVES, GREEK STYLE

ΠΩΣ ΝΑ ΕΤΟΙΜΑΣΗΣ ΤΗΣ ΕΛΑΙΕΣ   (pos na etemasis tis elyes)

If you own an olive tree and do not want to go through the complicated process of leaching olives with chemicals, follow one of these ancient Greek methods to get rid of the bitterness.

SALTING METHOD: Place washed olives in a wicker basket or a plastic container with holes. Cover with medium-coarse salt. Set basket in sun and protect with a cheesecloth cover. Twice a day for a week, toss olives to redistribute them, until the bitter fluid is drawn from them. Bring olives in at night to prevent mold.

WATER METHOD: Cover washed olives with a solution of salt water—1 cup salt to each quart water—in a crock or glass jar. Place a weight, such as a small plate or washed rock, to keep olives submerged. Olives may remain in this brine for months. Marinate in Olive Marinade before serving.

GREEK BREADS
AND ROLLS

ΕΛΛΗΝΙΚΑ ΨΩΜΙΑ-ΚΟΥΛΟΤΡΕΣ-ΚΟΥΛΟΤΡΑΚΙΑ
(ellenyka psomia-kouloures-koulourakia)

When you start your day with rolls and coffee, you are following an ancient Greek custom. The Greeks, three thousand years ago, breakfasted on freshly baked rolls and buns called *kollikia* and *kallaboi*. Many of these breads are baked today, among them a great variety of yeast breads made from wheat, barley, rye, rice, spelt and groats. In small villages, the method of baking in communal ovens, some of them bee-hive shaped outdoor charcoal ovens, is still practiced. Breads and pastries are prepared at home, then taken to the community baker who charges a small fee for his service of stoking the fire and tending the oven.

Greek bread is traditionally round, with a hole in the center like a doughnut. The top is usually braided and covered with sesame seeds. These loaves are called *kouloures* and come in all sizes. The smaller sweet rolls are called *koulourakia*.

The arrangement in Greek bakeries of those rolls, piled high, one on top of the other, a round stick through the holes in the centers, dates back to Sparta. The poor and orphaned, who could not afford to donate food to the communal tables, were required to bring a reed on which to carry the *kollikia* as their contribution.

Molded breads, especially those made in Crete, are lavishly decorated with bread animals, flowers, leaves and other designs. Hot cross buns are found in Greece, and the ancient pagan symbol for the four quarters of the moon is still used on these, so the next time you buy them, say a few words of respect for Demeter, the earth goddess, who made the wheat grow.

For other bread recipes, see Archaic Greek Bread (page 14) and Church Bread, Prosphoron (page 207).

GREEK BREAD

ΑΡΤΟΣ ΕΛΛΗΝΙΚΟΣ   (artos ellenehkos)

Greek bread has a firm texture and a thick crust. This recipe will make 2 rectangular loaves.

2 tablespoons dry or cake yeast
¼ cup warm water
7 cups unsifted flour, white, whole-
    wheat or rye
2 tablespoons sugar

3 tablespoons oil or melted butter
2 cups warm water or milk
1 egg (optional)
¾ teaspoon salt

Soften yeast in ¼ cup warm water. Put 5 cups flour in large bowl. Mix sugar, salt, oil and egg in 2 cups water and pour over flour. Add yeast mixture and start mixing, using spoon or paddle. Mixture will look like paste. Add remaining 2 cups flour leaving about 2 tablespoons in measuring cup to use on hands and board. Knead the dough in the bowl for 5 minutes then transfer to board and continue kneading for 15 minutes until dough is smooth and does not feel sticky.

Place dough in a greased bowl. Cover with towel dampened with hot water and keep in a warm place until dough has doubled in bulk. Punch bread down. Shape into 1 large loaf or 2 loaves and put in greased baking pans. Set aside to rise once again in a warm place, uncovered, about 2 hours. Bake in a preheated oven at 375° F. for 45 minutes. Brush top with melted butter upon removal from oven.

KOULOURA ROLLS AND BUNS

ΚΟΤΛΟΤΡΑ ΚΑΙ ΚΟΤΛΟΤΡΑΚΙΑ   (kouloura kai koulourakia)

This recipe is the traditional twisted bread with sesame seeds on top which every Greek cook bakes. The smaller sweeter rolls, *koulourakia,* meaning "little rolls," can be made from this same recipe.

2 tablespoons dry or cake yeast
½ cup warm water
2 cups warm milk
3 tablespoons sugar (or 5 if making
    koulourakia)
3 tablespoons butter, margarine, or
    oil

¾ teaspoon salt
7 cups all-purpose flour, unsifted
1 egg

TOPPING:
1 egg yolk
¼ cup sesame seeds

Melt yeast in warm water. Set aside. Bring milk to boil. Add sugar, butter, and salt. Allow milk to cool slightly.

Put flour in a large bowl leaving about a tablespoon of it in the measuring cup for hands and make a hole in the center. Pour liquid into it. Add yeast and egg. Start mixing with spoon or paddle, pushing flour from all sides into center. Dough will be sticky until flour is absorbed. Begin kneading dough in the bowl and then transfer it to a lightly floured board. Continue kneading until dough is smooth and elastic, about 20 minutes.

Place dough in a greased bowl. Cover with towel dampened with hot water. Set aside in a warm place to rise until bulk has doubled, about 4 hours.

Punch down in the middle. Knead for a few minutes and shape into a round loaf or into individual rolls (see below). Using fingers, rub top with egg yolk and sprinkle with sesame seeds. Place in greased baking pans. Let rise once more, uncovered, in a warm place, approximately 1 hour.

Bake in a preheated oven at 375° F. for 45 minutes. Remove from oven; allow to cool 10 minutes before removing bread from pan.

To Shape Traditional KOULOURA

Divide dough into 3 long ropes. Braid together. Place braid in a greased tube pan or a large round baking pan. Stretch dough to make ends meet. Use egg yolk to stick ends together.

To Shape Koulourakia Rolls

Pinch off pieces of dough. Roll on board with the palms of your hands to make a rope 6″ long. Twist it into a hairpin, coil the ends around each other and stick the tips together with a dab of egg yolk. Or coil it like a snake, round and round; or roll into small round balls using the palms of your hands. Do not flatten or press down as you roll.

CRESCENT ROLLS

ΚΡΟΣΣΑΝΤ   (krossan)

The crescent shape, a reminder of the Turkish occupation, comes from the moon symbol on the Ottoman flag. The Greeks still use this shape, and the quick easy method for rolling them has been taken from the secrets of professional bakers.

2 tablespoons dry or cake yeast	1 egg
¼ cup warm water	
6½ cups all-purpose flour, unsifted	TOPPING:
½ teaspoon salt	¼ pound butter
2 tablespoons sugar	1 egg white
2 cups hot milk	½ cup sesame seeds
2 tablespoons butter or oil	

Sprinkle yeast in warm water. Set aside. Put 4 cups flour in a large bowl. Make a hole in center. Sprinkle salt and sugar over flour. Heat milk, add fat, and allow milk to cool slightly.

Pour into flour well and start mixing, adding egg and yeast mixture as you mix. Add 2 cups flour leaving a ½ cup of it in the measuring cup to use for hands and board. The mixture will ball up quickly. Knead on a lightly floured board for 15 minutes to make a smooth dough. Resist the temptation to add more flour. Shape crescents and place on oiled baking pan 2″ apart. Let rise until double in bulk in a warm draft-free place for 1½ hours.

Bake at 400° F. for 20 minutes. Will make 24 small rolls or 18 large ones.

To Shape Crescent Rolls

Pinch off a small amount of dough, the size of a plum. Flour board lightly. Roll out dough into a round circle, about 6″ wide. Cut into four or six wedges like a pie. Put 3 or 4 dabs of cold butter on top of each triangle. Roll each triangle, starting from the wide edge toward the point. Lay each roll on oiled baking sheet with point tucked underneath and curve into a crescent. Dip fingers in lightly beaten egg white and rub on top of rolls. Sprinkle with sesame seeds.

SWEET CRESCENT ROLLS

ΓΛΤΚΑ ΚΡΟΣΣΑΝΤ   (glika krossan)

FILLING:
1 cup fruit preserves, any kind,

or

1 cup brown sugar
1 teaspoon cinnamon
½ cup chopped nuts
¼ pound chopped cold butter or
   margarine

Follow recipe for Crescent Rolls. While shaping rolls, add filling in center before rolling. Omit sesame seeds on top and sprinkle with coarse sugar instead.

SUNDAY BREAD

ΤΣΟΤΡΕΚΙ   (tsoureki)

This sweet and spicy bread which Greek women bake for Sundays, holidays, and religious festivals is known as *tsoureki*. For New Year's Day, it is called *vasilopitta* and baked with money inside. It is *christopsomo*, "Christ's bread," at Christmas and decorated with a cross; on Easter, *lambropsomo*, and topped with dyed red eggs.

2 tablespoons dry or cake yeast
¼ cup warm water

FLAVORINGS:
½ teaspoon each: cinnamon, anise
   seeds, orange peel
1 bay leaf
¼ teaspoon mahaleb (optional)
4 grains mastic or 1 ounce ouzo
   (optional)
½ cup water

7 cups all-purpose flour, unsifted
½ cup sugar
½ teaspoon salt
½ cup hot milk
¼ pound butter or 6 tablespoons oil
3 eggs

TOPPING:
egg yolk
¼ cup sesame seeds

Dissolve yeast in warm water and set aside. Put flavorings in ½ cup water in pan and bring to a boil. Set aside to steep and cool. Put flour, sugar, and salt in a large bowl. Heat milk; remove from fire, add butter or oil, and allow to cool slightly.

Make a hole in the middle of flour and mix in eggs, yeast, milk, and flavored water having removed the bay leaf. Use spoon or paddle to push flour from sides into center. Finish by kneading on lightly floured board until dough is smooth, about 20 minutes. Place in an oiled bowl. Cover with towel dampened with hot water and set aside in a warm draft-free place until bulk has doubled, about 4 to 6 hours.

When doubled, punch down and knead for 5 minutes. Pinch off two pieces of dough, each the size of a small apple, to make the Byzantine cross. Shape remaining dough into one round loaf or two rectangular loaves and place in greased baking pans. Glaze with egg yolk and decorate top with Byzantine cross (see below). Glaze cross with egg yolk. Set aside to rise once again, about 2 hours. Do not cover with towel. Bake in preheated oven at 350° F. for 1 hour.

To Make Byzantine Cross

Roll each ball of dough into a long rope, 12″ to 16″ long. Slit the ends down 5 inches. Coil each slit in opposite directions. Form a cross with the two ropes on top of loaf which meets at the exact center. Do not press flat.

EASTER BREAD TSOUREKI

ΛΑΜΠΡΟΨΩΜΟ   (lambropsomo)

Follow directions for Sunday Bread, adding an extra ½ cup sugar. Place a hard-boiled egg dyed red in the center of the loaf before the second rising. Glaze with egg yolk and sprinkle with sesame seeds. Bake as above.

NEW YEAR'S DAY BREAD

ΒΑΣΙΛΟΠΗΤΑ   (vasilopitta)

Follow directions for Sunday Bread, adding an extra ½ cup sugar. Wrap coins of any denomination in aluminum foil and put into dough when kneading it. Shape into one large round loaf. Decorate with walnuts, cherries, or almonds. Set aside to rise in a warm place. Bake as above. The belief is that he who finds the coin or coins will have luck the coming year.

CRETAN WEDDING BREAD

ΚΡΗΤΗΚΟ ΨΩΜΙ ΤΟΥ ΓΑΜΟΥ   (Kretiko psomi tou ghamou)

Follow directions for Sunday Bread. Cut off two balls of dough the size of oranges. Knead the remaining dough into a long rope, and make ends meet. Place on greased round baking pan. Rub top and sides of dough with a mixture of 1 egg white and 1 table-spoon of water.

Take the two orange-size balls of dough, break off bits and shape into leaves, roses, birds, crosses, circles, exercising your imagination for new designs. Pile them lavishly on top and sides of rope. Brush on more egg white. Set aside to rise for 45 minutes. Do not cover.

Bake at 350° F. for 50 minutes.

This bread is cut after the marriage ceremony and the groom receives the first piece according to ancient custom.

SWEET TOAST RUSKS

ΠΑΞΗΜΑΔΑΚΙΑ   (paxemadakia)

This sweet toast rusk, often called by its German name "zwie-back," has been a favorite Greek recipe since the fifth century B.C. The crumbs are used as a base for cheese pies and cakes in recipes which also date back for centuries. (See Athenian Cheese Cake.) Sweet toast rusks are delicious at breakfast, luncheon, or tea time.

½ pound butter or ⅔ cup oil	2½ cups flour, unsifted
3 large eggs	3 teaspoons baking powder
1 cup sugar	⅛ teaspoon salt
1 teaspoon anise seeds	¼ cup sesame seeds

Cream butter until light and thick. Add eggs, sugar, and anise seeds beating all the while. Sift flour and baking powder and mix in well. Add salt if using oil.

Dough will be a sticky batter. Oil one long loaf pan or 3 half-sized ones and scoop batter into them. Sprinkle top with sesame seeds. Bake in preheated oven at 350° F. for 45 minutes. Remove and allow to cool. Serve as sweet bread or dry into rusks.

Slice loaves ½″ to ¾″ thick. Place slices on ungreased cookie sheets and dry slowly in 250° F. oven for 30 minutes, turning the toast over once. Allow to cool before storing in tightly closed plastic bag.

For other bread recipes, see:

Easter Tsoureki (page 44).

Archaic Greek Bread (page 14).

Church Bread Prosphoron (page 207).

GREEK CHEESES

ΤΥΡΙΑ   (terya)

Greek cheeses, usually made from rich goat's or sheep's milk, have strong pungent distinct flavors. In a land where refrigeration is primitive or nonexistent in many areas, turning milk into cheese is an excellent way to preserve milk. Every family, no matter how poor, is able to own a goat to produce this basic vital food. Crete and Epirus are famous for their particular cheeses.

Feta, ΦΕΤΑ, is salty, white, moist cheese that crumbles easily with a fork. It is eaten sliced as a table cheese or crumbled into salads, most often combined with eggs. It is a common cheese, found all over Greece and made by every peasant. Feta is best when fresh, and must be stored in a brine solution of 1 teaspoon salt per cup of water. In recipes in this book, a reasonable substitute for Feta cheese is hoop cheese. Add 1 teaspoon salt per 8-ounce package of hoop cheese, in recipes which require Feta. See: Balkan Egg Puff (page 51), Cheese Pie (page 148), Cheese Trigona (page 148), Lettuce and Cheese Salad (page 73).

GRAVIERA, ΓΡΑΒΙΕΡΑ, similar to Gruyère cheese, comes from Crete and Skyros in the Northern Sporades. Made of cream and very rich it is a cheese to be sliced and eaten as an appetizer or dessert.

HALOUMI, ΧΑΛΟΥΜΙ, is a favorite cheese from Cyprus, similar to Feta.

KASERI, ΚΑΣΕΡΙ, is a firm, white, aged cheese, mild in flavor, similar to Italian Provolone. It is sliced as a table cheese and, because it doesn't melt quickly, fried as an appetizer.

KEFALOTERI, ΚΕΦΑΛΟΤΗΡΙ, a hard, cream-colored, aged cheese with a strong pungent flavor, often grated into vegetables, meat, and spaghetti recipes. Roman or Parmesan cheeses are quite similar, and may be used as substitutes.

KOPANISTI, ΚΟΠΑΝΙΣΤΗ, a soft, creamy, pungent cheese, has a peppery butter taste and is good for spreading on canapés, etc. Mykonos has an excellent one.

MANOORI, ΜΑΝΟΥΡΙ, is a soft white cheese from Crete and Macedonia. When flavored with dill, Cretan cheese is called ANTHOTYRO, ΑΝΘΟΤΥΡΟ· The Kretiki islanders eat it with honey. This delicious combination can be tried with other cheeses.

MEZITHRA, ΜΕΖΙΘΡΑ, is a firm, white, mild cheese, delicious when fresh and used as a grated cheese when aged.

TELEMES, ΤΕΛΕΜΕΣ, is another unusual Greek cheese that comes from Thrace. Lamia Cheese from the Roumeli area is also generally recognized for its superior qualities.

GREEK COTTAGE CHEESE

ΦΡΕΣΚΟ ΤΥΡΙ   (fresko teree)

½ cup powdered skim milk
1 quart fresh milk, preferably goat's
    milk

1 junket or rennet tablet
2 tablespoons crushed Feta cheese
    (optional)

Add powdered milk to fresh milk and heat to 100° F. Do not allow to get too hot or the cheese will not clabber. Dissolve junket or rennet tablet in a small amount of warm milk, add Feta cheese if desired, and mix into remaining milk. Place in glass jar.

Put jar in a pan of hot water, under 120° F., and put in a warm place away from draft. Keep covered. Let set until a solid clabber is formed. Put into cheesecloth bag or large strainer and drain whey. Add salt if desired. Store in covered bowl in refrigerator.

For other recipes using cheese, see: Athenian Cheese Cake (page 160), Balkan Egg Puff (page 51), Cheese Pie (page 148), Cheese Roll Tarts (page 148), Spinach Cheese Pie (page 148), Feta Cheese Buns (page 28), Lettuce and Feta Cheese Salad (page 73), Meat and Macaroni Pastitso (page 62), Baked Eggplant Moussaka (page 88), Peasant's Fried Cheese (page 28), Spaghetti, Greek Style (page 62).

YOGURT

Yogurt no longer is considered an exotic food from the Middle East, eaten only by the gourmet or the health food enthusiast. Today, plain as well as fruit-flavored yogurt are sold side by side with milk in every grocery store in the United States.

Yogurt is made from whole or skim milk and the enzyme action of a bacteria, a process similar to the making of cheese, and it can be made at home quite easily. It has the flavor of sour cream without the calories, a boon to dieters. An electrical appliance for making yogurt, which maintains the even temperature required, may be ordered from any health food or appliance store.

YOGURT

⅓ cup powdered skim milk
1 quart fresh milk, whole or skim

¼ cup prepared yogurt, room-temperature, to use as starter (mayia) (Remove yogurt starter from refrigerator 1 to 2 hours ahead of time.)

Mix powdered milk into fresh milk and heat to 112° F. which is hot enough to stick a finger in. Remove from fire. Dilute prepared yogurt with ½ cup warm milk, and stir into milk. Pour into a jar or covered bowl.

Wrap it in a Turkish towel. Set in a warm place away from drafts for 6 hours. A gas oven with pilot is often just right. Otherwise, place a saucepan filled with hot water in the oven to raise the temperature. When prepared, store in refrigerator.

Serve yogurt plain in individual bowls. Serve as a sauce over Rice Pilaf (page 59), baked or mashed potatoes, fresh fruit, or fruit preserves. Mix with cucumbers for Tsatziki (page 72), or put into recipes such as Yogurt Salad Dressing (page 70), Yogurt Cake (page 166), Yogurt Meze (page 28).

FRESH YOGURT CHEESE

ΤΥΡΙ ΓΙΑΟΥΡΤΗ   (teree yaourti)

This cheese tastes like Feta cheese and makes a reasonable substitute.

1½ cups powdered skim milk   **¼ cup yogurt, room-temperature**
1 quart water

Mix powdered milk with water. Heat slightly. Mix ½ cup of warm milk with prepared yogurt (which should have been out of the refrigerator at least 2 hours).

Follow same procedure as for making yogurt. Let stand 12 hours or more. Put cheese in large strainer or cheesecloth bag over pot to drain. Add 1 teaspoon salt, or more to taste. Store in glass jar in refrigerator.

EGGS

ΑΤΓΑ   (avgha)

Eggs are usually the third course, following the fish and soup in a formal Greek dinner. The traditional and most frequent recipe is a light fluffy omelet, or perhaps an airy souffle. Hard-boiled eggs, however, are more often dressed with oil and vinegar and served as an appetizer or *meze* (snack), or in a salad.

OMELET

ΟΜΕΛΕΤΤΑ   (omeletta)

A true omelet should be cooked in less than a minute.

1 tablespoon butter   salt and pepper to taste
2 or 3 eggs   1 tablespoon water

Heat small skillet. Add butter and swirl around pan until well melted. Beat eggs slightly with a few whisks of a fork, adding salt, pepper, and water. Slide eggs gently into hot pan and let set over high heat for 30 seconds. Shake pan, sliding it back and forth as omelet forms. Using spatula, fold eggs over. Do not turn over. In less than a minute, omelet is ready. Serve hot.

BALKAN EGG PUFF

ΑΤΓΑ ΧΤΤΠΗΤΑ ΜΕ ΤΤΡΙ   (avgha xhtipita meh teree)

The ancient Greek cooking pot with a false bottom, recognized today as a double boiler, is still used to make these fluffy eggs.

1 tablespoon butter   salt and pepper to taste
3 to 6 eggs   ¼ cup crumbled cheese, such as
½ cup milk   Feta or Cheddar

Bring water to a boil in bottom of double boiler. Melt butter in top and coat sides with it. Using whisk, mix all ingredients but cheese. Pour into double boiler and sprinkle in cheese. Cover, reduce heat to medium, and cook 15 minutes.

GREEK RESTAURANT SCRAMBLED EGGS

ΑΥΓΑ ΧΤΥΠΗΤΑ ΜΕ ΝΤΟΜΑΤΑ   (avgha xhtipita meh domata)

The Greek recipe for scrambled eggs with its slivers of green pepper and onions has become a favorite in the United States and is often served in restaurants and coffee shops disguised as a Western or Denver sandwich.

1 tablespoon butter
2 tablespoons onion or scallions,
   chopped
2 tablespoons slivered ham
   (optional)
1 tablespoon green pepper, slivered

1 tomato, chopped
4 eggs
salt and pepper, marjoram or sweet
   basil to taste
1 tablespoon water

Melt butter in a hot small skillet. Add onion, pepper, ham and tomato and a tablespoon of water, cover and cook 3 minutes.

Beat eggs with fork or whisk, adding seasonings and water. Pour eggs over vegetables in pan. Cook on high heat, using spatula to turn eggs over once. Serve immediately.

For other egg recipes, see: Arcadian Eggs (page 29), Byzantine Eggs (page 29), Easter Eggs (page 208), Egg and Lemon Sauce, Avgholemono (page 67).

A FINE KETTLE OF
SOUPS

ΣΟΥΠΕΣ   (soupes)

Greek soups are hearty and filling, unusual yet inexpensive and simple to make. If you feel making soup is really too much bother, this introduction to typical Greek soups will change your attitude. To pass up Egg and Lemon Soup Avgholemono or Lentil Soup Agathocles is never to know the taste of a real Greek soup.

CHICKEN SOUP

ΚΟΤΟΣΟΥΠΑ   (kotosoupa)

Greek women were not the only ones to start boiling chicken for soup at the first sign of illness. In every land and climate, chicken soup is considered an excellent remedy for fevers, colds, hangovers, queasy appetites, bad tempers, chills, and pregnancy.

1 chicken, or chicken parts (exclude livers)	2 teaspoons salt
	pepper to taste
3 quarts water	½ cup rice

Wash chicken with cold running water. Cover with water, add salt, and bring to a boil. Skim off the froth that floats to the top. Cover, reduce heat, and simmer 2 hours. Remove chicken from pot to a dish.

Pour broth over strainer into another clean pot. Bring strained broth to a rolling boil, add rice, stirring it in. Reduce heat to simmer for 40 minutes. Rice should be extra soft. Season with pepper if desired. Slice chicken, serve separately.

CHICKPEA SOUP

ΣΟΤΠΑ ΡΕΒΤΘΙΑ   (soupa revithia)

The yellow chickpea has been a favorite in Greece for so many centuries that the early Greeks thought the secret of preparing them had been revealed by Poseidon, god of the sea. Xenophanes of Colophon's idea of a romantic picture which he described in his play *The Parodies* was that of lying by the fire on a soft couch, sipping wine and munching roasted chickpeas. In this recipe the peas are made into a thick hearty purée.

1 pound chickpeas or garbanzo beans	2 teaspoons salt
3 onions, chopped	pepper to taste
1 bay leaf	¼ cup olive oil
2 quarts water	cruet of oil and vinegar

Cover chickpeas with cold water and bring to a boil. Reduce heat and simmer 15 minutes. Drain into colander and run cold water over peas. Transfer to a fresh bowl of water. Peel skins off by rubbing chickpeas gently between palms of hands. The skins should float to the top; remove and discard skins.

Cover skinned chickpeas, onions, and bay leaf with 2 quarts water and bring to a boil. Reduce heat and simmer slowly for 2½ hours, or until tender. (Add more water if a thinner soup is desired.) Add salt and oil the last 10 minutes of cooking time. Remove bay leaf. Blend soup in blender for 1 minute to make a thick smooth purée. Serve with cruet of olive oil and vinegar for individual seasoning at the table.

EGG AND LEMON SOUP AVGHOLEMONO

ΑΤΓΟΛΕΜΟΝΟ ΣΟΤΠΑ   (avgholemono soupa)

The secret of this famous Greek soup is in the Egg and Lemon Sauce that is mixed into it minutes before it is served. The trick is in mixing the sauce and avoiding its curdling when it hits the hot broth (explained here).

1 or 2 quarts Chicken Soup or canned chicken soup (diluted according to directions)	SAUCE: 3 eggs 2 lemons, juice only salt and pepper to taste

Bring soup to boil. Remove kettle from heat. Pour hot soup into a large bowl or tureen, to reduce the temperature. Beat eggs until thick and light. Add strained lemon juice slowly, beating all the while. Pour 1 cup hot soup into the egg mixture, stirring quickly with a spoon. Add a second cup. Pour egg sauce into soup, mixing it in quickly. Serve immediately. Do not cover. Do not boil again. If necessary to reheat, use the lowest heat possible. Serve with wedges of lemon and buttered toast.

GREEK VILLAGE BEAN SOUP

ΦΑΣΟΛΛΔΔ (fasolada)

This is the authentic Greek way of making bean soup, considered a complete meal in itself.

1 cup dried beans: white, broad, lima, lupines, or yellow or green split peas	2 carrots, chopped (optional)
	1 bay leaf
2 quarts cold water	¼ cup olive oil or 1 tablespoon butter
4 stalks celery, chopped	2 teaspoons salt
2 onions, chopped	pepper to taste

Bring beans to a boil in water. Reduce heat and simmer 1 hour. Add remaining ingredients, except salt and pepper, and simmer 1½ hours more or until beans are tender. Add salt the last 10 minutes of cooking time, and pepper to taste. Serve with crackers or toast and a cruet of olive oil and vinegar for individual seasoning.

BEAN PURÉE

ΠΟΤΡΕ (poureh)

Follow directions for Greek Village Bean Soup. When beans are tender, purée in blender or sieve and add liquid in which beans were boiled. Serve hot or cold, garnished with fresh chopped green onions. Serve with cruet of olive oil and vinegar for individual seasoning.

LAMB SOUP WITH EGG AND LEMON SAUCE

ΣΟΥΠΑ ΑΡΝΙΖΩΜΟΣ, ΑΥΓΟΛΕΜΟΝΟ   (soupa arnizomos avgholemono)

This tasty version of a Greek Easter soup, *mayeritsa,* is made during the year and is less complicated than the traditional version.

½ pound lean lamb meat and bones
½ pound lamb liver (optional)
2 quarts water
2 teaspoons salt
pepper to taste
1 cup rice or pasta: *orzo* (Rosa
   Marina) or *fides*

1 tablespoon dill, fresh preferably
   (optional)
1 teaspoon spearmint flakes

SAUCE:
3 eggs
2 lemons, juice only

Bring meats to a boil in salted water. Skim off froth and fat which floats to top. Reduce heat and simmer 2 hours. Remove meat and chop into fine pieces; discard bones.

Strain broth, return to clean pot and bring to a boil. To remove all fat, place broth in refrigerator until fat congeals on top and can be lifted off easily with a spatula. Add rice or pasta, salt, pepper, and herbs. Reduce heat and simmer on medium heat for 40 minutes. Add chopped meat to hot soup, and pour into a large bowl or tureen.

Make sauce by beating eggs until thick. Add lemon juice to eggs, beating all the while. Add 1 cup broth to sauce. Mix sauce into soup quickly and serve immediately.

LEEK SOUP ROUMELI

ΠΡΑΣΣΟΣΟΥΠΑ   (prassosoupa)

2 leeks, sliced, stems and bulbs included
2 potatoes, diced
¼ pound mushrooms, sliced
2 tablespoons olive oil or butter

2 quarts chicken broth, or water
   flavored with chicken base
1 egg
2 tablespoons milk or cream

Rinse leeks and mushrooms in running water. Brush off tops and stems of mushrooms with brush; do not peel. Slice leeks into 1″ inch pieces and separate rings in basin of water to rinse thoroughly. Peel potatoes and dice.

Heat oil in a deep pot, cook vegetables over medium heat for 5 minutes, stirring all the while. Add water and chicken base (or broth) and bring to a boil. Reduce heat. Cover and cook on medium heat for 30 minutes. Remove from heat. Whisk egg and milk with fork and stir into soup.

LENTIL SOUP AGATHOCLES

ΣΟΥΠΑ ΦΑΚΗ   (soupa faki)

The cook who introduced lentils to Agathocles of Sicily in the 3rd century B.C. received great honors and so should the modern cook who makes this delicious dish. Try to purchase the tiny red lentils grown in Lagovouni, southeast of Kertezi, Peloponnesus. Be as the Stoic philosophers suggested, "The wise man will do all things right, including the seasoning of lentil soup."

1 cup lentils	1 bay leaf
1 quart water	2 teaspoons salt
2 onions, chopped	pepper to taste
1 tablespoon olive oil	vinegar and olive oil

Examine lentils for bits of sticks and tiny pebbles. Wash in cold water. Drain. Bring all ingredients, except salt, to a boil. Reduce heat to low; cover and simmer for 2 hours. Add salt the last 10 minutes of cooking time. (For a thinner soup, add more water.) Season each bowl with 1 teaspoon vinegar and 1 teaspoon olive oil, or serve cruet for individual seasoning, accompanied with toast, crust bread, or soda crackers; Greek olives and cheese.

LITTLE MEAT BARRELS SOUP

ΣΟΥΠΑ ΓΙΟΥΒΑΡΛΑΚΙΑ   (soupa youvarlakia)

Meat balls are traditionally shaped in the form of barrels or little fingers rather than balls. You will recognize the egg and lemon sauce that gives this meat soup its piquancy.

1 pound ground beef or lamb	1 cup flour to roll meatballs
1 onion, chopped fine	2 quarts water
¼ cup rice	1 tablespoon butter
1 teaspoon salt	
pepper to taste	SAUCE:
1 teaspoon spearmint flakes	3 eggs
1 cup parsley, finely chopped	2 lemons, juice only

Mix meat, onion, rice, salt, pepper, spearmint, and parsley and form tiny meatballs in the shape of little barrels. Roll in flour.

Bring water and butter to a rolling boil and drop meatballs gently into water. Reduce heat, cover, and simmer 1 hour.

Remove pot from fire. Make sauce: beat eggs until thick, add lemon juice and 1 cup of hot broth to eggs, and stir sauce into soup quickly. Serve immediately.

SPLIT PEA FAVA

ΦΑΒΑ Η ΣΟΥΠΑ ΜΕ ΜΠΙΖΕΛΙΑ   (fava e soupa meh bizelia)

Follow directions for *Greek Village Bean Soup,* page 55, substituting yellow or green split peas and using 1 quart water. Puree when cooked. Blend for 1 minute in blender or mash tender peas through sieve.

GREEK VEGETABLE SOUP

ΧΟΡΤΟΣΟΥΠΑ   (hortosoupa)

There is no word in Greek that corresponds to the English word "vegetables." The nearest word is "green groceries," *horta* meaning greens. Despite this problem of semantics, Greek women make a delicious vegetable soup.

1 pound soup bone with meat, or 2 tablespoons butter	2 onions, chopped
2 quarts cold water	2 potatoes, cubed
2 teaspoons salt	2 fresh tomatoes
3 carrots, chopped	1 bay leaf
4 celery stalks with leaves chopped	1 tablespoon flour

Make broth by boiling bones, water, and salt for 1 hour. Skim off frothy scum which floats to top. Strain broth and return to clean pot. If using butter to flavor broth, eliminate these first steps.

Add all vegetables and boil 1 hour. Dilute flour in ½ cup cold water and add to broth to thicken.

FARINACEOUS FOODS, CRACKED WHEAT, RICE, AND PASTAS

ΣΙΤΑΡΙΚΑ ΚΑΙ ΡΥΖΙ   (sitarika kai ryzi)

The ancient Greeks believed the gift of wheat, barley and other grains that came from Demeter, the goddess of fruitfulness, was the reason men did not live like wild animals. Greece has always been an agricultural country of peasants and herdsmen. Even today in the small villages each family grows its own wheat, corn, and barley, sowing, reaping and threshing it themselves, on pieces of land called *stremata* ΣΤΡΕΜΑΤΑ, a *strema* being about one quarter of an acre. The wheat is ground into a semolina from which egg noodles, trahana, and other pastas are made, as well as into flour for the basic staple of bread. Groats of both barley and wheat are pounded in mortars into fine, medium or coarse grinds and are boiled in broth or in sweetened milk as puddings.

Rice was introduced to Greece during the time of Alexander the Great (330 B.C.), who brought it from Persia. It had originated in India but the ancient Greeks at that time thought it came from Africa and called it the "Ethiopian grain that looked like melon seeds."

BOILED RICE PILAF

ΠΙΛΑΦΙ   (pilafi)

The Near East is united in agreement on this recipe (if on nothing else), and whether it is called *pilaffe* by the Persians, *pilau* by the Indians, or *pilav* by the Turks, the consensus is the same: each kernel of boiled rice must be separate from the others.

2 cups water or broth, meat or chicken	1 teaspoon salt
	white pepper, to taste
1 teaspoon chicken base or butter, if using water	1 cup rice, long grain converted

Always measure carefully. The proportions remain constant: For 2 cups rice, it becomes 4 cups water, etc. If using other kinds of rice, rinse with cold water first.

Bring seasoned water or broth to a rolling boil. Add rice slowly. Stir once or twice. Reduce heat, cover and simmer 25 minutes. The rice will be moist, tender, with each kernel separate. Serve with roast chicken or lamb.

TOMATO PILAFI

ΠΙΛΑΦΙ ΜΕ ΝΤΟΜΑΤΑ   (pilafi meh domata)

Missing from this delicious Mediterranean *paella* is saffron, the spice from the orange-red stigma of the saffron crocus, which the Spanish and French cooks use so profusely. At one time, saffron was a favorite perfume of the hetaeriae of ancient Greece and used in their scented salves. The Greeks used saffron in medicines rather than food.

2 tablespoons each butter and oil	pepper to taste
2 onions, chopped	1 teaspoon sugar
1 clove garlic, minced	1 pound raw or cooked meat:
½ green bell pepper, slivered	chicken, beef, pork, etc.
1 cup tomatoes, canned or fresh	2 cups rice, preferably long grain
3 cups chicken broth	1 pound or 2 cups mixed seafood, raw
½ cup wine	or cooked: shrimp, lobster, crab,
2 teaspoons salt	clams, etc.

Heat butter and oil in large skillet. Fry onions, garlic, and green pepper for 5 minutes over medium heat. If meat is raw, cut in small pieces and add at this time. Fry for 10 minutes. Add tomatoes, broth, wine, and seasonings. Bring to a boil. Add rice. Stir once or twice and cover. Reduce heat to simmer for 20 minutes. Stir once or twice to avoid sticking. Add seafood and cooked meat and cook 10 minutes more. SERVES 8. Serve hot with salad.

For other rice recipes, see: Byzantine Dolmathes (page 89), Egg and Lemon Soup Avgholemono (page 54), Greek Rice Pudding (page 175), Lamb Soup (page 56), Macedonian Rice Stuffing (page 124), Taverna Chicken with Tomato Sauce and Rice (page 67), Roast Lamb with Rice (page 138), Spinach and Rice Stew (page 95), Stuffed Cabbage (page 84), Stuffed Squid Piraeus (page 108).

CRACKED WHEAT

ΣΙΤΑΡΙ/ΠΛΥΓΟΤΡΙ   (sitari/pligouri)

Cracked wheat may be used wherever rice or pasta is suggested and is delicious as a pilafi, simmered in meat or chicken broth.

1 cup cracked wheat
3 cups broth, chicken or meat
½ teaspoon salt

white pepper to taste
grated Kefaloteri or Parmesan
cheese

Cover cracked wheat with cold water to soak for 1 hour. Bring seasoned broth to a boil and add wheat, stirring it in. Reduce heat and simmer for 25 minutes. Serve grated cheese separately as topping.

MANI WEDDING WHEAT

ΜΑΝΙΑΤΙΚΟ ΣΙΤΑΡΙ ΤΟΤ ΓΑΜΟΤ   (maniatiko sitari tou gamou)

Few tourists visit that part of Greece known as the "Bad Mountains" where the Maniotes live, and even fewer receive an invitation to partake in their wedding festivities. These stern people have a reputation to match the rugged Peloponnesus mountains where the forbidding Laconian crags of Morea provide a natural fortress to protect their primitive way of life. Their pride is so fierce that they are known as *kakovoulia* meaning "bad advice," and their resistance to new ideas is legendary; they were the last of the Greek people to embrace Christianity, and were converted as late as the ninth century.

1 cup cracked wheat
¼ cup olive oil
1 pound lamb meat, in 2" chunks
1 onion, chopped
1 clove garlic, minced

1 teaspoon salt
⅛ teaspoon pepper
1 teaspoon each, fresh or dried,
  spearmint, oregano, and thyme
4 cups water

Cover cracked wheat with water to soak for 1 hour. Meanwhile, heat oil and brown meat, onion, and garlic for 10 minutes. Add seasonings and herbs and 2 cups water. Simmer 1½ hours until meat is tender.

Add 2 more cups hot water, bring to a rolling boil, and add strained cracked wheat. Cook 30 minutes or longer, until soft. Serve with yogurt.

SPAGHETTI WITH BROWN BUTTER SAUCE

MAKAPONIA ME BOTTTPO   (makaronia meh kafto voutiro)

The Greeks learned the art of making pasta when the Italians came to Greece in the 1300s. It was a secret which Marco Polo had brought from the Far East. Greeks serve macaroni with its many variations frequently, often as an accompaniment to roasted meat or fowl.

1 pound spaghetti or any other macaroni product	**½ cup Kefaloteri or Parmesan grated cheese**
½ pound butter	

Fill a large deep pot ¾ full with water. Add salt and bring to a rolling boil. Add pasta slowly, without breaking the boil. Cook 10 minutes. Place a colander in sink and turn pasta into it. Rinse under hot running water, allowing the water to drain through the spaghetti.

Heat butter in a small saucepan to a honey brown. Watch it carefully for these few minutes; it burns quickly and suddenly. Return spaghetti to large pot and dribble hot butter over it. Sprinkle with half the cheese and toss gently to mix.

Transfer to a large ovenproof platter, sprinkle top with more cheese and bake for ten minutes at 350° F. Serve hot.

MEAT AND MACARONI PASTITSO

ΠΑΣΤΙΤΣΟ   (pastitso)

This Greek version of baked macaroni is a favorite recipe for family or holiday meals. You'll also find it served frequently on Greek ships as part of the elegant buffet suppers.

2 teaspoons salt
1 pound elbow macaroni or other
   pasta
¼ pound butter or ½ cup olive oil

FILLING:
1 pound ground beef or lamb
2 onions, chopped
½ teaspoon salt
pepper to taste
⅛ teaspoon cinnamon
1 teaspoon oregano
½ cup red wine (optional)
½ cup tomato sauce

2 cups hot water

WHITE SAUCE:
3 tablespoons cornstarch
½ cup cold water
3 cups milk
¼ teaspoon salt
4 eggs, beaten

TOPPING:
2 cups grated cheese, such as
   Kefaloteri, Parmesan, or Cheddar
cinnamon

Fill a large pot ¾ full with water and bring to a rolling boil. Add salt and pasta and cook 10 minutes. Drain in colander and rinse under hot running water.

Melt 2 tablespoons butter in skillet and fry meat and onions on medium heat for 5 minutes. Add remaining filling ingredients and cover. Cook for 15 minutes.

Make white sauce: (page 69). Beat in all the eggs at one time.

Pour half of the remaining melted butter in a square baking pan and swirl to cover bottom. Add half of the pasta, spreading it evenly. Add the meat filling, distributing it evenly, and sprinkle 1 cup grated cheese. Add the second layer of pasta. Pour cream sauce over top. Sprinkle evenly with remaining cheese, any remaining butter, and cinnamon. Bake 45 minutes at 350° F.

NOODLES MESSINIA

ΧΤΛΟΠΗΤΕΣ   (hilopittes)

A common sight in Kalamara, near Kalamata, is that of noodle dough drying out in the hot sun. You can make a smaller batch with far less work and once you discover how simple it is to make this recipe, you won't buy packaged noodles ever again.

2 large eggs
½ teaspoon salt
2 tablespoons water

1½ cups flour, or cream of wheat
   (farina, semolina)

Mix eggs, salt and water together with fork or whisk. Add flour and knead into a firm smooth dough. Put into a plastic bag and let ripen at room temperature for one hour.

Divide into 2 pieces and roll out each piece, using a rolling pin or a wooden dowel, as thinly as possible. Flour board and hands lightly. As you finish each layer, set aside or hang it over a towel on a chair for one hour to dry a little.

Return layers to cutting board. Roll each layer up loosely as for a swirl roll and cut across with sharp knife into strips ¼" or ½" wide.

To Cook: Bring 2 quarts of chicken broth or salted water to a boil. Add noodles. Boil 8 to 10 minutes, or until tender.

NOODLES TRAHANAS

ΤΡΑΧΑΝΑΣ   (trahanas)

Shepherds originated these sun-dried noodles as an instant food. While tending their flocks, they could quickly prepare a filling soup by dropping a handful of yogurt noodles into boiling water. Packaged under the name "Trahana," they can be purchased in shops which carry foods of the Middle European countries. There are two kinds of Trahana: "sweet," made with milk and "sour," made with yogurt.

1 egg
½ teaspoon salt
½ cup yogurt (for sour) or milk (for sweet)

1½ cups farina, cream of wheat (semolina)

Mix in a bowl with fork or whisk the egg, salt, and liquid. Add farina and knead into a stiff dough. Roll between palms and break into tiny pieces or press dough through a sieve onto a dry baking pan. Bake in a slow oven at 200° F. for 2 to 3 hours. After the first hour remove pan from oven and with spatula break up the noodles and turn over. Break up any large pieces between palms. Return to oven and continue drying. After turning off oven, allow to dry overnight.

Grind with blender or crush with rolling pin into a coarse meal. Cook immediately or store in a jar to use at a later time; it keeps indefinitely.

To Cook: Bring a quart of water to a boil. Add ⅛ teaspoon salt or chicken base and boil for 10 minutes or until tender. Use as any other noodles. When you serve it with egg and lemon sauce it becomes TRAHANAS LAMIA.

MANESTRA

ΜΑΝΕΣΤΡΑ   (manestra)

Manestra, also known as *orzo,* is a pasta, shaped like cantaloupe seeds. It can be boiled and served buttered with cheese or cooked in meat sauces. This is a typical recipe, cooked in all regions of Greece but particularly favored in the islands.

1 tablespoon oil
1 pound beef or lamb stew meat (or
  pieces of chicken) (optional)
2 onions, chopped
1 cup tomato sauce or 1 tablespoon
  tomato paste
1 teaspoon salt

⅛ teaspoon pepper
⅛ teaspoon cinnamon
1 teaspoon spearmint flakes
4 cups boiling water
1 cup *manestra* (*orzo*) or other small
  pasta
1 cup grated cheese

Heat oil in large saucepan and brown meat and onions for 10 minutes over medium heat. Add tomato, seasonings, and 2 cups water. Cover and simmer for 1½ hours until meat is tender.

Add remaining water and bring to boil. Add *manestra.* Stir once or twice. Simmer 20 minutes more. Serve hot with grated cheese.

For other recipes using pasta, see: Lemon Chicken with Manestra (page 116), Greek Lamb with Manestra (page 138), Taverna Chicken with Tomato Sauce and Pasta (page 119), or Lamb Soup (page 56).

SAUCES AND SALAD DRESSINGS

ΣΑΛΤΣΕΣ   (saltses)

Greek cooking does not involve complicated sauces. Often the pan juices of cooked meat or fowl, flavored with lemon juice, will be the only sauce served as an accompaniment. Vegetables are never creamed, although they are often cooked in a tomato sauce and served in the same sauce in which they were cooked. If there is a national sauce of Greece, it is Egg and Lemon Sauce— an ancient recipe which in all probability was the precursor of mayonnaise. This sauce is poured over soups, meats, fish, fowl, and vegetables.

BROWN BUTTER

ΚΑΤΤΟ ΒΟΤΤΤΡΟ   (kafto voutiro)

The secret of this sauce is in knowing when the melting butter has reached the right color, which can best be described as "medium toast." Turn your back on it to reach for something and that second may be too late.

½ pound butter (to serve four)

Melt over medium heat, watching it as it goes from a golden yellow oil with a white foam on top to a tan, then a deeper tan. Stir with a spoon for even cooking. Take pan off fire before it darkens too deeply. Use as a sauce over boiled pasta, rice or wheat, and as a dip for boiled artichokes, asparagus, and seafood.

EGG AND LEMON SAUCE

ΣΑΛΤΣΑ ΑΓΓΟΛΕΜΟΝΟ   (saltsa avgholemono)

This famous Hellenic sauce can transform ordinary chicken soup and boiled vegetables into extraordinary fare.

3 eggs   1 cup hot broth
juice of 2 lemons, strained

Beat eggs until thick and light yellow, at least 5 minutes, with an electric beater or 10 to 15 minutes by hand. Use your drink mixer if you have one. Add juice slowly, beating all the while. Mix 1 cup hot broth from prepared soup or stew into beaten eggs, stirring it in quickly with spoon so heat will not curdle the eggs. Transfer hot food for which sauce is being prepared into a serving bowl and pour sauce over it.

Serve immediately. Do not cover pot or dish. Do not reboil. If you must reheat, do so at very low heat. For recipes using this sauce, see: Chicken Soup (page 53), Easter Soup, Mayeritsa (page 209), Lamb Soup (page 56), Stuffed Grape Leaves (page 89), Little Meat Barrels Soup (page 57), Lamb and Celery Stew (page 139).

GREEK TOMATO SAUCE

ΣΑΛΤΣΑ ΝΤΟΜΑΤΑ   (saltsa domata)

The tomato is a comparative newcomer to Greek cooking. It was introduced at the turn of the 20th century by French and Italian cooks and today this vegetable from South America forms the base for countless Greek recipes.

2 tablespoons oil   1 teaspoon sugar
1 onion, chopped   2 teaspoons salt
1 clove garlic, minced   ⅛ teaspoon pepper
1 can tomatoes or tomato purée   ½ teaspoon each: sweet basil,
2 ounce can tomato paste   oregano, cinnamon, parsley, spear-
   (optional)   ment flakes
4 cups water   1 bay leaf
½ cup wine or 1 tablespoon vinegar

Heat oil in pan. Fry onion and garlic for 3 minutes. Add remaining ingredients. Bring to a boil, reduce heat to low, and simmer 45 minutes. Stir occasionally. Serve as a sauce for pasta or rice or use as a base for casseroles.

TOMATO SAUCE WITH MEAT

ΣΑΛΤΣΑ ΜΕ ΚΡΕΑΣ   (saltsa meh kreas)

Add 1 pound ground beef or lamb with the onion in above recipe and continue as directed.

GARLIC SAUCE

ΣΚΟΡΔΑΛΙΑ   (skordalia)

This sauce is considered to be an excellent cold preventative. It's not difficult to understand why; no one will come near you after you eat it.

¼ cup water
5 cloves garlic
½ teaspoon salt
1 cup mashed potatoes or 4 slices
   fresh bread

½ cup walnuts, pine nuts or almonds
   (optional)
2 tablespoons vinegar and ½ cup
   olive oil, or ½ cup mayonnaise and
   1 teaspoon vinegar

Put ingredients in order listed in blender and blend until smooth. Serve chilled as a sauce over fish, meat, or vegetables.

NATURAL PAN GRAVY

ΣΑΛΤΣΑ   (saltsa)

The Greek cook never throws away the natural drippings of juices from baked, broiled, or fried meats, fowl or fish. Crusty Greek bread is always delicious for dipping in this gravy, family style.

juice of 1 lemon   dash of salt and pepper to taste
½ cup boiling water

After removing cooked meat, fish, or fowl from pan, add above ingredients to the drippings and return to fire for 3 minutes. Pour over meats or serve in separate bowls with slices of bread for family-style dipping at the table.

OIL AND LEMON DRESSING

ΛΑΔΟΛΕΜΟΝΟ, ΛΑΔΟΞΕΙΔΟ   (ladolemono) (ladoksitho)

Restaurants often list foods with this dressing as *à la Grecque.* It occurs over and over in Greek cooking.

½ cup olive oil (or diluted olive oil if   ¼ teaspoon salt
  preferred)   dash of white pepper, to taste
juice of 1 lemon or 2 tablespoons   ¼ teaspoon oregano
  vinegar

   Mix ingredients with a few whisks of fork just before ready to serve. Use over hot or cold vegetables, fresh greens, fish, olives. It is also an excellent marinade for meats and fish.
   Variation for salad greens: Mix in 1 egg and 2 tablespoons grated Parmesan, Kefaloteri or blue cheese.

WHITE SAUCE

ΛΕΥΚΗ ΚΡΕΜΑ   (lefke crema)

White sauce, first whipped up by a Greek *maygeros* (chef) named Orion 3000 years ago, is one of the world's classic recipes. The ancient Greeks used it frequently over fish, vegetables and various meats but the modern Greek prefers it only as a topping on casseroles.

2 tablespoons cornstarch   1 tablespoon butter
½ cup cold water   1½ teaspoons salt
2 cups milk   1 egg, well beaten

   Dilute cornstarch in cold water and set aside. Bring milk, butter, and salt to a boil over medium heat. Add diluted cornstarch, stirring as it thickens. Remove from heat. Add some sauce to beaten egg, then add egg to sauce, mixing it in well. Use in recipes such as Meat and Macaroni Pastitso (page 62), Baked Eggplant Moussaka (page 88), Custard Pie (page 156).

CHEESE SAUCE

ΚΡΕΜΑ ΜΕ ΤΥΡΙ   (krema meh teree)

Recipe for White Sauce
½ cup grated cheese, either
**   Kefaloteri, Parmesan, Cheddar, or**
**   other**

Follow recipe for White Sauce. Add cheese to sauce after adding cornstarch and stir in until melted and blended. Continue as above.

YOGURT SALAD DRESSING

ΓΙΑΟΥΡΤΗ ΜΑΓΙΟΝΝΕΖΑ   (yaourti mayoneza)

This is a tart, tangy dressing for lettuce and other greens. Try it over endive.

1 cup yogurt   **½ teaspoon each: mustard (dry);**
1 teaspoon vinegar   **   oregano, salt, sugar**
1 clove garlic   **dash of pepper to taste**
2 oz. blue cheese (optional)

Blend ingredients together. Let stand 1 hour before serving. Keep refrigerated. Use on any leafy fresh vegetable, endive, or cooked vegetables.

GREEK SALADS

ΕΛΛΗΝΙΚΕΣ ΣΑΛΑΤΕΣ   (ellenehkes salates)

Greek salads are the heart of a Greek meal. The high regard for salad vegetables can be understood when one realizes that although the Greeks have a word for everything, the word for vegetable is ΣΑΛΑΤΙΚΑ (*salatica*), which translates literally as "salad vegetables." All vegetables, hot or cold, raw or boiled, with or without dressings, are considered *salatica,* and a meal without a vegetable is no meal at all.

VEGETABLES, GREEK STYLE

ΣΑΛΑΤΙΚΑ ΛΑΔΟΛΕΜΟΝΟ   (salatica ladolemono)

The addition of olive oil, lemon juice or vinegar, and a bit of crushed oregano will turn any boiled vegetable into a Greek salad. In Greece, it is the most common way of eating vegetables. Use any canned, fresh, or frozen vegetable:

artichokes, hearts
asparagus, whole or pieces
beans, boiled
green beans, sliced
beets, whole or sliced
broccoli, flowerets
Brussels sprouts, whole
cabbage, chopped
cauliflower, flowerets
eggplant, pieces (see directions below)
leeks, sliced
okra, whole
sweet green peppers, slivers (see directions below)
spinach, chopped or leaf

all green leafy vegetables such as Swiss chard, dandelions, mustard, kale, collards, etc.
summer squash, preferably zucchini
tomatoes
salt and pepper to taste
¼ cup chopped onions or scallions
1 teaspoon oregano
1 teaspoon spearmint flakes
¼ cup olive oil and juice of ½ lemon
Oil and lemon dressing (see page 69),
                              or
Yogurt Salad Dressing (see page 70)

If using fresh vegetable, boil it in salted water until soft. Drain liquid. If using frozen, follow directions on package and add 4 minutes to the recommended cooking time. Vegetables must be soft for eating in the Greek way.

To prepare eggplant and green peppers, bake in a shallow baking dish in 375° F. oven for 30 minutes, or until tender. Then plunge into cold water to loosen skin, and peel carefully. Sprinkle vegetable with scallions, oregano and mint and choice of dressing. Serve warm, tepid, or slightly chilled.

CUCUMBER SALAD WITH YOGURT

ΤΣΑΤΖΙΚΙ   (tsatziki)

Here is a cool and refreshing salad, popular in Greece where there are many hot days.

2 or more cucumbers, peeled and
   thinly sliced

DRESSING:
1 cup yogurt

1 teaspoon vinegar
1 teaspoon spearmint flakes
1 teaspoon scallions, chopped
½ teaspoon sugar
salt and pepper to taste

Mix cucumbers in sauce and serve chilled.

GREEK LETTUCE SALAD

ΜΑΡΟΥΛΟΣΑΛΑΤΑ ΑΝΑΜΙΚΤΗ   (maroulosalata anamikti)

All the vegetables in a true Greek salad are finely cut with a knife, never torn. The secret of making a crisp salad is in the timing. Serve it immediately after adding the oil dressing.

1 head firm Iceberg lettuce, finely cut
¼ onion or 4 scallions, finely
   chopped
¼ green bell pepper, slivered
¼ cup parsley, finely cut with
   scissors
6 radishes, sliced
2 tomatoes, cubed
1 cucumber, peeled, cut thin
2 stalks celery, finely chopped

DRESSING:
¼ cup olive oil
1 tablespoon vinegar
⅛ teaspoon salt
pepper to taste
1 teaspoon oregano

GARNISHES:
8 Greek olives
3 anchovies or boneless sardines
   (optional)
½ cup cubed Feta cheese

Cut lettuce in half from top to base. Lay flat on board and cut across for medium shredding. Put into large bowl, preferably wooden, and add vegetables.

Mix oil and vinegar and pour over salad. Sprinkle with salt, pepper, and oregano. Crush oregano by pinching between fingers. Toss once or twice. Serve immediately in individual bowls and place garnishes on top. Or, if serving buffet, serve in large bowl with garnishes on top but wait until the last possible moment to add dressing. Be generous. Do not worry about tossing it—guests will do that as they help themselves.

LETTUCE SALAD WITH FETA CHEESE

ΜΑΡΟΥΛΟΣΑΛΑΤΑ ΜΕ ΦΕΤΑ   (maroulosalata meh feta)

Diphilus, the respected Ancient Greek physician, considered lettuce inhibiting to the sexual drive but that didn't stop the hedonistic philosopher Aristoxenus, who thought pleasure in living to be the total sum of life, from watering the lettuce in his garden with wine and honey.

1 head crisp lettuce, finely cut   **¼ cup olive oil**
¼ pound Feta cheese, crumbled   **salt and pepper to taste**

Cut lettuce in half from top to base. Lay flat on board and cut across for medium shredding. Cut vertically once more into fine pieces. Put into a bowl. Sprinkle with remaining ingredients and toss. Serve in individual bowls with crisp hot bread or toast.

TOMATO SALAD SANTORINI

ΝΤΟΜΑΤΟΣΑΛΑΤΑ   (domatasalata Santorini)

On a hot summer day, there is nothing more inviting than this easy-to-prepare salad. Try it when tomatoes are plentiful and ripe, or when visiting Santorini where the rich volcanic soil produces the sweetest tomatoes in all Greece.

8 medium-size ripe tomatoes   **salt and pepper to taste**
½ onion or 5 scallions, chopped   **1 teaspoon oregano**
1 cucumber, peeled, thinly sliced   **¼ cup olive oil**

Peel tomatoes, if you are in the mood, but it's not necessary.

(To make peeling an easier chore, plunge the tomato into hot water for a minute.) Cut into small pieces directly into a bowl.

Add remaining ingredients and toss lightly. Let stand 10 minutes before serving at room temperature—this salad is best when it is not chilled. Serve in individual salad bowls with slices of bread for dipping into sauce, family style. This salad is especially good with broiled chops.

PICKLED VEGETABLE SALAD

ΤΟΥΡΣΙ   (toursi)

This piquant vegetable salad recipe can be made with great variety, depending on the different kinds of vegetables used.

Include any or all of the following kinds of raw vegetables in any amount you wish:

artichokes, hearts
asparagus, pieces
broccoli, flowerets
carrots, strips
cauliflower, flowerets
celeriac, chunks
celery, strips
eggplant, chunks
mushrooms, sliced or buttons
okra, whole
onions, tiny whole

radishes, sliced or halved
sweet bell peppers, strips
gherkins or sliced sweet pickles
olives, both green and black
salted water to cover, proportion: 1
    teaspoon salt to 1 cup water
vinegar to cover
3 garlic cloves, split in threes
1 tablespoon mixed pickling spices
1 or more cups olive oil

Clean and prepare vegetables. Bring salted water to a boil in a large pot and plunge vegetables into boiling water for 2 minutes. Drain in colander. Place in bowl or into clean jar and fill with vinegar to the ¾ mark. Add garlic, spices, and olive oil.

Cover or seal and set aside to marinate for a few days or a week. Once in a while, stir with spoon or, if packed in jars, turn jars over to distribute oil and spices. Serve slightly chilled.

WILD BULBS SALAD VORVI

ΒΟΡΒΙΑ ΣΑΛΑΤΑ   (vourvia salata)

Wild grape hyacinths, *muscari,* grow profusely on the rocky terrain of Greece. You'll see bright blue flowers four or five inches high growing everywhere. The bulbs of this delicate plant are considered edible. They have a slightly bitter although refreshing flavor.

During the spring, fresh bulbs are imported from Greece and can be bought in the United States in Greek specialty food shops. Bottled *vorvi* can be found all year round.

1 pound grape hyacinth (*muscari* variety) bulbs, (vorvi)
4 scallions, chopped
¼ cup olive oil

1 tablespoon vinegar or lemon juice
1 teaspoon each oregano and spearmint flakes (optional)
salt and pepper to taste

Peel and clean bulbs. Cover with salted water and boil for 45 minutes, until tender. Drain. Sprinkle with scallions, dressing and remaining ingredients. Serve warm or slightly chilled.

BOILED WILD GREENS

ΒΡΑΣΤΑ ΑΓΡΙΑ ΧΟΡΤΑ   (vrasta agria horta)

During a Sunday drive in the country, you may have noticed a neat well-dressed old lady, perhaps in black, digging in fields by the roadside. She works alone while the occupants of a nearby car wait for her. Chances are you have witnessed the spring rite of a Greek woman. She has discovered a patch of tender mustard greens (*sinapia*) or dandelions (*radikia*) or perhaps some other favorite wild greens native to her countryside; *paparonis, strouthula, galafthia, melalithria, mironia, vlita,* and *lapata* at their most delicious moment, before they flower and become too bitter to cook. The tender plants are dug up, sometimes roots and all, and taken home to be boiled that very night.

1 bunch of any of the following wild greens:
Dandelions ΡΑΔΙΚΙΑ (radikia)
Mustard ΣΙΝΑΠΙΑ (sinapia)
        or
1 pound of the following domestic greens:
Beet greens or tops ΠΑΤΖΑΡΟΦΥΛΛΑ (patzarofila)
Cress ΚΑΡΔΑΜΟ (kardamo)
Endive or escarole ΑΝΤΙΔΙΑ (antidia)
Sorrel ΞΥΝΙΘΡΑ (ksinithra)

Spinach ΣΠΑΝΑΚΙ (spanaki)
Swiss chard ΣΕΣΚΟΤΛΑ (seskoula)

1 quart water	**olive oil**
¼ teaspoon salt	**quartered lemon slices**
pepper to taste	

Cut the root system of each plant at the base so leaves will separate. Fill a sink with cold water and wash leaves thoroughly by agitating the water with your hands. Take greens out and drain water from sink. Fill sink twice again with fresh cold water and rinse greens a second and third time.

Put wild greens in a l rge kettle filled with plenty of salted water. Use 1 cup of water fo domestic greens. Cover and boil rapidly for 20 minutes, or until tender. Drain. Serve hot or cold with cruet of olive oil and quartered slices of lemon for individual seasoning.

THE MEDITERRANEAN VEGETABLES

ΧΟΡΤΑΡΙΚΑ (hortarika)

Many of these vegetables originated in the Mediterranean regions or in Asia and have spread from there to Europe and on to the rest of the world. The Greeks have even personalized certain vegetables within the idiom of their language. Instead of saying "Rubbish!" they will say, "Squash with oregano!" ΚΟΛΟΚΗΘΙ ΜΕ ΡΙΓΑΝΙ (kolokithe meh rigani). There's a phrase to describe something that is worthless: "It's not worth one cucumber" ΔΕΝ ΑΞΙΖΕΙ ΕΝΑ ΑΓΓΟΥΡΙ (den ahxeasy ena ahngouree). To belittle the pretentious, or cut someone down to size, a Greek will say, "How magnificent is the cabbage." ΣΠΟΥΔΑΙΑ ΤΑ ΛΑΧΑΝΑ (spoutheya ta lahana).

These recipes are served either hot or tepid; rarely are they chilled. In planning a menu, you will discover that these dishes are interchangeable and may be used as a salad, as side dishes or as the main vegetable dish. A stew or a bean recipe may be the main course.

ARTICHOKES PELOPONNESUS

ΑΓΚΙΝΑΡΕΣ   (aginares)

The magnificent coastline of Western Peloponnesus from Patras to Pyrgos is filled with the silvery foliage of globe artichokes. Each town in this region has its own way of preparing this delicious sweet, green vegetable. The edible parts of the fresh artichoke are the stem, the white fleshy part at the base of the leaves and the heart. The inedible parts are the tips of the leaves which have thorns, and the fuzz over the heart which is called the "choke." Select firm crisp artichokes, the tips of which are curled tightly together.

To Prepare

Cut off ¼ inch from bottom of stem. Snap off at least eight outer leaves at the base, going once around the whole artichoke. Lay artichoke on wooden board. Slice off top, about 1" down from top, using sharp knife or kitchen scissors. Cut in half, from top through stem. Using a small paring knife, trim off fuzz. (Do not cut too deeply or you will be wasting some of the heart.) Cut away some of the tiny purplish leaves surrounding the heart; the tips have sharp thorns. To keep artichokes from discoloring while you prepare them, put the cleaned halves in a bowl of water with lemon juice and 1 tablespoon of flour.

To Parboil Artichokes

Cover prepared artichokes with salted water and lemon juice and boil rapidly for 30 minutes. Drain. Use in Fried Artichokes (page 79) or Fried Artichoke Patties (page 79).

BOILED WHOLE ARTICHOKES

ΒΡΑΣΤΕΣ ΑΓΚΙΝΑΡΕΣ   (vrastes aginares)

1 artichoke per person
1 cup water per artichoke
1 teaspoon salt
1 tablespoon lemon juice, or vinegar

Recommended sauces:
Brown Butter Sauce (page 66)
Oil and Vinegar Dressing (page 69)
Yogurt Dressing (page 70)
Mayonnaise
Cruet of olive oil and lemon wedges

Rinse artichokes. Leave whole. Cut stems off at base so they can sit upright on plate. Arrange artichokes in pot and partially cover with salted water and lemon juice or vinegar. Bring to a boil, cover and cook for 35 to 45 minutes, until tender.

Drain well. Serve individually on plates, with leaves pointing upwards. Serve small cup of melted butter sauce, mayonnaise or cruet of oil and lemon wedges, according to preference.

To eat: peel off each leaf, dip the bottom end in sauce and bite off the tender part. Pile discarded leaves on one side of plate or on extra dish. Serve hot as a vegetable, cold as a salad. Artichoke plates are available, specifically designed to hold the artichoke, the discarded leaves, and the sauce.

FRIED ARTICHOKES

ΑΓΚΙΝΑΡΕΣ ΤΗΓΑΝΙΤΕΣ   (aginares tiganistes)

If you have never tasted artichokes prepared in this manner, you have a treat in store.

Allow 1 or 2 small or medium artichokes, per person; or 2 packages frozen artichoke hearts	2 cups bread crumbs, finely crushed
	1 cup oil
2 eggs, well beaten	2 tablespoons butter
	salt and pepper to taste

Clean and parboil artichokes in manner described on page 78. If using frozen artichokes, parboil 10 minutes only. Drain well.

Roll each half in beaten egg, then in bread crumbs. Combine oil and butter in skillet, and heat. Fry breaded artichokes on both sides until brown over medium heat about 15 minutes total cooking time. Remove from oil, using slotted spoon. Drain. Salt and pepper while hot.

FRIED ARTICHOKE PATTIES

ΑΓΚΙΝΑΡΕΣ ΚΕΦΤΕΔΕΣ   (aginares keftedes)

The Greek woman from Argos who thought this was her secret will be surprised to discover how many Greeks know this delicious recipe.

6 artichokes or 3 packages frozen artichokes (or zucchini squash or spinach may be substituted)	1 clove garlic, pressed
	5 scallions, chopped or 1 onion, finely cut
3 eggs	½ cup chopped parsley
¼ teaspoon salt	1 cup fine bread crumbs
pepper to taste	1 cup oil for frying

Clean and parboil artichokes as described on page 78. Drain. Put artichokes or spinach or squash in a bowl and chop into small pieces. Add eggs, seasonings, scallions and parsley. Mix well. Make flat patties and roll in bread crumbs. Fry in hot oil 7 to 10 minutes, turning when golden brown. Drain on paper towels. Serve hot.

STUFFED ARTICHOKES

ΑΓΚΙΝΑΡΕΣ ΠΑΡΑΓΕΜΙΣΤΕΣ   (aginares parayemistes)

Allow 1 large artichoke per person. Use as filling: Greek Stuffed Vegetables (page 97) or Byzantine Dolmathes (page 89). Prepare as directed.

TOPPING: **½ cup grated cheese, Kefaloteri or**
1 cup bread crumbs   **Parmesan**
                                       Juice of 1 lemon

Use large artichokes. Cut off 12 outer leaves and stem at base. Parboil in salted water with 1 teaspoon vinegar for 20 minutes. Drain well. With a sharp spoon scoop out the choke or center part, leaving a well. Stuff with cooked prepared filling and top with combined bread crumbs and cheese. Place in baking pan. Add two cups water and lemon juice and bake 45 minutes at 350° F.

For other recipes with artichokes see: Greek Roast Lamb with Artichokes (page 138), Artichokes in Byzantine Pot Roast (page 131), Artichokes in Hellenic Pot Roast (page 131), Artichokes in Meat Stew with Egg and Lemon Sauce (page 132), Artichokes in Pickled Vegetable Salad (page 74).

ASPARAGUS

ΣΠΑΡΑΓΓΙΑ   (sparangia)

Wild asparagus was a favorite vegetable among the ancient Greeks who had a saying, "Let it be done quicker than you would cook asparagus."

1 bunch fresh asparagus   **cruet of olive oil**
2 cups water   **wedges of lemon**
salt and pepper to taste

Rinse asparagus in cold water. Snap off ends. Put asparagus with tips facing the same direction in a frying pan large enough to accommodate their full length. Add water and salt, cover and boil on high heat for 5 minutes. Turn off heat and leave in covered pan for a few minutes more if a softer texture is desired.

Place on oval platter, or asparagus dishes, tips facing same direction. Serve Greek style with cruet of olive oil and wedges of lemon for individual seasoning. Other suggested sauces are: Brown Butter Sauce (page 66) and Cheese Sauce (page 70).

BEANS

ΦΑΣΟΛΙΑ   (fasolia)

Despite all other instructions you have ever read, there is no need to soak dried beans overnight before cooking. Nor do you need to attend a Bean Boiling Festival in the month of *Pyanopsia* (October) as the ancient Greeks did when they honored the new crop of beans, to be assured they are fresh. You can be certain the beans you buy in today's markets are of this year's crop. The real secret of softening beans to a delicious tenderness is a slow simmer without salt. Use any dried beans in the legume family in these recipes:

Black-eyed, broad, ceci, fava, garbanzo, haricots, lentils, lupines, lima, mungo, navy, peas, yellow or split, pinto, red, red kidney, white, small and large.

BOILED BEANS PIAZI

ΒΡΑΣΤΑ ΦΑΣΟΛΙΑ ΠΙΑΖΙ   (vrasta fasolia piazi) (gigantes plaki)

2 cups beans, white, navy or pea (or any variety preferred)
1½ quarts cold water
1 teaspoon salt

2 or more chopped scallions or thinly sliced onion
pepper to taste
olive oil and vinegar to taste

Put beans in a pot and cover with cold water. Bring to a boil. Reduce to simmer, cover and cook for 2½ hours. Add salt the last 10 minutes. Drain. Mix beans with 1 tablespoon olive oil, and serve a cruet of olive oil and vinegar for individual seasoning.

BEAN PURÉE

ΦΑΣΟΛΙΑ ΠΟΤΡΕ   (fasolia poureh)

1 cup boiled beans, canned, or prepared according to directions on
  page 81
1 cup liquid from beans
¼ cup olive oil

salt and pepper to taste
1 tablespoon vinegar
¼ cup chopped scallions
1 teaspoon chopped dill

Follow recipe for boiling beans. When tender, blend beans in a blender for 30 seconds or force through a press. Mix in oil, salt, and vinegar with spoon and sprinkle dill and scallions on top. Serve hot or chilled with yogurt on the side.

Variation: Add 1 cup Tahini in blender with above ingredients for Tahini Bean Purée.

GREEK BAKED BEANS

ΦΑΣΟΛΙΑ ΠΛΑΚΙ   (fasolia plaki)

2 or more cups cooked beans

SAUCE:
¼ cup oil
2 onions, chopped
1 clove garlic, minced (optional)
2 tablespoons tomato paste or 1 cup
  tomato purée

2 tablespoons vinegar
3 tablespoons honey
2 cups hot water
1 bay leaf
2 whole cloves
¼ cup cheese, Kefaloteri or
  Parmesan

Boil beans according to directions on page 81. Drain.

Make sauce: Heat oil in a saucepan and fry onions until soft. Add remaining ingredients and bring to a boil. Mix sauce with beans and pour into a shallow pan. Bake 30 minutes in 375° F. oven. Sprinkle top with grated cheese.

BEETS

ΠΑΤΖΑΡΙΑ   (patzaria)

The ancient Greeks held this native Mediterranean vegetable in such high esteem that they made replicas of beets in silver. As for turnips, that vegetable was designed out of lead. Gold was reserved for radishes.

To prepare fresh beets: Cut off tops and set aside to boil separately. Wash whole beets in cold running water. Put in large pot, cover with salted water and bring to a rapid boil. Reduce heat to medium. Cover and cook 45 minutes, or until tender. Drain. Peel by slipping skins off. Slice or cut in cubes, and cover with a marinade of ¼ cup olive oil and ¼ cup vinegar.

BEET GREENS

ΠΑΤΖΑΡΟΦΥΛΛΑ   (patzarofila)

Rinse beet tops in water and follow recipe for Boiled Greens (page 75).

BROCCOLI

ΜΠΡΟΚΟΛΑ   (brokola)

This vegetable is native to eastern Mediterranean regions and is another food which the Greeks introduced to the Romans. Follow recipe for Vegetables, Greek Style (page 71).

CABBAGE, GREEK STYLE

ΛΑΧΑΝΟ   (lahano)

The Greeks have always believed that boiled cabbage had medicinal qualities. In ancient Athens it was prepared as an antidote for women in childbed. The Sybarites, renowned for their opulence and luxury throughout the ancient world of sixth century B.C., used to eat cabbage before drinking to prevent that "morning after" feeling which was inevitable from the kind of powerful undiluted wine they drank.

1 head of cabbage   **1 teaspoon salt**
water to cover   **cruet of olive oil and lemon wedges**

Cut a head of cabbage in half, then in thirds, making 6 sections altogether. Cover with water. Bring to a boil and cook 40 minutes. Add salt the last 10 minutes. Drain. Pass cruets of oil and lemon slices for seasoning at the table. Serve with sesame seed bread and slices of Feta or other cheeses as an accompaniment.

CABBAGE DOLMATHES

ΛΑΧΑΝΟ ΝΤΟΛΜΑΔΕΣ   (lahano dolmades)

The Celts stole this recipe from the Greeks in one of their invasions, 600 B.C., and gave this Greek vegetable its French name
of Caboche, meaning head.

1 head of cabbage

FILLING:
1 pound ground beef
1 onion, finely chopped
½ cup rice
1 egg
½ cup parsley, chopped
½ cup tomato sauce or juice

½ teaspoon salt
pepper to taste

SAUCES:
Tomato Sauce (see page 67)
or
**Egg and Lemon Sauce (see page
67)**

Cut out core from base of cabbage. Plunge whole cabbage
into boiling water and cook 10 minutes. Remove from water and
allow to cool a few minutes. Peel cabbage leaves off, one by one,
carefully. Trim off some of the thick stem, using a paring knife.
Lay each leaf on counter.

Mix ingredients for filling. Place a tablespoon of filling on each
leaf, near the end of the stem. Bring right side of leaf, then left
side, towards the center. Pick up stem and roll away from you, as
tightly as possible, covering filling with all the leaf. The rolls
should look like fat sausages.

Pack rolls snugly side by side in large skillet. Place plate on top
as weight. Add 3 cups water. Cover pot. Bring to a boil. Reduce
heat to simmer and cook 45 minutes. Serve plain or with suggested sauce.

CARROTS AND HONEY

ΚΑΡΡΟΤΟ ΜΕ ΜΕΛΙ   (karroto meh meli)

Centuries before Christianity, Diphlius, a noted Greek physician,
warned that eating carrots would arouse sexual desire. In spite of
this advice, or perhaps because of it, Greeks have continued to
add this native Mediterranean vegetable to their soups, stews and
in this favorite recipe.

**1 or 2 pounds carrots, peeled and
sliced; if tiny leave whole**
water to cover
salt and pepper to taste

½ cup honey or orange preserves
¼ cup butter
1 teaspoon mint

Cover carrots with water. Bring to a boil. Cover. Reduce heat to medium, cover, and cook for 20 minutes, or until soft. Drain. Melt butter and honey until it bubbles. Add carrots and mint and ladle syrup over them. Transfer to serving dish.

CAULIFLOWER, GREEK STYLE

ΚΟΥΝΟΥΠΙΔΙ   (kounoupidi)

In 1586, cauliflower was called Cyprus cabbage or colewort in England after its introduction there but boiled cauliflower was not a new recipe to Cyprus where it had originated thousands of years before.

1 head of cauliflower or 2 packages frozen 2 cups water ¼ teaspoon salt	Any *one* of the following sauces: Oil & Lemon Dressing (page 69) Brown Butter Sauce (page 66) Cheese Sauce (page 70) Egg and Lemon Sauce (page 67)

Make 6 cuts, 2″ deep into the stem of a head of cauliflower. Break apart into flowerets. Bring water to a boil. Add salt and vegetable. Cover pot and boil rapidly on high heat for 15 minutes, 8 minutes if frozen. Drain. Serve with any dressing listed.

PICKLED CAULIFLOWER TOURSI

ΚΟΥΝΟΥΠΙΔΙ ΛΛΔΟΞΕΙΔΟ   (kounoupidi ladoksido)

Follow recipe for Pickled Vegetables Toursi (page 74) using only the following vegetables: cauliflower, onion, carrots, green and red sweet peppers.

See also, Vegetables, Greek Style (page 71).

CELERY WITH EGG AND LEMON SAUCE

ΣΕΛΙΝΟ ΑΥΓΟΛΕΜΟΝΟ   (selino avgholemono)

Wild celery, a native Mediterranean vegetable, was used originally as a tonic. Celery tonic, concocted by Homer, 900 B.C., is still prescribed today for jangled nerves and an upset stomach.

---

1 whole stalk of celery, peeled and   ½ teaspoon salt
  cut into 2" lengths   Egg and Lemon Sauce (page 67)
2 cups water

Cover celery with water and add salt. Bring to a boil, cover, and reduce heat to medium. Cook 10 minutes, or until tender. Make sauce and pour over celery. Serve immediately.

STREET VENDOR'S CORN ON THE COB

ΑΡΑΒΟΣΙΤΟΣ, ΚΑΛΑΜΠΟΚΙ   (aravositos, kalamboki)

America's Indian corn has been adopted by the Greeks with great enthusiasm. They do not share the opinion of some Europeans, including the French, who think fresh corn is fit only for fodder. Street vendors of Greece sell this delicious vegetable hot from their portable braziers.

Allow 2 cobs per person   salt to taste
butter

Place corn covered with husks in water for 5 minutes. Peel. Place corn over hot charcoal brazier for 10 minutes, turning it frequently. Serve with butter and salt.

EGGPLANT

ΜΕΛΙΤΖΑΝΕΣ   (melitzanes)

The eggplant originated in India and has become the queen of vegetables in all Near Eastern cooking from Greece to Persia. There are more ways to cook this vegetable than any other in the Greek vegetable kingdom. The most elaborate and famous eggplant recipe is an eggplant and meat casserole with the exotic name of Moussaka (page 88).

Eggplants come in various sizes. The smallest ones, 2" long, are used for appetizers or a sweet preserve. Those averaging 4" to 6" long are stuffed, see page 88. Large fat eggplants are sliced and baked or fried in oil.

EGGPLANT BYZANTINE

ΜΕΛΙΤΖΑΝΕΣ ΒΥΖΑΝΤΙΟΥ   (melitzanes vizantiou)

1 large eggplant, sliced ½″ thick
   slices
salt
½ cup oil or melted butter

SAUCE:
1 cup tomato purée or tomato sauce
1 cup yogurt or cream cheese

1 cup water
1 teaspoon oregano
1 onion, finely chopped
¼ teaspoon salt
pepper to taste
½ cup grated cheese, Kefaloteri or
   Parmesan

Wash eggplant. Slice. Salt slices of eggplant generously and set aside for 15 minutes. Rinse well in cold water. Place slices on oiled broiler pan and brush tops with oil or melted butter. Broil on each side for 5 minutes.

To make sauce, blend all ingredients except grated cheese in a blender for ½ minute.

Lay one layer of eggplant in a casserole baking dish. Spread half of the sauce over it. Arrange second layer of eggplant and cover with remaining sauce. Sprinkle with grated cheese, salt and pepper. Bake 45 minutes at 350° F.

FRIED EGGPLANT WITH GREEK SAUCES

ΤΗΓΑΝΙΤΕΣ ΜΕΛΙΤΖΑΝΕΣ ΜΕ ΣΑΛΤΣΕΣ   (tiganites melitzanes meh saltses)

1 eggplant, sliced ¼″ thick
salt
1 cup flour
¼ cup grated cheese, Kefaloteri or
   Parmesan
2 eggs, beaten
1 cup oil for frying

SAUCES:
Any one of the following:
Garlic Dressing (page 68)
Tomato Sauce (page 68)
Yogurt or Yogurt Dressing (page
   70)

Wash and slice eggplant. Sprinkle slices generously with salt. Let stand 15 minutes. Rinse with cold water and pat dry. Dip in combined flour and cheese, coating both sides, then dip in egg. Repeat. Fry in hot oil until light brown on both sides, about 10 minutes. Serve with any sauce listed.

STUFFED EGGPLANT

ΜΕΛΙΤΖΑΝΕΣ ΠΑΡΑΓΕΜΙΣΤΕΣ   (melitzanes parayemistes)

Allow 2 small eggplants, or 1 medium size per person.

FILLING: either from Greek Stuffed Vegetables (page 97) or Byzantine Dolmathes (page 89). Prepare as directed.

TOPPING:
1 cup bread crumbs
½ cup grated cheese, Kefaloteri or Parmesan

Cut off tops of eggplant. If small and fat, scoop out insides with grapefruit knife. Be careful; try not to cut through the skin. Large sized eggplant may be halved lengthwise and scooped out. Chop pulp and add to partially cooked prepared filling. Fill hollow shells. Sprinkle top with combined bread crumbs and cheese. Set eggplants straight up in pan or lay gently on sides. Add two cups water and bake 45 minutes at 375 F.

BAKED EGGPLANT MOUSSAKA

ΜΟΥΣΑΚΑ   (moussaka)

The most famous eggplant recipe in all of the Near East is called *moussaka*. It's origin is lost in time, but most probably it was carried to Greece by the Arabs when they introduced the eggplant in the Middle Ages. It is a very elegant dish and when your hostess serves it to you, be assured she has gone to great lengths to prepare it.

1 large eggplant
salt
½ cup oil
¼ pound butter or margarine

FILLING:
1 pound ground lamb (or beef)
2 onions, chopped
1 clove garlic, pressed
½ cup parsley, chopped
½ cup tomato sauce
½ cup wine
1 cup water

WHITE SAUCE: (see page 69)
2 cups milk
2 tablespoons cornstarch
½ teaspoon salt
4 eggs, slightly beaten

TOPPING:
1 cup grated cheese, Kefaloteri or Parmesan
¼ teaspoon cinnamon

Wash eggplant. Cut into ½" thick slices. Sprinkle with salt and let stand in a bowl for 10 minutes..Rinse with cold water. Dry with a towel. Place slices close together, side by side, on an oiled cookie sheet. Melt oil and butter together and brush tops lightly with some of it. Bake in pre-heated oven at 350° F. for 10 minutes. Remove from oven.

Prepare filling: Heat a tablespoon of butter-oil mixture in a frying pan and cook the meat, onions, and remaining ingredients for 7 minutes.

Oil the bottom and sides of a square or rectangular cake pan. Lay one layer of eggplant. Spread with meat filling. Add the remaining eggplant on top. Brush with some butter-oil mixture. Prepare white sauce (see page 69). Add eggs and pour over top of eggplant. Sprinkle with cheese, cinnamon and any remaining butter-oil. Bake at 325° F. for 45 minutes. Cut into squares like a cake and serve immediately.

BOILED ENDIVE, GREEK STYLE

ΒΡΑΣΤΑ ΑΝΤΙΔΙΑ   (vrasta antidia)

Endive was one of the earliest vegetables the Greeks cultivated, and was undoubtedly their favorite. It grew wild and was eagerly sought in the fields, but soon the Greeks had their own garden plots of this tender, bright green, leafy vegetable. It is always boiled and served in this manner.

2 heads of endive   **cruet of olive oil and lemon juice**
¼ teaspoon salt

Cut off roots and discard. Rinse endive at least three times in sink. Place in a large pot. Sprinkle with salt. Cover and steam on high heat for 25 minutes. Serve with cruet of oil and lemon juice.

BYZANTINE DOLMATHES

ΝΤΟΛΜΑΔΕΣ ΒΥΖΑΝΤΙΝΟΙ, ΓΙΑΠΡΑΚΙΑ   (dolmathes VIZANTIN) (yaprakia)

Dolmathes, sometimes called *dolmas,* describes the little rolls made from leaves stuffed with rice or meat and steamed until cooked.

Early Greeks used fig leaves and leaves from the mulberry and hazelnut trees but this recipe was born when Alexander the Great demolished Thebes and food was so scarce the Thebans had to cut the little bit of meat they had into mincemeat and roll it in grape leaves. The ornate Byzantine world refined this recipe further to include nutmeats, currants, and spices common in Persia and India.

1 jar of grape leaves, or freshly cut
  vine leaves

FILLING:
2 tablespoons oil
1 pound ground meat, beef or lamb
2 onions, finely chopped
1 clove garlic, pressed
2 cups water
½ cup tomato sauce
1 cup rice
1 teaspoon each spearmint flakes and
  parsley

½ teaspoon salt
pepper to taste
⅛ teaspoon cinnamon
½ cup currants
¼ cup port wine (optional)
¼ cup pine nuts or walnuts
2 cups water
juice of 1 lemon

SAUCE:
Egg and Lemon Sauce (page 67) or
  plain Yogurt

If using canned grape leaves, rinse off brine by floating leaves in a basin of cold water. Prepare fresh vine leaves by pouring a cup of boiling water over them in a bowl. Drain. Spread 5 or 6 leaves out at a time on a flat surface. Lay leaf stem side up. Snip off stem with kitchen shears.

MAKE FILLING: Heat oil in large frying-pan. Fry meat, onions and garlic on medium heat for 5 minutes, mixing it as it cooks. Add water and remaining ingredients. Bring to a boil. Cover. Reduce heat to simmer and cook 10 minutes, until water is absorbed. Set aside until cool enough to handle. Put 1 teaspoon of filling near stem. Bring left side of leaf towards center, then bring right side towards center. They will not always meet. Pick up stem end of leaf, tucking in the filling. Roll away from you. It will be an oblong roll like a sausage.

Line the bottom of a large skillet with 4 leaves. Place each roll so that the tucked under end is on the bottom. Arrange each roll snugly, one next to the other, until all the leaves (except 3), and filling are gone. Place these leaves flat on top of rolls. Place a flat dish on top of rolls also to prevent their unraveling during cooking.

Add water and lemon juice. Bring to a boil. Cover. Reduce heat to simmer and cook 45 minutes. When done, remove pot from fire. Make Egg and Lemon Sauce and add to broth immediately or serve without sauce either cold as an appetizer or as a hot entree.

LEEKS, GREEK STYLE

ΠΡΑΣΣΑ   (prassa)

To prepare leeks: Slice into ½″ rounds and wash well in basin of cold water. Cook in salted water for 20 minutes over high heat. Serve with cruet of olive oil and vinegar for individual seasoning or egg and lemon sauce (page 67).

BOILED MALLOW GREENS

ΜΟΛΟΧΙΑ   (moloha)

Mallow greens (*malva neglecta*) are uncommon in the United States, though they are a favorite vegetable in Greece. When boiled, they produce a glutenous sauce used as a remedy for sore throats and colds. The round leaves look like spinach and cook quickly.

1 pound mallow greens, chopped or whole	1 clove garlic
2 cups water or broth	SAUCES:
½ teaspoon salt	Oil and vinegar, or lemon, to taste; or
2 or 3 coriander seeds	yogurt

Wash leaves well in cold water. Bring broth to a boil and add greens. Boil 5 to 10 minutes, stirring all the while to prevent sticking. Serve hot with preferred dressing.

FRIED MUSHROOMS

ΜΑΝΙΤΑΡΙΑ ΤΗΓΑΝΙΤΑ   (manitaria tiganita)

The wild mushrooms of Greece are considered a treasure and the women and children search for them in the fields. It is a rare Greek who does not recognize the edible mushroom. They are dried and threaded on raffia and hung in the kitchen to be used as needed. The flavor of mushrooms was considered too delicate to be ruined by sauces so stated Poliochus, the 3rd century B.C. comedy poet, "a braised mushroom and if there's a little dew we'd catch a snail."

½ pound fresh mushrooms	½ teaspoon lemon juice
1 tablespoon butter	salt and pepper to taste

Wash well in a basin of cold water. Separate caps from stems.

Heat butter in skillet. Add mushrooms, sprinkle with lemon juice and seasonings. Cover immediately for 2 minutes. Remove cover and fry 2 or 3 minutes more.

OKRA WITH TOMATOES

ΜΠΑΜΙΕΣ ΜΕ ΝΤΟΜΑΤΕΣ   (bamies meh domates)

Okra, also known as gumbo, is a vegetable that came to Greece by way of Ethiopia and is used often in Greek cooking, boiled and pickled or put into meat stews. Sometimes the seeds are used as a substitute for coffee, especially around Istanbul where it is grown. Some villagers still use it for poultices and medicinal reasons.

1 pound fresh okra or 2 packages
  frozen
1 tablespoon oil or butter
1 cup chopped onion, scallions or
  leeks
1 cup chopped tomatoes, canned or
  fresh

1 cup water
1 lemon, juice only
1 bay leaf
salt and pepper to taste

Prepare fresh okra by cutting off stems. Try not to expose the seeds. Cover with water, 1 teaspoon of vinegar and salt and let stand 15 minutes. Drain. Heat butter or oil, add onions and cook for 5 minutes. Add remaining ingredients. Cover, reduce heat to medium and cook 25 minutes. Serve hot with crusty bread.

OKRA GREEK STYLE

See Vegetables Greek Style (page 71). Okra with Meat, see Byzantine Pot Roast (page 131), and Hellenic Pot Roast (page 131).

PEAS POLITA

ΑΡΑΚΑ (ΜΠΙΖΕΛΙΑ) ΠΟΛΙΤΑ   (araka [bizelia] polita)

Peas have been found in the archeological diggings on the site of Troy which was built twelve thousand years before Christ. Polita means "that's the way it's cooked in the City." Some people think the city referred to is Constantinople (Istanbul), which was the largest city in the word for over a thousand years.

1 pound small whole onions (about 10)
6 small whole potatoes, peeled
1 package frozen artichokes (canned or fresh)
3 cups water (or liquor from canned vegetables if using them)

¼ teaspoon salt
2 lemons, juice only
pepper to taste
1 package frozen peas (canned or fresh)
¼ cup olive oil
1 tablespoon dill

In a saucepan or frying pan with cover, bring water or vegetable liquor to a boil with salt, juice of one lemon, and pepper. Add onions, potatoes, and fresh artichokes only. Cover and cook over medium heat for twenty minutes. Add fresh peas and continue cooking for ten minutes, until all vegetables are tender and soft. Add olive oil the last five minutes. Do not add more water unless it's necessary to keep from scorching. (If using frozen or canned vegetables, add to pot after the potatoes and onions are soft.)

Arrange vegetables on a round platter separately, with the artichokes around a mound of peas. Sprinkle with dill, more lemon, and olive oil. Allow to cool in its own liquor if planning to use as salad.

STUFFED QUINCE

ΚΥΔΟΝΙΑ ΠΑΡΑΓΕΜΙΣΤΑ   (kidonia parayemista)

Quince is a fruit that is treated like a vegetable. Like squash, it can be hollowed out and stuffed, or like an apple, it can be preserved with sugar and candied. It must always be cooked to be edible.

Allow 2 quinces per person

FILLING:
See Greek Stuffed Vegetables (page 97). Prepared as directed

1 cup water
juice from 1 lemon

Cover quince with water and parboil for 10 minutes. Drain. Scoop out pulp, being careful not to cut through skin. Add pulp to partially cooked prepared filling and mix in. Fill quince shells with filling and arrange in baking pan with or without other stuffed vegetables. Add water with lemon juice and bake at 375° F. for 45 minutes.

DRACHMA FRIED POTATOES

ΤΗΓΑΝΙΤΕΣ ΠΑΤΑΤΕΣ   (tiganestes patates)

One of the greatest surprises to the returning native who visits his homeland after many years is the popularity of fried potatoes in Greece. No matter what you order, invariably it will be accompanied by these fried potatoes, cut into round shapes like the Greek silver coin, the drachma.

2 large potatoes, per person   **salt**
2 cups oil for frying

Peel potatoes and slice into ½″ rounds. Dry with towel. Heat oil in a large frying pan until hot. Gently place potatoes in oil and fry 10 minutes or until ready.

For very crisp potatoes, fry only 5 minutes. Remove from oil and place in the refrigerator to chill. Reheat oil until hot again and place chilled, partially cooked potatoes in oil to finish frying for 5 minutes more.

Use a slotted spoon to turn potatoes over and to remove from oil. Drain. Sprinkle with salt while hot. Serve immediately.

GREEK POTATO PANCAKES

ΠΑΤΑΤΟΚΕΦΤΕΔΕΣ   (patatokeftehes)

This recipe comes from the potato farms of Kyperounda in Cyprus where the women turn left-over mashed potatoes into delicious pancakes called *patatokeftethes.*

2 cups cold mashed potatoes   **¼ cup grated cheese, Kefaloteri or**
2 eggs   **Parmesan**
2 scallions, or 1 tablespoon onion,   **½ cup oil for frying**
  chopped   **or**
3 tablespoons flour   **¼ pound melted butter, if broiling or**
1 teaspoon parsley   **baking**
salt and pepper to taste

Mix all ingredients in a bowl except fats and cheese. Make patties. Dip in grated cheese and fry in hot oil until brown on both sides, about 10 minutes. Use a wide spatula to turn over.

If broiling or baking is preferred, lay patties in buttered pan, sprinkle with grated cheese and bake at 450° F. for 15 minutes, or broil until brown for approximately 10 minutes. Serve plain, with yogurt or Garlic Sauce (page 68).

TAVERNA POTATO SALAD

ΠΑΤΑΤΟΣΑΛΑΤΑ   (patatosalata)

The potato, originally from South America, has been made a Greek citizen with a baptismal of olive oil, vinegar, and a sprinkling of oregano. The secret of this recipe is to marinate the onions in the dressing before mixing them into the hot potatoes.

8 potatoes, unpeeled
1 quart water
1 teaspoon salt

1 onion finely chopped

DRESSING:
½ cup olive oil
2 lemons, juice only
½ teaspoon salt
pepper to taste
2 teaspoon oregano
½ teaspoon sugar

Boil whole potatoes in salted water until soft, about 45 minutes. Peel potatoes while hot. (Spear with a fork to make handling an easier chore.) Cube.

Mix dressing while potatoes are boiling. Add onions. Let stand 15 minutes, or more.

Pour mixture over hot potatoes and toss well. Serve while still warm.

SPINACH AND RICE STEW

ΣΠΑΝΑΚΟΡΙΖΟ   (spanakorizo)

Spinach, the wallflower of vegetables, is a prima donna in the Greek kitchen. Of Persian origin, unknown to the ancient Greeks, it was brought to Greece and to Europe by the Moors. In this recipe, spinach is mated with rice to make a tasty vegetable dish.

2 pounds fresh spinach or 3 packages
   frozen
2 tablespoons oil or butter
1 onion, finely chopped

½ cup rice, preferably long grain
2 cups water
½ teaspoon salt
pepper to taste

Wash fresh spinach in three rinses of cold water. If frozen, partially defrost. Heat oil in saucepan and fry onion on medium heat for 3 minutes.

Add spinach. Sprinkle rice over spinach. Add water and seasonings. Bring to a boil. Cover. Reduce heat and cook on low heat for 35 minutes. Stir once or twice with spoon to avoid scorching and sticking to the bottom. Add another cup of water if more sauce is desired. Serve with crusty bread.

For other recipes using spinach, see: Lenten Vegetable Stew (page 97). Spinach Pie Spanakopitta (page 149). Vegetables Greek Style (page 71).

BOILED SUMMER SQUASH GREEK STYLE

ΒΡΑΣΤΑ ΚΟΛΟΚΥΘΑΚΙΑ   (vrasta kolokithakia)

This recipe comes from Attica where the peas, zucchini, and squash are grown that fill the markets of Athens in late summer.

1 pound of summer squash,   salt and pepper to taste
  preferably zucchini   Oil and Vinegar Dressing (page 69)
1 cup water   or Garlic Sauce (page 68)
¼ teaspoon sugar   1 teaspoon mint or dill

Wash and cut off ends of squash. Do not peel. Slice into 1″ rounds. Put squash in a pan and add water and salt. Cover and boil until soft, approximately 15 minutes. Serve with sauce above, or with cruet of olive oil and wedges of lemon for individual seasoning.

STUFFED SQUASH

ΚΟΛΟΚΥΘΑΚΙΑ ΠΑΡΑΓΕΜΙΣΤΑ   (kolokythakia parayemista)

Allow 2 zucchini squashes per per-   TOPPING:
  son. Select small sizes, about 4″   1 cup bread crumbs
  long, and fat, if possible.   ½ cup grated cheese, Parmesan or
                                         Kefaloteri
FILLING: 2 cups water
See Greek Stuffed Vegetables (page   juice from 1 lemon
  97) or Byzantine Dolmathes (page
  89). Prepared as directed.   SAUCE:
                                       Garlic Sauce (page 68), or plain
                                         yogurt

Cut off tops. If small and fat, scoop out insides, using grapefruit knife. If large, cut in half and scoop out shells. Chop pulp and add to partially cooked filling. Fill hollowed shells. Sprinkle with combined bread crumbs and cheese. Set straight up in pan or lay on sides. Add water and lemon juice. Bake 45 minutes at 350° F. Serve with selected sauce.

GREEK STUFFED VEGETABLES

ΕΛΛΗΝΙΚΗ ΠΑΡΑΓΕΜΗΣΙ ΑΠΟ ΡΥΖΙ ΚΑΙ ΚΡΕΑΣ
(elleneke parayemisi apo rizi kai kreas)

In many Athenian *tavernas,* particularly in Plaka, a section of old Athens, it is the custom to go into the kitchen to choose your meal. Invariably on the stove there will be a pan of stuffed vegetables, a colorful arrangement of tomatoes, bell peppers, squash, eggplant, artichokes, and quince. If you can't speak the language, just point to your selection.

Allow two tomatoes or peppers (or any vegetable listed) per person

FILLING:
1 tablespoon each oil and butter
1 pound ground meat (lamb or beef)
1 onion, chopped
1 cup water or tomato juice
1 cup rice, preferably long grain
1 teaspoon salt
⅛ teaspoon pepper
1 tablespoon parsley

1 teaspoon spearmint flakes
1 teaspoon oregano
¼ cup each currants and pine nuts (optional)

TOPPING:
1 cup bread crumbs
½ cup grated cheese, Kefaloteri or Parmesan
2 cups water
juice of 1 lemon

Use firm tomatoes and large fat bell peppers with squat bottoms so they'll sit up in the baking pan. Cut off tops and save. Scoop out pulp from tomatoes and set aside to add into filling later. Scoop out seeds of bell pepper and discard.

Heat oil and butter combined, in a skillet. Fry meat and onions for 5 minutes. Add remaining ingredients for filling, including pulp, and cook 10 minutes, stirring once or twice. Fill shells. Sprinkle with combined bread crumbs and cheese. Replace tops. Arrange stuffed vegetables in pan, placing them close together. Add 2 cups hot water and lemon juice. Bake 45 minutes at 350° F.

LENTEN VEGETABLE STEW

ΓΙΑΧΝΙ ΝΗΣΤΙΣΙΜΟ   (yahkni nistismo)

Slight differences in cooking exist in various regions of Greece, but the basic approach to stewing vegetables is the same. No matter what regional food preferences are, a lenten stew always excludes meat. This is a very old and rare Greek recipe.

Use fresh or frozen vegetables. Canned vegetables should not be substituted in this particular recipe.

2 tablespoons olive oil
1 tablespoon butter
½ pound green beans, whole or
    halved
3 zucchini squash, cut in 2" slices
2 potatoes, peeled and quartered
1 bunch scallions, cut in 1" lengths
1 or 2 cups celery leaves, chopped
½ pound fresh washed spinach or 1
    package frozen

4 tomatoes, quartered
1 cup parsley, chopped
6 squash blossoms (optional)
2 tablespoons each fresh oregano
    and spearmint leaves, or 1 tea-
    spoon of dried herbs
1 teaspoon salt
pepper to taste
1 bay leaf
4 cups water

Heat oil and butter in a large pot on medium heat. Add all ingredients in order listed and toss with large spoon to coat vegetables with oil. Add water and bring to a boil. Reduce heat. Cover
and cook on medium heat for 45 minutes. Check stew after 20
minutes and stir to avoid sticking at the bottom of pan. Serve hot
with crusty bread.

THE FISH OF
GREECE

ΨΑΡΙΔ ΤΗΣ ΕΛΛΑΔΟΣ   (psaria tis elados)

The symbol of the fish appears constantly in Greek art. Greeks drew simple fish designs on dishes and pots long before the Gnostics, an early sect of Christians, took it as a symbol for a secret password.

The Greeks have evolved many ways to cook and serve fish and seafood. Anyone, including a child, is able to identify, clean, and prepare anything that is caught in the Mediterranean or Aegean seas. Some of the most common are:

CARP, ΦΑΓΚΡΙ (faghree); COD, ΜΠΑΚΑΛΙΑΡΟΣ (bakaljaros); PORGY, ΤΣΙΠΟΤΡΑ (tsipoura); MACKEREL, ΣΚΟΤΜ BPI (skoumbree); ISTANBUL MACKEREL, ΚΟΛΙΟΣ (koleeos); RAY FISH or SKATE, ANGEL FISH, ΒΑΤΟΣ (vatos) ΠΙΝΑ (reena); RED MULLET, ΜΠΑΡΜΠΟΤΝΙ (barbounee); RED SNAPPER, GOURMAND, SEA BASS and HALIBUT, ΣΤΝΑΓΡΙΔΑ (sinagritha); ROCKFISH, ΠΕΤΡΟΨΑΡΟ (petropsaro), or ΡΟΤΦΙΟΣ (rufios); SARDINES, ΣΑΡΔΕΛΛΕΣ (sardelles); SEA BREAM, ΛΙΘΡΙΝΙΑ (lithrinia); SMELTS, SPRATS, WHITE BAIT, ΜΑΡΙΔΕΣ (marithes), or ΑΘΕΡΗΝΟΤΣ (atherinous) or ΓΟΤΠΤΕΣ (goupies); SOLE, ΓΛΩΣΣΑ (ghlossa); SMALL SOLE, ΚΑΤΣΟΤΛΕΣ (katsoules); SWORDFISH, ΞΙΦΙΑΣ (ksifios); TROUT, ΠΕΣΤΡΟΦΑ (pestrofa); TUNNY FISH, ΛΑΚΕΡΔΑ (lakareda).

Some transplanted Greeks insist fish from the cold waters of North America cannot compare with the fish from the Mediterranean and Aegean. Some Greeks in California lament the fact that the fish from the Pacific Ocean cannot match those from the Atlantic Ocean. This sort of complaint seems to be standard among Greeks even in ancient times, when the fish from the waters of Byzantium were considered to be far superior to those from Greek waters.

In the following recipes, do not be dismayed if you cannot find the kind of fish that is recommended. Substitute another kind and the results will be the same, providing your fish or seafood meet the first requirement—freshness. A fish cooked within minutes of being caught cannot be ruined; but a stale fish cannot be redeemed by even the greatest recipe and the best cook in the world.

AEGEAN SEA CHOWDER

ΨΑΡΟΣΟΥΠΑ ΚΑΚΑΒΙΑ   (psarosoupa kakavia)

All Greece knows this ancient recipe and the ingredients change each time it is made depending upon the fisherman's catch that day. Making a small amount of this chowder is difficult, but since it is even better a few days later, prepare and enjoy it for more than one meal, or freeze it for later use.

1 pound of white fish, cut into 2" pieces
½ pound each of any or all of the following seafood; fresh, canned or frozen: clams, crab, lobster, oysters, scallops or mussels and shrimp
½ pound baby octopus (optional)
¼ cup olive oil
3 onions, chopped

2 garlic cloves, pressed
2 pound can of peeled tomatoes, including liquid
1 cup chopped mushrooms
4 stalks celery, chopped
2 teaspoon salt
⅛ teaspoon cayenne pepper
1 bay leaf
½ cup wine, red preferably
4 cups water

Prepare fish and shellfish by cleaning and cutting into bite-size pieces. Heat oil in a large pot. Fry onions and garlic on medium heat for 5 minutes. Add remaining ingredients, except seafood and bring to a boil. Reduce heat and cover. Cook one hour.

Add fish and octopus, and cook 20 minutes. Add shellfish and simmer 5 minutes more. Serve hot with crusty bread and crisp salad.

BAKED FISH MYKONOS

ΨΗΤΟ ΨΑΡΙ ΜΥΚΟΝΟΥ   (psito psari)

The people of the delightful sunbathed island of white Mykonos in the Aegean Sea prepare a delicious baked fish with aromatic herbs which is impossible to forget.

Whole fish, approximately 2 to 3 pounds	**juice of 2 lemons or ½ cup white wine**
	1 teaspoon salt
MARINADE:	**⅛ teaspoon pepper**
½ cup olive oil	**¼ teaspoon each: tarragon, rosemary, thyme, parsley**

Rinse fish and lay full length in a shallow pan. Mix marinade and ladle over fish. Let stand in refrigerator 30 minutes. Turn over and marinate the other side for another 30 minutes. Spoon off some of the marinade to use as a basting sauce.

Bake 25 minutes at 375° F. Allow 10 minutes per pound. Baste frequently with sauce while baking.

Serve whole with garnishes, such as black olives, Feta cheese, or raw vegetables.

BAKED FISH SALONIKA

ΠΛΑΚΙ ΘΕΣΣΑΛΟΝΙΚΗΣ   (plaki)

This prized recipe was brought to the United States in 1912 from Salonika when that city was still part of Turkey. The touch of cinnamon and mavrodaphne (or port wine) will remind you of all the Mediterranean seaports you have ever visited.

2 pounds boneless whitefish, filet of halibut, ray, bass, or cod, sliced	**½ cup parsley, chopped**
¼ cup olive oil	**1 teaspoon oregano**
4 onions, thinly sliced	**⅛ teaspoon cinnamon**
1 clove of garlic, pressed	**1 teaspoon salt**
2 cups tomatoes, or 1 cup tomato purée diluted with 2 cups water	**pepper to taste**
	½ cup red wine, preferably mavrodaphne or port

Rinse fish with cold water. Oil baking pan with half of the oil. Place slices of fish on pan.

Sauce: Heat remaining oil in frying pan, and fry onions and garlic on medium heat for 5 minutes. Add remaining ingredients and cover. Cook 10 minutes.

Pour sauce over fish. Bake 45 minutes at 375° F. Serve with crusty bread and a crisp salad.

SALTED CODFISH

ΜΠΑΚΑΛΙΑΡΟΣ   (bakalyaros)

The odor of salted cod is strong and admittedly repellent. You may be one of those people who believe it should be given a decent burial. Not only would Greeks give you an argument on this point of view, they would also tell you about the many delicious ways of preparing it. Dried cod must be brought to life by soaking it in cold water for at least 24 hours, before it can be prepared and cooked, but for many people who live away from the sea, the salted cod may be the only kind of fish they can buy.

BOILED CODFISH

ΒΡΑΣΤΟΣ ΜΠΑΚΑΛΙΑΡΟΣ   (vrastos bakalyaros)

Cover dried codfish with cold water and soak 24 hours, keeping it in the refrigerator. Rinse twice with cold water. Cut into pieces or slices, and put in a pot. Cover with water and boil for 30 minutes or until tender. Serve hot or chilled with any of the following sauces: Oil and Lemon Dressing (page 69), plain yogurt or Yogurt Dressing (page 70), Garlic Sauce (page 68) or Greek Tomato Sauce (page 67).

BAKED CODFISH PLAKI

ΠΛΑΚΙ   (plaki)

Soak and prepare fish as in Boiled Codfish. Drain and pat dry. Follow recipe for Baked Fish Salonika (page 101).

FRIED CODFISH WITH GARLIC SAUCE

ΜΠΑΚΑΛΙΑΡΟΣ ΣΚΟΡΔΑΛΙΑ   (bakalyaros skordalia)

Soak and prepare fish as in Boiled Codfish. Cut into bite-size pieces or slices 2″ long and roll in flour. Fry in a cup of hot oil until crisp and brown on both sides for 5 minutes. Serve with Fish Marinade (page 106) or Garlic Sauce (page 68).

CAVIAR TARAMA

ΤΑΡΑΜΟΣΑΛΑΤΑ   (taramosalata)

Tarama, carp roe, is sometimes called red caviar. The best red caviar, called brik, comes from the river Evros in Macedonia and is readily available in the United States. No special occasion is needed to serve this recipe, nor is its cost prohibitive. If, despite an aristocratic background you dislike caviar, you will find the recipe for MILD TARAMA more to your liking.

MILD
1 jar tarama (4 ounces)
2 cups fresh bread crumbs
1 package cream cheese (4 ounces)
1 cup mayonnaise
1 lemon, juice only
¼ small onion, finely chopped

TRADITIONAL
1 jar tarama (4 ounces)
¼ cup water
1 cup fresh bread crumbs
2 lemons, juice only
1 cup olive oil
½ onion, finely chopped

Blend all ingredients in order listed, using blender or electric mixer, into a smooth paste. Chill. Use as a dip or a spread. Serve in a bowl with water biscuits, toasted bread, or raw vegetables, such as green peppers or celery sticks.

If making canapés, butter crackers or toast before spreading the salad to prevent the moisture from making the bread soggy.

CAVIAR TARAMA MOLDED SALAD

ΦΟΡΜΑΡΙΣΜΕΝΗ ΤΑΡΑΜΟΣΑΛΑΤΑ   (formarizmeno taramosalata)

One of the pleasures of traveling to Greece by ship is being able to taste the cuisine before you arrive. The chefs aboard make Caviar Tarama into a molded fish mousse and present it elegantly in the form of a decorated fish on the buffet table.

FILLING:
1 jar Tarama (4 ounces)
1 cup mayonnaise
1 tablespoon lemon juice
1 cup fresh bread crumbs
dash cayenne pepper
½ cup grated onion
dash of salt
2 tablespoons gelatine

2 cups boiling water
pimento (1 ounce can)
4 black olives, pitted
1 package cream cheese (8 ounces)

GARNISH:
2 cups chopped parsley
whole olives
pickles

Put a metal fish mold in freezer to chill.

Sprinkle gelatine in ¼ cup cold water to soften. Add 2 cups

boiling water and stir until gelatine dissolves. Set aside in refrigerator to cool, about 5 minutes.

Blend the filling ingredients in blender or electric mixer. Mix 1
cup gelatine liquid into filling and set aside in refrigerator.

Cut olives into slices and pimentos into narrow strips. Pour ¼
cup of gelatine liquid into fish mold and tip it to spread into all
crevices. Arrange slices of olives and pimento as scales, eyes,
tail, etc. Return mold to freezer for 15 minutes. Pour ¼ cup more
of gelatine mixture over decorated mold and return to freezer.

Beat or blend cream cheese and add remaining ½ cup gelatine
liquid to beaten cheese. Set aside to cool in the refrigerator for 15
minutes. Do not let it jell completely. Spread cheese mixture in
bottom and sides of mold. Return to freezer for 15 minutes to set.
Fill mold with Tarama mixture. Place in refrigerator to set about 4
hours or overnight. Place serving platter in refrigerator to chill
also.

To serve: Dip mold in hot water. Place serving platter over
mold and turn mold over quickly. Garnish with chopped parsley
around the fish. Add olives, pickles and any other vegetables desired.

DODECANESE FISH CHOWDER IN THE SHELL

ΠΛΑΚΙ ΣΕΡΒΙΡΙΣΜΕΝΟ ΜΕΣΑ ΣΕ ΟΣΤΡΑΚΟΝ
                          (plaki servirismeno mesa se ostrakon)

This classic *plaki* recipe from the Dodecanese Islands, the most
famous of which is Rhodes, is served in scallop shells. The liberal
use of tomato is a remnant of Italian influence from the time these
islands were a possession of Italy, 1912 to 1948.

**Use any one of the following: 1 pound
   boneless fish, cut into 1" cubes;
   shrimp or scallops, cut and
   quartered.**

SAUCE:
2 tablespoons oil
2 onions, chopped
1 clove garlic
1 cup tomato sauce

½ teaspoon salt
⅛ teaspoon pepper
1 cup water
½ cup wine, red or white
1 tablespoon flour
1 teaspoon each basil and parsley
1 cup chopped mushrooms
1 cup bread crumbs
½ cup grated cheese, Kefaloteri or
   Parmesan

Prepare fish or seafood by rinsing with cold water, cleaning
and cutting into bite-size portions. Put ingredients for sauce in a

blender for a few seconds. Bring sauce to a boil and cook on medium heat for ½ hour, until sauce is thick and hot.

Add seafood and mushrooms. Cover pot and cook for 15 minutes. Pour a spoonful or two into each scallop shell. Sprinkle with bread crumbs and grated cheese. Bake in hot oven at 375° F. for 10 minutes just before serving.

EEL EPIRUS

ΧΕΛΙ ΣΤΟ ΧΑΡΤΙ   (heyli sto harti)

The eel is a delicious, delicately flavored fish and has been considered so for thousands of years, but its resemblance to a snake has kept it out of many American kitchens. Like lobster, it must be kept alive until the last possible moment before preparation; therefore, it is usually sold smoked or frozen.

To prepare fresh eel

Remove undesirable layer of fat underneath the skin by broiling it under high heat on all sides until the skin blisters and peels easily. Trim and cut any fat that doesn't come away with the skin. A tasty white flesh will be left.

Use in any of the following recipes: Baked Fish Salonika (page 101), Baked, wrapped in paper, see Stolen Chickens (page 121), Fried Fish (page 105), Baked Fish Mykonos (page 101).

FRIED FISH VOLOS

ΤΗΓΑΝΙΤΑ ΨΑΡΙΑ   (tiganita psaria)

Fried fish should be cooked in a matter of minutes and for the woman who overcooks these small whole fish, the men of Volos have a few words: ΟΛΑ ΣΤΙΓΝΑ ΚΑΙ ΤΗΓΑΝΙΤΑ, "all is dried and fried." This phrase also applies to anything else that is ruined, be it fried fish, a woman's beauty, or an unsuccessful business deal.

This is a recipe for trout or porgy (tsipoura) but any small whole flat fish such as mullet, perch, pike, smelt, or sole is suitable. Allow ½ pound or 2 fish per person.

1 teaspoon salt   1 cup flour
1 lemon, juice only   1 cup oil

Wash scaled fish under cold water. Place whole fish on platter, sprinkle with salt and lemon juice. Put flour on another flat dish.

Heat oil on high heat in a large frying pan. While oil is heating, flour both sides of each fish, flipping it over from one side to the other. Slip fish into hot oil and fry on each side until crispy brown, about 5 to 10 minutes total cooking time. Remove and drain on paper towel. Serve with lemon slices, plain yogurt, Garlic Sauce (page 68) or Fish Marinade (see below).

FISH MARINADE

ΨΑΡΙΑ ΜΑΡΙΝΑΤΑ   (psara marinata)

1 cup vinegar   1 teaspoon thyme, marjoram or
1 clove garlic, pressed   tarragon

After all the fish has been fried in recipe for Fried Fish Volos, remove from frying pan, add the listed ingredients to the hot oil and stir until smooth. The flour from the fish will thicken the sauce. Add 1 teaspoon more of flour if a thicker sauce is desired.

Pour sauce over fish and serve immediately. Fish improves in flavor if allowed to marinate in this sauce for a few hours. Serve at room temperature or chilled.

FRIED SMELTS

ΜΑΡΙΔΕΣ ΤΗΓΑΝΙΤΕΣ   (marithes tiganites)

Even if you can't go to the small village of Old Phaleron outside of Athens for these delicious hot smelts called *marides,* or to Lesbos for fresh sardines from the Gulf of Kalloni, you can duplicate this easy recipe at home.

1 pound smelts or sardines   ⅛ teaspoon pepper
1 cup flour   1 cup oil for frying
1 teaspoon salt

Put fish, flour and salt in a bag. Shake bag to coat fish. Heat oil in a large frying pan. Take out fish and slip into hot oil. Fry on high heat until browned on all sides, 5 minutes total cooking time. Serve plain or with Fish Marinade (page 106).

SKEWERED FISH GRI-GRI

ΨΑΡΙΑ   (psaria)

Being able to eat fish that is caught minutes before makes a simple recipe as this one for broiled fish over *karvouna* (coals) especially memorable. In Greece, the colorful fishing boats, called *caiques,* go out to sea or in the bay, in families of boats like a mother duck and ducklings, with the largest boat towing a smaller one filled with nets followed by a chain of five smaller boats called *gri-gri* which have lamps hanging over their bows that twinkle at night like fireflies or another city in the bay. The modern Greek fisherman is not afraid of fishing at night as was his Greek predecessor in ancient times who feared Scylla and Charybdis.

Allow ½ pound of fish per person. Use a variety with firm flesh such as: cod, halibut, swordfish, rockfish, octopus, squid, scallops or shrimp.

½ cup oil   ½ teaspoon thyme or oregano
2 lemons, juice only   salt and pepper to taste

Cut fish into squares. Place fish on skewers. Dip into oil, sprinkle with lemon juice, thyme and seasonings and broil under hot flame or over charcoal beach fire for 5 minutes on each side. Serve with retsina wine and Greek bread.

OCTOPUS

ΧΤΑΠΟΔΙ   (oktapodi)

The general opinion that the best place for an octopus is in an aquarium is not held by the Greek islanders. The cowardly octopus is formidable in appearance and the legends about its ferocity hasn't helped it either. A Greek fisherman will pound his catch against the rocks, and spread its legs to dry out in the sun before it is grilled over hot coals.

Octopus is sold canned, frozen, dried and sometimes it is available fresh. The tiny octopi are very tender, suitable for quick frying. The larger ones require pounding to make the flesh tender, but are best for stews, fish chowders and grilled over coals.

To prepare fresh octopus

Rinse in several washes of cold running water. Drain. Pound gently with wooden mallet to soften flesh or hold the head and slap the legs on a hard surface forty times. Remove eyes, mouth, and discard. Drop head first into boiling water and simmer for 10 minutes, or until tender, depending upon the size. Cut tentacles and middle part of the body into bite size portions. The octopus is now ready to be added to a rice pilaf or floured and fried in oil. See recipe for Shellfish Pilafi (page 112), Aegean Sea Chowder (page 100).

OCTOPUS MEZES

ΧΤΑΠΟΔΙ ΜΕΖΕΣ   (oktapodi mezes)

Drain boiled octopus. Cut into small pieces. Place in a clean sterile jar, with vinegar to cover. Add ½ cup olive oil. Seal and allow to marinate a week in refrigerator. Serve as appetizer.

GRILLED OCTOPUS MOUDROS

ΧΤΟΠΟΔΙ ΤΗΣ ΣΧΑΡΑΣ   (octopodi tis skaras)

The Robinson Crusoe of Greek legend, Philoctetes, was marooned on the island of Limnos, in the northern Aegean Sea, where large octopus is caught in the land locked bay of Moudros. The people there prepare it in the fisherman's manner, grilling pieces of it over hot coals.
1 octopus frozen, fresh or dried, cut into pieces.
If canned, drain and pat octopus dry with towel. Oil grill rack or pan to avoid sticking and broil over hot coals or flame for 5 minutes. Salt and pepper and serve hot, as appetizers. (If using dry octopus, dip pieces in wine before grilling.)

FRIED SQUID OR CUTTLEFISH

ΤΗΓΑΝΙΤΑ ΚΑΛΑΜΑΡΑΚΙΑ/ΣΟΥΠΙΕΣ   (tiganita kalamarakia/soupyes)

Fried baby squid or cuttlefish, succulent inside and crisp on the outside, is a speciality of the islands off the shores of Argolid, particularly in Hydra, Aegina and Spetsai in the Argo-Saronic Gulf. You may use fresh, frozen, or canned squid to duplicate this recipe.

Allow 4 squids, or young cuttlefish	**½ teaspoon salt**
(calamarakia), per person	**pepper to taste**
1 cup oil	**½ teaspoon thyme**
1 cup flour	**dash of garlic powder (optional)**

To clean fresh squid. Wash thoroughly in cold water. Pull off head. Remove bones, ink sacs, and pull out black skin. Remaining edible part will look like a little bag.

Heat oil until hot. Put combined flour and seasonings in a flat dish and flip squids on all sides until completely coated. Slip into hot oil and fry on both sides until light brown, about 3 minutes total cooking time. Serve with Oil and Lemon Dressing (page 69) or Garlic Sauce (page 68).

STUFFED SQUID PIRAEUS

ΚΑΛΑΜΑΡΑΚΙΑ ΠΑΡΑΓΕΜΙΣΤΑ ΠΕΙΡΑΙΩΤΙΚΑ   (kalamarakia parayemista)

Squids are perfect for stuffing and baking. They are formed into little bags by nature. This recipe from Athens' port of Piraeus is so tasty it is difficult to remember these sea creatures are related to the legendary monster of the deep. The texture and flavor of the squids are like scallops.

Allow 3 squids per person:	**1 clove garlic, pressed**
	¼ cup pine nuts
FILLING:	**¼ cup currants or grapes**
1 cup rice	**¼ cup melted butter or oil**
1 cup tomato juice	**½ cup water**
½ teaspoon salt	**juice of 1 lemon**
dash of cayenne pepper	

Prepare squids for stuffing by cleaning and rinsing. Cook rice for 30 minutes in remaining ingredients. Allow to cool slightly.

Fill sacs of squids with rice mixture. Spread remainder of rice in an oiled baking dish and lay stuffed squids on bed of rice. Brush tops with oil. Bake at 350° F. for 10 minutes.

THE SHELLFISH
OF GREECE

ΘΑΛΑΣΣΙΝΑ (thalassina)

The waters of Greece abound in an amazing variety of shellfish. The list of shellfish eaten by the Greeks given by Aristotle in his work entitled ZOOLOGY, ΠΕΡΙ ΖΟΙΚΟΝ (peri zoikon) remains the same today: pinnas, oysters, mussels, scallops, razor fishes, conches, limpets, ascidium, barnacles, periwinkles, purple shells, sea urchins, twisted snails, cockles, whelks, nereids; not forgetting the most important, crabs, lobsters, and shrimp. All the shellfish in Greek waters are considered edible.

CRAB

ΚΑΒΟΥΡΙΑ (kavouria)

It is the European crab, *Cancer Pagurus,* which has the honor of having a northern constellation named after it, not the delicate ladylike blue crab of the eastern seaboard of the United States or the great Dungeness crab of the Pacific coast. But for a particularly exquisite taste, you must go to Greece in April to try the delicious river crab, *Potamon Edulis,* which is called the Lenten crab. It is tiny and succulent, and not always available.

To prepare fresh crab

Fresh crab, like lobster, should be alive when plunged into boiling water. Boil for 10 minutes. Crack shell. Pick white meat from main body area to which legs are attached and from main claw. Serve with Brown Butter Sauce (page 66), Oil and Lemon Dressing (page 69), or mayonnaise.

GREEK ISLAND LOBSTER

ΑΣΤΑΚΟΣ ΒΡΑΣΤΟΣ   (astakos vrastos)

By some accident of local climate the tastiest Greek lobsters are caught on the island of Skyros, in the Northern Sporades, which enjoys in Greece the same fame for its lobsters as Maine does in the United States.

To prepare fresh lobster

Plunge live lobster into boiling water and simmer 20 minutes, longer for large ones. Drain. Crack shell. Pick meat from tail, claws and the edge of the main body where the small legs are attached.

To prepare frozen lobster

Do not defrost. Cover lobster with cold water and simmer slowly for 15 minutes.

To broil lobster

Split and clean a fresh live lobster. Place under broiler or on hot coals for 15 minutes. Serve hot, with any sauce listed below.

Serve with Brown Butter Sauce (page 66) or with Oil and Lemon Dressing (page 69).

Add to Shellfish Pilaf (page 112) or Aegean Sea Chowder (page 100).

OYSTERS AND MUSSELS

ΣΤΡΕΙΔΙΑ, ΚΑΙ ΜΥΔΙΑ   (streidia, kai mydia)

At one time, an oyster or mussel shell called *Ostrakon*, was used by the democratic Greeks as a ballot. The voter inscribed his choice of candidates with a sharp point on the mother-of-pearl inside the shell. These ancient Greeks prized the Hellespont oysters which came from the Dardanelles, now named Canakkale Boğazi. The same precaution must be followed for all shellfish: Unless bottled and frozen, they should be alive when purchased. If the shell is closed tightly, it is fresh and alive. If the shell is slightly open, tap on shell; if it closes, it is alive, and good to eat.

To prepare: Scrub shells. Cover with cold water for 8 hours to rinse out the sand. Put shells in 1 cup salted water for 2 minutes. Drain. Remove meat from shell. Trim beard on oysters. Serve in shells with any sauce desired. Suggested sauces: Oil and Lemon Dressing (page 69) or mayonnaise.

MUSSELS

ΜΥΔΙΑ   (media)

To the islanders, who live in the paths of storms, a big wind does blow some good. After a storm the beaches are littered with mussels which have been dredged up by the churning sea. Whole populations of the villages by the sea can be seen at the water's edge picking up these delicious fruits.

Discard any shells which are not tightly closed.

Fried Mussels: the most popular way of preparing these delicious bivalves is very simple. Trim the beard after rinsing. Dip in beaten egg and flour and fry in hot oil for 4 minutes, total cooking time.

Serve with any sauce desired or with Garlic Sauce (page 68) or Oil and Lemon Dressing (page 69).

SEA URCHINS

ΑΧΙΝΙΟΣ   (ahinie)

Even those people living on the sea coast of the United States do not approach the spiny formidable looking sea urchin with delight. This is not the case with the islanders of Ikaria, famous for its therapeutic hot springs, where the sea urchin has been considered a delicacy for centuries.

To prepare sea urchins: Look for the ones which are under water at low tide. They must be eaten fresh and raw. Slice top off with sharp knife. Drain. Rinse in sea water. Eat the yellow roe that clings to the inside of the shell. A sprinkle of parsley or sweet pickle is especially good with it.

SHELLFISH PILAF

ΠΙΔΑΦΙ ΜΕ ΘΑΛΑΣΣΙΝΑ   (pilafi meh thalassina)

The *pilafi* which is made in Mytilene includes both mussels and shrimps as well as the local olive oil considered one of the best in Greece. In ancient times, the island of Mytilene was known as Lesbos, the birthplace of Aesop who was a cook as well as a story-teller, and of Sappho, the first woman poet.

Use any one of the following kinds of seafood: 1 pound scallops, mussels, shrimp, octopus, crab, lobster or fish

PILAFI:
¼ cup oil
1 cup rice, long grain or small pasta
2 onions chopped

½ cup celery, chopped
½ cup parsley, chopped
1 tablespoon spearmint flakes
1 clove garlic (optional)
½ teaspoon salt
pepper to taste
1 cup tomatoes or tomato juice
1 cup water

Rinse and prepare shellfish by cutting into bite-size pieces. Heat oil in a large skillet, and fry rice for 5 minutes. Add onions, celery, spearmint flakes and garlic and fry 5 minutes more, stirring all the while. Add remaining ingredients. Bring to a boil. Reduce heat. Cover and simmer 30 minutes until rice or pasta is tender. Add seafood the last 5 minutes of cooking time.

SHRIMP CASSEROLE SARANIKOS

ΓΑΡΙΔΕΣ   (gharithes)

Hundreds of bays, called *Kolpos,* which punctuate the coastline of Greece provide a sweet shrimp, called *garithes,* which are all the more delicious cooked in this manner.

1 pound raw shrimps
2 tablespoons butter or olive oil
3 tomatoes, peeled and chopped
1 onion, or chopped scallions
1 garlic clove (or garlic powder
   equivalent)

1 tablespoon brandy
1 tablespoon red wine
¼ lb. Feta cheese (optional)
salt and pepper to taste

To prepare fresh shrimp. Use a small sharp knife to pick off shell. Slit shrimp down the back. Pick off the black vein down the back. Rinse.

To boil shrimp: Bring 1 cup water or white wine to a boil. Add shrimp, cover and cook 1 minute.

Melt butter in a frying pan and fry shrimps over medium low heat for 3 minutes until pink. Remove to a casserole dish. Add chopped tomatoes, onions, garlic to frying pan and cook for 5 minutes, adding the salt, pepper and liquor during this time. Pour sauce over shrimps and arrange thin slices of cheese over it.

Serve immediately or place under broiler for 2 minutes to toast cheese. Serve hot.

Aegean Sea Chowder (page 100).
Dodecanese Fish Chowder in Shell (page 104).
Shellfish Pilaf (page 112).
Skewered Shrimp (page 107).
Tomato Pilaf (page 60).
Shrimps, see Prawns Pamvotis (page 114).

PRAWNS PAMVOTIS

ΓΑΡΙΔΕΣ   (garides)

If you have ever visited Yoannina in Epirus, and sat in an open air
café under the canopy of the plane trees along the shores of Lake
Pamvotis, you will remember the sweet flavor of the lake prawns,
cooked in a white wine from the vineyards of near-by Zitsa.

6 large shrimp or prawns, per person	salt and pepper to taste
2 tablespoons flour	¼ cup oil
1 tablespoon grated dry cheese	½ cup wine, dry white or champagne
pinch of garlic powder	

Mix flour, cheese and seasonings. Dip shrimp in egg. Roll
shrimps in flour mixture. Heat oil in skillet. Fry for 2 minutes on
both sides, or broil, if preferred. Remove shrimp. Add wine to pan
and stir until it bubbles and a thick sauce forms. Pour over shrimp.
Serve hot.

SNAILS, WINKLES, PERIWINKLES

ΚΟΧΛΙΕΣ   (kohlies)

This seafood is eaten by those Greeks and Europeans who know
them and can find them at the seashore. Winkles are a tiny mol-
lusk that have brown-colored spiral shells and live along the
coastline in Greece as well as the United States. They are eaten
raw like oysters, or cooked like cockles or scallops. The meat is
extracted from the shell with a pin after steaming for 1 minute.

THE LITTLE CHICKENS

ΚΟΤΕΣ ΚΑΙ ΚΟΤΟΠΟΥΛΑ   (kotes kai kotopoula)

Whether it be the tiniest bird, the tender fryer or the fat old hen the Greek cook will sprinkle it with oregano and lemon juice and make a most delectable dish. The Greeks no longer eat peacocks, swans, francolins or cranes, as Aristotle described, but they do still consider a plump partridge, a fat little pigeon or dove fair game and supreme delicacies. The wild dove shooting held on Strofadia in the Ionian Sea attracts people from all over the world, including Greek sportsmen.

Roast duck and goose made crisp with honey and lemon basting are not as common as roast turkey which, surprisingly enough, is quite popular throughout Greece. It is stuffed with unusual dressings which add to the enjoyment of this tasty bird.

BAKED LEMON CHICKEN OREGANO

ΨΗΤΗ ΚΟΤΑ ΜΕ ΛΕΜΟΝΙ ΚΑΙ ΡΙΓΑΝΗ   (psiti kota meh lemoni kai rigani)

A hospitable Greek will invite you with the words, "Come to my house for a proper *trapezi* (meal). We will kill a chicken for you." If he is a villager, that is exactly what he will do to honor you. Sprinkled with lemon juice and oregano it will be baked in the Greek way.

1 roasting chicken or two broilers, whole or disjointed	⅛ teaspoon pepper
	1 tablespoon oregano
¼ pound butter	2 lemons, juice only
¼ cup oil	3 cups boiling water
2 teaspoons salt	2 tablespoons flour or cornstarch

Wash chicken under cold running water. Heat butter and oil together until hot. Pour half of it into a shallow baking pan, spreading it to cover bottom. Lay pieces or whole chicken in pan. Sprinkle with salt, pepper, and oregano. Mix remaining butter mixture with strained lemon juice and baste fowl. Bake 1½ hours at 375° F., basting 3 or 4 times during baking. When cooked, remove to platter.

Lemon Chicken Gravy: Add boiling water to drippings in pan. Use a spatula to scrape bottom and mix. Dilute flour or cornstarch in ½ cup cold water and stir into pan. Bake 5 minutes at 475° F.

Serve separately as sauce for mashed potatoes or Rice Pilaf (page 59); or add any kind of parboiled potatoes or rice and bake in sauce alongside chicken for the last ½ hour of cooking time, providing your baking pan is large enough. If it is not large enough, see following recipe, Lemon Chicken With Pasta, Potatoes, or Rice.

LEMON CHICKEN WITH PASTA, POTATOES, OR RICE

ΨΗΤΗ ΚΟΤΑ ΜΕ ΠΑΣΤΑ, Η ΠΑΤΑΤΕΣ, Η ΡΥΖΙ
                                        (psiti kota meh pasta, e patates, e ryzi)

Use any *one* of the following: 6 or 8 potatoes, peeled and quartered
1 pound pasta, either noodles,   or, if tiny, leave whole
   manestra (*orzo*) spaghetti or   2 cups rice, long grain
   trahana (page 64)   water to cover

Follow recipe for Lemon Chicken Oregano (page 115). Parboil any one of above ingredients for 10 minutes. Drain. Remove baked chicken to a covered dish. Add boiling water and parboiled pasta, potatoes, or rice to juices in baking pan and spoon sauce over the top. Bake for 15 minutes at 400° F. Serve in a separate platter.

BYZANTINE CHICKEN STEW

ΚΟΤΟΚΑΠΑΜΑ   (kotokapama)

1 large chicken, disjointed
Ingredients as listed for Byzantine Pot Roast (page 131)

CHICKEN BREASTS WITH AVGHOLEMONO SAUCE

ΚΟΤΑ ΜΕ ΑΥΓΟΛΕΜΟΝΟ   (kota meh avgholemono)

A sizeable chicken industry in Astros Kynourias, Peloponnesus, now supplies the nearby larger cities of Argos, Nauplia, and Tripolis. The women of Astros combine the juices of the large lemons that grow on their farms with the chickens raised by their husbands and sons to make this Greek recipe.

2 tablespoons, butter or margarine	2 cups water
1 tablespoon oil	3 eggs
4 or 6 chicken breasts, deboned	2 lemons, juice only
½ teaspoon salt	1 tablespoon cornstarch or flour

Combine butter and oil in a large skillet and heat. Add chicken and brown on each side 10 minutes over medium heat. Add salt and water, bring to a boil. Reduce heat and cover. Simmer for 30 minutes or until tender.

Make Avgholemono Sauce by beating eggs until thick. Add strained lemon juice, cornstarch, and the liquid from the chicken.

Pour over chicken and remove from heat immediately. Allow it to set for 3 minutes before serving. Serve over a bed of Rice Pilaf (page 59), Boiled Cracked Wheat (page 61), or Boiled Noodles (page 63).

CHICKEN BREASTS WITH WALNUT SAUCE

ΚΟΤΑ ΜΕ ΣΑΛΤΣΑ ΤΟΥ ΚΑΡΥΔΙΟΥ   (kota meh saltsa tou karidiou)

Allow 2 chicken breasts per person	1 tablespoon parsley, chopped
¼ cup flour or more	1 cup mushrooms, chopped
¼ teaspoon salt	1 cup water
pepper to taste	1 ounce brandy (optional)
2 tablespoons, butter or margarine	1 cup yogurt or sour cream
1 tablespoon oil	½ cup ground walnuts
3 fresh scallions, chopped	

Flour chicken lightly and sprinkle with salt and pepper. Heat fats in a large frying pan and add chicken. Brown for 5 minutes on each side. Add scallions, parsley, mushrooms, and water. Bring to a boil, cover, and reduce heat. Cook over low heat for 25 minutes or until tender.

Remove chicken from pan. Mix in brandy, yogurt or sour cream and walnuts, adding a little more water if a more liquid sauce is desired. Pour over breasts and serve on a bed of Rice Pilaf (page 59) or Boiled Cracked Wheat (page 61).

CHICKEN TAVERNA WITH TOMATOES

ΚΟΤΑ ΜΕ ΝΤΟΜΑΤΕΣ   (kota meh domates)

A *tapsie* is a large shallow baking pan, one of the handiest cooking utensils found in the Greek kitchen. One sees it in *tavernas* where large amounts of food are cooked, but no Greek bride would consider her dowry complete without one. Not only is this recipe cooked in a *tapsie,* but so are all the sweet pastries such as baklava and Custard Pie Galactoboureko.

1 chicken or 2 broilers, disjointed	1 onion, thinly sliced
¼ pound butter	1 tablespoon oregano
2 tablespoons oil	1 teaspoon marjoram
juice of 1 lemon	1 teaspoon savory
1 teaspoon salt	1 bay leaf
⅛ teaspoon pepper	½ cup red wine
1 2-pound can whole tomatoes or 1 cup tomato purée diluted with 2 cups hot water	

Wash chicken well with cold water. Combine butter and oil and heat. Pour half of it into shallow baking pan and lay chicken in it. Mix strained lemon juice in remaining mixture and baste chicken. Sprinkle with salt and pepper. Bake at 400° F. for 30 minutes.

Put tomatoes and remaining ingredients in a pot, bring to a boil and pour over chicken. Reduce oven heat to 350° F. and continue baking for 1 or 1½ hours more. Serve over a bed of Rice Pilaf (page 59) or add any kind of parboiled pasta, potatoes, or rice with chicken and bake in sauce for the last ½ hour of cooking time. If your baking pan is not large enough, see following recipe: Chicken Taverna with Pasta, Potatoes, or Rice.

CHICKEN TAVERNA WITH PASTA, POTATOES, OR RICE

ΚΟΤΑ ΤΑΒΕΡΝΑΣ ΜΕ ΠΑΣΤΑ, Η ΠΑΤΑΤΕΣ, Η ΡΥΖΙ
(kota tavernas meh pasta, e patates, e ryzi)

Use any *one* of the following:
1 pound pasta, either noodles,
  ***manestra (orzo)*, spaghetti or**
  ***trahana* (page 64)**

6 or 8 potatoes, peeled and
  quartered
2 cups rice, long grain
2 cups hot water

Follow recipe for Chicken Taverna with Tomatoes (page 118). Parboil pasta, potatoes, or rice for 10 minutes. Drain. Remove baked chicken to a covered dish. Add hot water to juices in roasting pan and drained pasta, potatoes, or rice. Spoon the sauce over the top of potatoes, etc. Bake 15 minutes at 400° F.

CRETAN CHICKEN PITTA

(page 150).

HELLENIC CHICKEN POT STEW

same as Hellenic Pot Roast (page 131).

CHICKEN WITH MANESTRA

(page 65).

CHICKEN STIFATHO

ΣΤΙΦΑΔΟ ΚΟΤΑ   (stifatho kota)

The aroma of this chicken stew is irresistible. It is also a magnificent recipe for wild duck or woodcock.

1 chicken or duck, disjointed
¼ cup olive oil
2 pounds, tiny whole onions, or, if
  large, quartered
3 cloves garlic, whole
2-ounce can of tomato paste
1 cup hot water

2 tablespoons vinegar
1 teaspoon salt
⅛ teaspoon pepper
1 tablespoon pickling spices
1 teaspoon orange rind
4 cups boiling water

Rinse chicken with cold water. Heat oil in a large pot. Brown meat, onions, and garlic on high heat about 10 minutes, stirring with a large spoon. Dissolve tomato paste in 1 cup of hot water, add vinegar and salt and pour into pot. Add remaining ingredients. Bring to a boil, cover and reduce to a slow simmer. Cook 2 to 2½ hours until fowl is tender and sauce is thick. Check stew midway through cooking to make sure meat is not sticking to the pot. If it is, you are cooking it too fast. Serve with mashed potatoes.

GREEK OVEN CHICKEN

ΤΗΓΑΝΙΤΗ ΚΟΤΟ ΣΤΟ ΦΟΥΡΝΟ   (tiganiti kota sto fourno)

The original recipe for crisp chicken called for the use of a frying pan, the *teganon.* The shape of it and its name are 3000 years old and so is the Greek lullaby to sleeping chickens and children that goes, "NANNI, NANNI, ΣΤΟ ΤΕΓΑΝΙ" *Nanni, Nanni, stou tegani.* "Sleep, sleep, in the frying pan." The same delicious blending of herbs and spices is used to coat the pieces of chicken but it is baked in a hot oven instead of frying to achieve the same kind of crunchy crust.

Allow 1 fryer for 3 persons
2 cups flour
1 teaspoon salt
¼ teaspoon pepper

½ teaspoon each: poultry seasoning, paprika, oregano, parsley, marjoram, thyme, garlic powder, and spearmint flakes
¼ pound butter
½ cup oil

Wash disjointed chicken with cold water. Put flour and seasonings in a strong bag. Shake bag to distribute flour and seasonings before adding pieces of chicken, a few at a time. Shake bag to coat each piece.

Melt butter and oil in pan until hot. Pour half of it into a large shallow baking pan. Lay pieces of chicken side by side. Brush remaining oil mixture on top. Bake at 450° F. for 1 hour, basting twice during baking. Turn pieces over to crisp on the other side during the last ½ hour. Remove chicken to dish and serve.

Add 2 cups boiling water to pan and stir to make a gravy for dipping bread or if planning to accompany with Rice Pilaf or mashed potatoes.

STOLEN CHICKENS

ΚΛΕΦΤΕΣ ΚΟΤΕΣ /ΕΞΟΧΙΚΟ   (kleftes kotes/eksohiko)

Throughout Greece you will be served succulent fowl, meat, or even fish baked with vegetables inside a paper wrapping. This recipe originated with a small band of Greeks who took to the hills to wage guerrilla warfare against the Turks in the 1500s. They lived in the mountains of Thessaly, harrying the Turks by night and hiding by day, forced to cook their food in earth pits to avoid being discovered. They became known as ΚΛΕΦΤΑΙ (kleftai), the thieves. After fighting to liberate Greece in the revolution of 1834, some of them degenerated into brigands, stealing from their own countrymen and demanding tribute. The author's grandfather was killed by these outlaws when he organized village resistance against them in 1900. They were finally routed in 1912 by the Greek army and all that remains of this terrorist group is a recipe for chicken.

1 small fryer, or any kind of fowl:
   partridge, pigeon, rock cornish
   hen, or lamb shanks, slices of leg
   of lamb or whole fish.
Any of the following, peeled: tiny
   carrots, mushrooms, onions and
   potatoes, Feta cheese

1 teaspoon salt
½ teaspoon pepper
1 teaspoon oregano
1 teaspoon thyme
1 teaspoon parsley
2 tablespoons butter

Wash fowl (or meat or fish) under cold water. Peel and cut vegetables into small pieces. Lay a generous piece of oiled parchment, or doubled oiled paper bag in a baking pan. Rub fowl with seasonings and herbs. Place butter and vegetables inside cavity, and around fowl. Wrap doubled paper snugly around fowl folding top over. Tie or seal with a paper clip. Bake at 325° F. for 2 hours or more, depending on the size of your roast. Serve on a bed of Rice Pilaf (page 59) or allow each person to open his own.

ROAST GOOSE WITH MACEDONIAN RICE STUFFING

ΨΗΤΗ ΧΗΝΑ ΜΕ ΠΑΡΑΓΕΜΙΣΤΗ ΜΕ ΡΥΖΙ
(psiti hena meh parayemisi meh rizi)

The wild mountainous area of Macedonia, around Kastoria, a town in the middle of a lake, provides good shooting sport for wild duck, goose and woodcock in January. This recipe comes from that region.

1 young goose or duck	½ cup honey
1 teaspoon salt	juice from 1 lemon
pepper to taste	Macedonian Rice Stuffing (page 124)

Prepare goose or duck by rinsing with cold water and patting dry. Sprinkle with salt and pepper. Mix honey and strained lemon juice. Set aside.

Make stuffing and fill cavity. Do not pack too tightly.

Baste goose with half of honey mixture, saving the remainder to use as basting sauce during baking. Bake at 400 F. for 2 hours, basting and turning goose often until it is crisp and golden brown on all sides.

GREEK MOUNTAIN ROAST TURKEY WITH PELEPONNESUS DRESSING

ΨΗΤΗ ΓΑΛΟΠΟΥΛΑ ΜΕ ΠΑΡΑΓΕΜΙΣΤΗ ΜΕ ΚΑΣΤΑΝΑ
(psiti galopoula meh parayemisi meh kastana)

The turkey may be a traditional North American bird but when he fluffs his feathers, his resemblance to the white-shirted red-fezzed Evzone of the Palace Royal Guards is unmistakable. The fat chestnuts grown in Peleponnesus gives this delicious recipe double citizenry.

1 large turkey, approximately 12 to 20 lbs.	1 tablespoon salt
¼ pound cold butter or margarine	1 tablespoon poultry seasoning
	Chestnut Dressing (page 124)

Pre-heat oven to 450° F. Rinse and prepare turkey. Cut butter into pats and with fingers push lumps of butter between skin and meat, next to breasts, legs and wherever you can. Try not to break through skin. Rub with salt and poultry seasoning inside cavity and out. Make dressing and stuff turkey. Save neck and giblets to be boiled into broth.

Place turkey in large roasting pan in preheated oven at 450° F. Bake 30 minutes.

Reduce heat to 350° F. and bake 4 hours. Cover during last 2 hours, to reduce drying out. Baste with drippings 4 or 5 times during baking. Cool 1 hour before slicing. Scoop out dressing and serve separately.

PICKLED FIGPECKERS (BECCAFICIA)

ΑΜΒΕΛΟΠΟΥΛΙΑ, ΣΥΚΑΛΙΔΕΣ   (ambelopoulia, sykalides)

The orphean warbler of southern Europe, called *ambelopoulia,* meaning bird of the grape vineyards, is quite meaty though only the size of a hummingbird. This recipe comes from Cyprus, where these birds migrate in great numbers when the figs and grapes are ripe for harvest.

Allow 5 or 6 figpeckers per person
2 cups water
½ teaspoon salt

MARINADE:
2 cups vinegar
1 cup white wine (optional)
½ teaspoon salt

Prepare by dipping bird in boiling water for a minute. Pluck feathers. Cut off heads and feet. Do not clean cavity.

Place birds in saucepan with cover, add 2 cups water and salt. Bring to a boil and boil for 5 minutes. Drain. Cool.

Mix. marinade. Allow birds to marinate 4 hours or longer. Chill before serving as appetizers.

ROAST BIRDS ON A SPIT

ΠΟΥΛΙΑ ΤΗΣ ΣΟΥΒΛΑΣ   (poulia tis souvlas)

Every young Greek village boy carries a sling shot but it's not the toy a casual observer would be likely to presume. These children learn at an early age to become accurate shots and downing a few sparrows, *ambelopoulia,* or turtledoves will turn dinner for the family into a minor feast with barbecued spitted birds over an open fire.

Allow 4 tiny birds per person: salt and pepper
   sparrows, figpeckers, turtledoves;   1 teaspoon oregano
   or larger birds such as pigeons,   ¼ cup butter or oil
   quail, or squab

Prepare birds by dipping in boiling water for 1 minute and plucking the feathers. Cut off heads and feet. Clean cavity.

Skewer 4 or 6 of the birds on a metal skewer. Baste with seasonings and melted butter or warm oil. Broil for 5 or 10 minutes turning skewer on all sides frequently. The small birds cook quickly. The larger ones will take 10 minutes more. Serve hot as appetizers and eat whole.

MACEDONIAN RICE STUFFING

ΠΑΡΑΓΕΜΙΣΜΑ ΜΕ ΡΥΖΙ   (parayemisma meh rizi)

Macedonia has produced one of the greatest conquerors of history, Alexander the Great. Macedonians are a proud and strong people, and their immediate proximity to the borders of Albania, Yugoslavia, Bulgaria and Turkey has brought a great variety into their foods.

2 tablespoons butter or oil   ½ teaspoon thyme
1½ cups rice, white or brown   ½ pound Feta cheese or Kefaloteri
3 cups boiling water   cheese, crumbled
½ teaspoon salt (less if using Feta)   ½ cup currants or raisins
⅛ teaspoon pepper   ¼ cup pine nuts or chopped almonds
1 teaspoon basil or marjoram

Melt butter in frying pan. Add rice and stir for 5 minutes to a golden color. Add boiling water, salt, pepper and herbs and cover. Simmer for 10 minutes. Allow to cool slightly. Add crumbled cheese. Mix in egg and remaining ingredients. Stuff any fowl such as chicken, duck or goose.

CHESTNUT DRESSING PELOPONNESUS

ΠΑΡΑΓΕΜΙΣΙ ΜΕ ΚΑΣΤΑΝΑ ΠΕΛΟΠΟΝΝΗΣΙΑΚΗ
                          (parayemisi meh kastana peloponnisiaki)

The mountains of the Peloponnesus produce large chestnuts and the people from Dholiana have developed many ways of using them. This Greek stuffing for barbecued roasts is equally delicious for the American Thanksgiving turkey.

3 tablespoons butter or oil
1 pound bulk pork sausage
5 onions, chopped
1 whole head celery, chopped, including leaves
1 bunch parsley, chopped
2 tablespoons poultry seasoning
1 tablespoon salt
⅛ teaspoon pepper

2 cups water or bouillon
3 loaves bread, fresh
2 eggs
1 pound chestnuts, peeled and cooked (see page 194) or canned chestnuts or chopped pecans
½ cup raisins
8 black olives (optional)

Melt butter in deep kettle. On medium heat, fry sausage, onions, celery and parsley for 5 minutes, stirring all the while. Add herbs and seasonings, and water. Cover and cook 15 minutes on low heat.

Make bread crumbs, using blender or chop into tiny pieces. Add to pot, toss, and mix well with onion mixture. Cover. Turn off heat and allow to steam 15 minutes. Mix in eggs and add chestnuts, raisins and olives last. Stuff turkey, chicken, lamb or suckling pig.

Bake any remaining dressing in covered dish at 350° F. for 1 hour.

THE SACRIFICIAL
ANIMALS

ΚΡΕΑΤΑ   (kreata)

To accuse the Greeks of appreciating only lamb is not to know them, though it is true they have a special way with it, using thyme, oregano, spearmint, garlic and lemon juice. Young spring lamb heralds the Easter season and is eagerly awaited for barbecuing, but no more than the suckling pig in late summer. Today in Greece the favorite meat seems to be veal, and recipes once confined to lamb are now likely to be made with veal. Beef is still rare because the raising of cattle has only recently begun in Greece and Cyprus with bulls from Scotland. Pork has been a festival meat since ancient times when it was offered as sacrificial meat to the Greek gods. Following the ceremonies, the pork was eaten by the priests or the people. Young goat or kid has a succulent meat which is often prepared over the glowing embers of outdoor barbecues.

Although the variety of smoked meats and sausages is limited, certain regions of Greece, particularly Cyprus and Levkas, are famous for the kinds which they prepare. *Kokkoretsi,* a sausage recipe thousands of years old, is still made.

BROILED STEAK, GREEK STYLE

ΚΡΕΑΣ ΤΗΣ ΣΧΑΡΑΣ   (kreas tis skaras)

A woman needs no other perfume to charm a man than the aroma she is wearing when she is in the kitchen broiling a good piece of prime steak. If she has also baked fresh bread that day, her conquest will be complete.

The major difference in broiling meat, Greek style, is that the juices are not allowed to drop away from the meat as they normally do on a slotted grill. Instead, a shallow pan is used to catch the juices, which are later served as a sauce with pieces of bread for dipping.

Allow ½ pound beefsteak (or pork, lamb or veal) per person
salt and pepper to taste
1 teaspoon oregano

3 pats of butter
juice of ½ lemon
½ cup boiling water

Place meat on shallow pan. Sprinkle with salt, pepper, and oregano. To crush oregano, pinch small portions between thumb and forefinger. Dot top with chunks of butter. Broil until done to taste on one side, approximately 5 minutes for medium rare; turn over and sprinkle with salt and more crushed oregano. Broil for another 5 minutes, or longer. Transfer meat to serving dish.

Working quickly, squeeze lemon into juices that remain in pan. Add hot water and return under broiler for 2 minutes. Pour juices into gravy boat. Serve with crusty bread, or pour over meat or potatoes.

SKEWERED STEAK SOUVLAKIA

ΣΟΤΒΛΑΚΙΑ   (souvlakia)

This recipe is more commonly known by its Turkish name, *Shiskebab,* but the actual origin of skewering meats and vegetables and broiling them antedates written history. In all probability, it began with shepherds who cooked strips of meat on twigs over open fires as they tended their flocks. About 500 B.C. the Greeks used a shallow clay brazier called an *eschara* which had lugs at either side so the spits could be turned easily to broil the *souvlakia* at the table.

½ pound meat per person: steak, beef or veal, pork, lamb, liver, kidneys
2 firm tomatoes, quartered
1 onion, quartered or tiny whole ones
1 green bell pepper, cut in 1" strips

8 mushrooms, caps and stems separated
salt and pepper to taste
oregano
1 lemon, juice only

Cube meat into 1" pieces. Wash and prepare vegetables. Skewer each one in the following order: green pepper, mushroom stem, onion, meat, tomato, and continue until skewer is ¾ full.

Cap with mushroom. Lay skewer flat in shallow pan. Do not crowd. Sprinkle with remaining ingredients.

Broil 5 minutes on one side, turn over and broil 4 minutes on other side. Do not overcook or they will taste dry. Serve immediately as appetizers or as main meat course on bed of pilaf.

ROAST BEEF, GREEK STYLE

ΨΗΤΟ ΒΩΔΙΝΟ   (psito voythino)

To cook roast beef without seasoning except for a little salt and, furthermore, not cook it beyond rare as preferred by so many people in the United States, is not an easy thing for a Greek cook to do. Because of all the foreign influences in Greece, roast beef is prepared in three different ways today. The nearest meat to America's favorite is called *moskhari psito* and is made from veal or young beef. *Doner Kebab* is beef roasted on a vertical spit called a *yiro,* and browned on all sides. Thick slices of meat are carved off this roast and sold in many restaurants and tavernas. It's an easy recipe to duplicate in the new stoves which have rotisserie attachments. *Roz Bif* is a delicous, spicy, highly flavored beef served with macaroni, a true Greek style of cooking.

ROZ BIF

ΡΟΣΜΠΙΦ, ΜΟΣΧΑΡΙ ΨΗΤΟ   (roz bif) (moshari psito)

5 pound roast of beef or veal (eye or round, rolled rump, rib roast, sirloin tip)
3 teaspoons salt
⅛ teaspoon cracked pepper
3 cloves garlic, halved
1 teaspoon each: oregano, savory and marjoram

1 onion, halved
3 cups boiling water
1 lemon, juice only
½ cup grated cheese, Kefaloteri, Parmesan or Romano
1 pound cooked macaroni or other pasta

Rub roast with seasonings and herbs, making slits in the meat for the garlic halves. Place onion on top and underneath roast in a shallow baking pan. Roast at 350° F. for 2 hours, or 2½ hours for well done. Remove meat to platter. Keep warm.

Add boiling water and lemon juice to pan. Add 1 pound of cooked macaroni or spaghetti to gravy in the pan. Toss to distribute sauce. Sprinkle with cheese and bake for 10 minutes at 375° F. Serve hot with slices of Roz Bif arranged around it.

ROZ BIF WITH POTATOES

ΡΟΖ ΜΠΙΦ ΜΕ ΠΑΤΑΤΕΣ   (roz bif meh patates)

Follow recipe for Roz Bif (page 128) and half-way through baking substitute 8 parboiled potatoes, sliced or quartered, instead of pasta, and continue cooking beef and potatoes together until done.

ROZ BIF WITH RICE

ΡΟΖ ΜΠΙΦ ΜΕ ΡΥΖΙ   (roz bif meh ryzi)

Follow recipe for Roz Bif (page 128), and substitute 2 cups cooked rice for pasta.

ROAST BEEF RARE

ΜΟΣΧΑΡΙ ΨΗΤΟ, ΜΙΣΟΨΗΜΕΝΟ   (moskhari psito misopsimeno)

5-pound roast of beef or veal   **pepper to taste**
2 teaspoons salt   **1 onion, quartered**

Rub roast with salt. Place onion on top and under roast. Do not add water to shallow pan. Cook at 325° F. for 1½ hours. *No more.* Do not cut immediately after taking it out of the oven. Slice beef thinly on a carving plate with a well to catch juices. The meat should be red and the juices bloody. This is the way many people in the United States prefer their roast beef.

BEEF STEW KALAMARA

ΣΤΙΦΑΔΟ ΚΑΛΑΜΑΡΑ   (stifatho Kalamara)

Once you have smelled stifatho cooking you will always remember it. Its aroma will beckon anyone in the neighborhood into your kitchen. This recipe has traveled from Greece to other lands. The Spanish call it *stifado* and the Hungarians know it as goulash, but no matter what it is named, every land has its version of this recipe.

2 pounds of lean meat: beef, or veal
2 pounds onions, tiny boiling onions
  or large ones, quartered
3 cloves garlic, peeled and halved
¼ cup olive oil
1 cup tomato sauce or 2-ounce can of
  tomato paste diluted in 1 cup hot
  water

2 tablespoons vinegar or ½ cup red
  wine
2 teaspoons salt
1 tablespoon pickling spices
1 teaspoon orange rind
3 cups boiling water

Cut meat into 1½" cubes. Peel onions, and quarter if large. (To make peeling onions easier, put them in a pan of hot water for a minute.) Peel and cut garlic cloves in half. Heat oil in a large pot until hot. Brown meat on all sides for 5 minutes on high heat. Use large spoon to stir and avoid sticking and scorching. Add onions and garlic and continue stirring for 5 minutes, until coated with oil. Add remaining ingredients, and mix in.

Cover, reduce heat and simmer over low heat for 2½ hours until meat is tender and sauce is thick. Check midway through cooking to make sure meat is not sticking to the bottom of the pot. If it is, add 1 cup of water and reduce heat.

CORFU STEAK

ΣΟΦΡΙΤΟ   (sofrito)

This recipe comes from Corfu and has become a favorite throughout Greece.

2 pounds round steak or rump roast
½ cup flour
½ teaspoon salt
pepper to taste
½ cup oil

2 cloves garlic
1½ cups vinegar
1 cup water
1 teaspoon sugar

Pound steak with mallet until thin. If using a small roast, slice into ¼ inch thickness. Place flour on a flat plate with salt and pepper. Flour steaks on both sides.

Heat oil in a large frying pan. Brown meat on medium heat for 5 minutes on each side. Add remaining ingredients. Bring to a boil. Reduce to simmer and cover. Cook 1½ hours. Serve with crusty bread.

HELLENIC POT ROAST

ΚΑΠΑΜΑ ΕΛΛΗΝΙΚΟ, ΓΚΙΟΤΒΕΤΣΙ   (kapama Elleniko, giouvetsi)

The Hellenic way of stewing meat in a covered pot, sometimes with vegetables added, other times not, is known as *kapama*. Another name for this encompassing recipe is *giouvetsi,* a Slavic word which Macedonians still prefer to use when making this stew. Thousands of years ago this ancient recipe was cooked in a shallow casserole clay pot, a *lopas,* placed over a cylindrical charcoal brazier.

2 pounds meat: beef, veal, lamb, kid, pork, chicken, or rabbit. Cut meat in 2" chunks or leave whole if using leg of lamb or chuck of beef
2 tablespoons oil or butter
2 onions, chopped
½ cup tomato sauce or 1 tablespoon tomato paste
3 cups water

SPICES:
2 bay leaves
½ teaspoon oregano or marjoram   It →
1 teaspoon salt
4 peppercorns

OPTIONAL:
Vegetables, any one *kind* or combination desired; fresh or frozen:
artichokes, quartered
celery, cut into 2" pieces
eggplant, peeled and cut into pieces
green beans
okra, destemmed
peas
summer squash, cut in 2" pieces or whole if small zucchini variety
quinces, peeled, quartered, parboiled
potatoes, peeled, quartered, parboiled

Prepare meat by cutting into pieces.

Heat oil in a heavy pot with cover (sometimes called a Dutch oven). Brown meat on all sides over medium heat. Add chopped onions and continue browning. Add tomato, water, seasonings and spices. Cover and simmer on top burners over stove on low heat until meat is tender, about 2 hours. (Or if preferred, bake at 350° F. for 2 hours.)

Add any fresh vegetables desired during the last 45 minutes of cooking time. If frozen, add the last 20 minutes of cooking time, and baste both meat and vegetables with sauce.

Variation

Byzantine Pot Roast: Add in with other spices and seasonings the following ingredients:

¼ teaspoon cinnamon
1 teaspoon orange peel
2 tablespoons currants
2 tablespoons pine nuts
½ cup red wine

½ pound parboiled pasta, either elbow macaroni, spaghetti or manestra (orzo) or 1 cup parboiled rice
1 cup hot water

1 lrg. eggplant   1 cup red wine
1 can beef consumme

When meat is cooked add parboiled pasta or rice and an extra cup of hot water to the juices in the baking pan and spoon some of it on top. Cook 15 minutes longer until soft alongside of meat unless your pan is not large enough to accommodate both. In that case, remove cooked meat first to a dish and keep warm.

MEAT STEW WITH EGG AND LEMON SAUCE

ΓΑΧΝΙ ΜΕ ΑΤΓΟΛΕΜΟΝΟ   (yahkni meh avgholemono)

The tangy sauce gives this Greek stew a refreshing piquant flavor. It can be made in many ways depending upon the kind of meat and vegetables desired.

2 pounds of beef or other kind of meat: veal, lamb, or pork	Brussels sprouts green beans
2 onions, coarsely chopped	1 tablespoon oil
5 stalks celery or 1 whole head, cut 1" pieces	1 tablespoon butter 1 teaspoon salt pepper to taste
Vegetables (optional): any one or combination desired; fresh or frozen:	3 cups boiling water Egg and Lemon Sauce, Avgholemono (page 67)
artichokes	3 eggs
broccoli	2 lemons, juice only

Prepare meat and vegetables by cutting into bite-size pieces. Heat oil and butter in a large pot. Add meat, celery, onions and brown on high heat for 5 minutes. Add remaining vegetables, seasonings, water and cover. Reduce heat. Simmer 1½ hours until tender. Remove from heat to a bowl.

Prepare sauce and pour over stew mixing in lightly. Serve immediately.

GREEK MEAT BALLS WITH MINT

ΚΕΦΤΕΔΕΣ   (keftethes)

These fried meat balls, *keftethes,* are crisp on the outside and moist on the inside, and are equally delicious hot or cold. The spearmint gives them a very unusual flavor.

1 pound ground beef (or lamb or veal)
4 slices bread
1 onion finely chopped, or a few
  green onions
½ cup parsley, finely chopped
1 egg

1 teaspoon spearmint flakes
1 teaspoon salt
⅛ teaspoon pepper
1 garlic clove, pressed (optional)
1 cup flour
½ cup oil

Put meat in a bowl. Dip bread in a bowl of water and squeeze out excess water. Crumble bread and add with remaining ingredients to meat. Mix together, kneading with your hands.

Put flour on a flat plate. Using a teaspoon, scoop out a small amount of mixture. With another teaspoon, push meat off the spoon onto the flour and roll into small balls covering all sides with flour. (Make these balls as large or as tiny as you prefer. For hors d'oeuvres, scoop out scant teaspoons of mixture.)

Heat oil in a large frying pan. Drop balls into hot oil and fry 10 to 15 minutes until crisp and brown on all sides.

GREEK MEAT BALLS WITH SAUCE

ΓΙΟΤΒΑΡΛΑΚΙΑ ΜΕ ΣΑΛΤΣΑ   (youvarlakia meh saltsa)

See Greek Meat Balls with Mint (page
  132)
½ cup rice
4 cups broth

SAUCE:
Any one of the following:
Egg and Lemon Sauce (page 67)
Tomato Sauce (page 68) with ½
  cup yogurt

Add rice to ingredients for Greek Meat Balls with Mint (page 132). Follow directions for mixing, and make floured balls as for frying. Bring broth to a rolling boil and drop meat balls into broth. Cover and simmer 45 minutes.

Prepare desired sauce. Remove meat balls from heat and mix sauce into it, stirring in lightly. If serving with tomato sauce, yogurt may be mixed in also at the same time.

MEAT PIE ROUMELI

(page 151).

MEAT AND MACARONI PASTITSO

(page 62).

MEZE SPERO

ΜΕΖΕ ΣΠΕΡΟ   (mehzeh spero)

This recipe is a Greek's way of catching all the juices from broiling meat. It makes an original open-faced sandwich. Any kind of sliced bread will do, although the ancient Greeks baked a special bread for sandwiches, called ΘΡΙΔΑΚΙΝΗ (thridakini).

For each serving:
2 ounces of ground beef
1 slice bread

salt and pepper to taste
Tomato sauce (page 68) or catsup

Pat raw meat on a slice of bread spreading it to the corners. Place under a hot broiler for 5 minutes. The meat is seared quickly and the juices seep into the bread as it cooks. Serve whole with knife and fork, or cut in quarters. Garnish with a dab of prepared tomato sauce or catsup.

SPICY SAUSAGES

ΣΟΥΤΖΟΥΚΑΚΙΑ   (soutzoukakia)

These spicy sausages are made by the people of Cyprus who flavor the meat with cumin or coriander and shape the sausage about the size of a finger.

1 pound ground coarse beef (lamb,
   pork or veal may be substituted)
1 cup bread crumbs or 3 slices of
   bread
1 teaspoon cumin
1 teaspoon coriander
2 cloves garlic, pressed
2 tablespoon parsley, chopped or 1
   teaspoon dried flakes
1 egg
1 teaspoon salt

⅛ teaspoon pepper
1 onion, chopped fine
½ cup tomato sauce
1 cup of flour for rolling
1 cup oil for frying

Recommended sauces:
Tomato Sauce (page 67)
Egg and Lemon Sauce (page 67)
Plain yogurt

Mix all ingredients except flour and oil, kneading with hands until well blended. Spoon out 1 generous tablespoon of mixture and make sausages about 4" long. Roll in flour. Fry in hot oil for 15 minutes until brown on all sides. Drain. Serve plain, hot or cold as appetizers, or with any one of the recommended sauces as the main meat course.

BREADED SWEETBREADS

ΓΛΥΚΑΔΙΑ   (glikadia)

If you have never been introduced to sweetbreads, this is a delicious way to start. The sweetbread is part of the thymus of a young calf and is soft yet firm. The contrast between a crisp crust and the cooked white meat is worth the effort of preparation.

2 pounds sweetbreads	2 cups bread crumbs or zwieback
water to cover	crumbs, fine
1 teaspoon salt	½ teaspoon salt
1 tablespoon vinegar	1 cup oil
2 eggs, beaten	2 tablespoons butter or margarine

Soak sweetbreads in water to cover with salt and vinegar, 1 hour or longer. Boil in fresh salted water 30 minutes. Drain. Plunge immediately into cold water. Clean by trimming off white membrane and thick part.

Slice into 2 or 3 slices, or cut in half. Dip in beaten eggs, roll in crumbs. Repeat once more. Heat oil and butter or margarine together in a large frying pan. Fry 10 to 15 minutes until golden brown on both sides. Drain on a paper towel.

To bake instead of frying: melt butter in a baking dish, add sweetbreads, baste tops with butter and bake 45 minutes at 375° F.

BROILED LAMB CHOPS, GREEK STYLE

ΜΠΡΙΖΟΛΕΣ   (brizoles)

1 tablespoon oregano	garlic powder (optional)
1 teaspoon spearmint flakes	Allow 2 lamb chops per person: rib
½ teaspoon garlic	or loin, or sliced ¾ inch thick off a
½ teaspoon thyme (optional)	leg
1 teaspoon salt	1 lemon
pepper to taste	

Mix herbs with salt and pepper in a smal bowl. Arrange chops on unslotted broiler pan. Sprinkle with some of the herb mixture. Broil 7 minutes on one side. Turn over and sprinkle tops with remaining herb mixture. Continue broiling 5 to 8 minutes more, depending on how well done you want them to be. Remove chops to a serving platter and squeeze half a lemon over them.

Add 1 cup of hot water to pan and squeeze the other half of lemon into it. Return under broiler for 3 minutes. Pour sauce into a gravy bowl and serve with crusty bread for dipping.

SKEWERED LAMB SOUVLAKIA

ΑΡΝΙ ΣΟΥΒΛΑΚΙ   (arni souvlakia)

The enlightened men of ancient Greece may not have used forks, knives or spoons but neither did they tear meat off large roasts when dining, as the Celts did. Instead Greek cooks, the magyerie, would cut meat into manageable pieces and cook it on skewers in braziers especially designed for this recipe.

Allow ½ pound lamb per person. Cut lean lamb from leg of lamb, into 1 inch cubes (veal, kid, rabbit or chicken may be substituted)

MARINADE:
½ cup olive oil

1 cup wine
1 teaspoon salt
⅛ teaspoon pepper
1 teaspoon oregano
1 teaspoon spearmint
1 clove garlic, pressed

Skewer lamb on metal or wood skewers, leaving a minimum of space between. Mix marinade and pour into a shallow pan. Lay skewered meat in it, and spoon marinade over meat. Marinate 2 hours, turning skewers over so all sides of meat will be in contact with sauce. Broil 10 minutes, turning as it cooks.

NEW SOUVLAKIA IN A BUN

ΝΕΑ ΣΟΥΒΛΑΚΙΑ ΜΕ ΨΩΜΙ   (nea souvlakia meh psomi)

Every country has its hamburger stands. In Greece, it is the new *souvlakia* stand, found on practically every street corner. The food is good, the price cheap and you meet everyone in town, townspeople and tourists. For fifteen cents you can get one of the most delicious dishes in the country—a flat bread, sort of baked pancake, crisp and puffy, filled with spicy barbecued lamb and onions, topped with fresh tomatoes and yogurt.

FLAT BREAD:
1 tablespoon dry or cake yeast
1 cup warm water
¾ teaspoon salt
2 cups flour, unsifted

FILLING:
1 pound lamb, chopped. See
Skewered Lamb Souvlakia (page
136).

1 teaspoon oregano
1 onion, chopped
salt and pepper to taste
1 tomato, chopped
½ lemon or 1 cup yogurt

Sprinkle yeast in water. Add salt and flour and mix until smooth. Cover and set aside in a warm place for 2 hours. Knead dough 15 minutes or more, filling it with air bubbles. Divide into 6 small balls the size of an orange. Pat each one into a round shape. Place on hot floured baking pan or cookie sheet and bake in a preheated oven at 550° F. for 5 minutes, until puffy.

Shape into a cone or slit tops and fill hollow with lamb filling. If flat breads are cool, place for 2 minutes in a hot oven or in a lightly oiled frying pan to heat before filling.

Filling: If lamb is uncooked, cut into small pieces, sprinkle with oregano and broil for 5 to 7 minutes. Put cooked meat into cone or hollow, salt and pepper lightly. Add a teaspoon of chopped onions and tomatoes and top with a squeeze of lemon or a dab of yogurt.

GREEK ROAST LAMB

ΑΡΝΙ ΨΗΤΟ   (arni psito)

Lamb is the meat of sacrifice in Greece and has been so since time immemorial. The priests of pagan Greece would sprinkle it with oregano and thyme that grew wild on the mountain side and anoint the animal with olive oil and lemon juice before roasting it as an offering to the gods. Women were not allowed to prepare this meat. To this day every male considers himself a *maygeiros* (chef) and will not hesitate to step into your kitchen to check whether the *buti* (leg) has been prepared properly.

1 leg of lamb
3 cloves garlic, peeled and halved
1 tablespoon salt
⅛ teaspoon pepper
1 tablespoon oregano

1 teaspoon thyme
1 tablespoon spearmint flakes
2 lemons, juice only
3 cups boiling water

Wipe meat and place in a shallow baking pan. With a small knife make four incisions and insert sliced cloves of garlic. Rub with salt, pepper, oregano and mint. Roast meat at 425° F. for 30 minutes. Reduce heat to 350° F. and continue baking 2 hours longer. Add lemon juice and water the last half hour and baste lamb with juice. Skim some of the floating oil that accumulates in the pan and use the remaining liquid as gravy. If desired, add parboiled potatoes, pasta or rice to juices in pan. See following recipe.

GREEK ROAST LAMB WITH PASTA, POTATOES, OR RICE

ΑΡΝΙ ΨΗΤΟ ΜΕ ΠΑΣΤΑ, Η ΠΑΤΑΤΕΣ, Η ΡΥΖΙ-ΓΙΟΥΒΕΤΣΙ
(arni psito meh pasta, e patates, e rizi-giouvetsi)

This recipe is often served in an earthenware pot, exactly as it was done thousands of years ago.

Recipe for Greek Roast Lamb
2 cups tomato juice (optional)
1 pound of any kind of pasta:
   macaroni, spaghetti, *manestra*
   (*orzo*) or noodles

or
8 potatoes, peeled and quartered
or
2 cups rice

Follow recipe for Greek Roast Lamb. During the last 45 minutes of roasting time, add tomato juice to pan if preferred. Parboil for 10 minutes, in water to cover, selected accompaniment from above list. Drain.

Remove lamb from pan, and add cooked pasta, potatoes, or rice to pan, spooning juices over the top. Return to oven for 15 minutes at 400° F.

GREEK ROAST LAMB WITH ARTICHOKES

ΑΡΝΙ ΨΗΤΟ ΜΕ ΑΓΚΙΝΑΡΕΣ   (arni psito me anginares)

Recipe for Greek Roast Lamb
8 artichokes, cleaned and prepared
   as described on page 78, or 3
   packages frozen artichokes

Follow directions for Greek Roast Lamb. Add parboiled or frozen artichokes to sauce in pan 30 minutes before lamb is done and finish baking with roast.

LAMB BAKED IN PAPER

ΑΡΝΙ ΨΗΤΟ ΣΤΟ ΧΑΡΤΙ/ΕΞΩΧΙΚΟ (arni psito sto harti/eksohiko)

leg of lamb or lamb shanks
2 ounces or more, Feta or Kasseri
   cheese
1 teaspoon each, thyme, spearmint
   flakes, oregano

2 cloves garlic
juice of two lemons
1 tablespoon salt
pepper to taste

Wipe meat with damp cloth. Make incisions with small sharp knife on all sides of leg or shanks. Insert pieces of garlic glove and cheese. Rub with lemon juice. Sprinkle with herbs, salt and pepper. Wrap securely in heavy paper twice. Use greaseproof paper such as cooking parchment or oil brown paper. (Do not use aluminum foil. It prevents browning.) Tie with string. Bake a leg for 2½ hours in 350° F. oven. Bake 2 hours if using shanks.

LAMB AND LEEKS MAHALA

ΑΡΝΙ ΜΕ ΠΡΑΣΣΑ ΜΑΧΑΛΑ (arni meh prassa mahala)

In the mountainous Roumeli region of Greece, near the city of Lamia, there is a little village called Mahala, where the women make a simple, tasty lamb dish with leeks.

2 tablespoons oil
2 pounds of lamb, cut in 2" pieces
1 clove garlic, peeled and halved
1 bunch leeks, washed and cut in
   pieces

2 teaspoons salt
pepper to taste
3 cups water

Heat oil and brown lamb on high heat for 10 minutes, stirring all the while. Add remaining ingredients, cover and reduce heat to simmer for 2 hours. Serve with crusty bread and retsina wine.

LAMB STEW WITH EGG AND LEMON SAUCE

Same as Meat Stew with Egg and Lemon Sauce (page 132).

BAKED LAMB HEADS

ΚΕΦΑΛΑΚΙΑ ΑΡΝΙΣΙΑ   (kefalakia arnisia)

Any rancher will tell you that barbecued calve's head makes "good eatin'." The same applies to the Greeks' version of baked lamb's head. They may be specially ordered at any butcher shop. The butcher should prepare them by halving them carefully and tying them together to keep the brains intact.

Allow 1 head per person

Soak heads in cold salted water for 2 hours.

Rinse. Place each half in baking pan with cut side up. Remove string. Baste with lemon juice, olive oil, salt, pepper, and oregano while baking. Bake at 350° F. for 45 minutes.

To eat: use forks to pick off meat. The soft baked brains are considered a delicacy, the tongue is meaty and tasty, and some people consider the eyes the most delectable.

LAMB KIDNEYS IN WINE SAUCE

ΝΕΦΡΑ ΜΕ ΣΑΛΤΣΑ ΚΡΑΣΙ   (nefra meh saltsa krasi)

2 pounds kidneys
1 tablespoon vinegar
2 tablespoons flour
2 tablespoons butter or margarine
2 tablespoons oil
1 clove garlic, pressed
salt and pepper to taste

1 teaspoon each: marjoram, oregano, parsley
1 bay leaf
1 cup mushrooms
1 cup wine or 1 tablespoon vinegar and 1 cup water

Prepare and rinse kidneys in cold water with vinegar. Remove skin, cut core, slice and flour. Melt butter and oil in large frying pan. Fry kidneys on medium heat until lightly browned, on both sides. Add remaining ingredients In order listed. Cover and simmer 20 minutes, stirring a few times.

SKEWERED MARINATED KIDNEYS

See Skewered Lamb Souvlakia (page 136).

BARBECUED KOKKORETSI ROUMELI

ΚΟΚΚΟΡΕΤΣΙ   (kokkoretsi)

If you are sightseeing in the streets of Athens or any other city of Greece, do not hesitate to buy some *kokkoretsi*. You are served a small piece of this sausage when you order a drink at a taverna, but the aroma will persuade you to buy some from street vendors barbecuing this three-thousand-year-old recipe on sidewalk grills. Everything that is edible from the inside of a young lamb or kid goes into this recipe, and the sausage is formed with the casing twined outside the filling, instead of the traditional way sausages are filled.

1 pound each of lamb's kidneys, liver, heart, lung and sweetbreads
water to cover
1 teaspoon salt
1 tablespoon vinegar

MARINADE:

½ cup olive oil
juice of 1 lemon
1 teaspoon each: oregano, cumin, garlic, thyme, salt
⅛ teaspoon pepper
1 pound intestines (special order from butcher)

Put meats in water to cover seasoned with salt and vinegar, for 10 minutes. Drain. Remove any membranes, and chop, or grind coarsely.

Mix marinade and mix into meat. Make a long sausage by skewering pieces of meat alternately.

Use washed intestines to tie meat securely to skewer, covering the meat by winding the intestines up and around back and forth. Or make sausage patties and place them on a broiler pan. Broil under slow fire or over charcoal fire until done.

BROILED PORK CHOPS GREEK STYLE

Same as Broiled Lamb Chops Greek Style (page 135).

SKEWERED PORK STEAK

Same as Skewered Steak Souvlakia (page 127).

PORK STEW WITH CELERY

Same as Meat Stew with Egg and Lemon Sauce (page 132).

JELLIED PORK PIKTI

ΠΥΚΤΗ   (pikti)

1 pound pigs knuckles, feet or head	2 teaspoons salt
1 pound lean pork	1 bay leaf
water to cover	1 cup vinegar or juice of 4 lemons
1 tablespoon mixed pickling spices consisting of a peppercorns, chili, pepper, bay leaf, clove, garlic, thyme	

Cover pork with approximately 2 quarts of water in a large pot. Add spices and salt. Bring to a boil, cover and reduce heat to simmer for 4 hours. Strain stock. Chop meat off bones. Add to stock. Mix in vinegar and chill. Meat and sauce will congeal and can be spooned out or sliced.

SAUSAGES MESSINIA

ΛΟΥΚΑΝΙΚΑ ΜΕΣΣΗΝΙΑΣ   (loukanika Messinias)

Pork recipes from Greece are rare even though pork is considered a great delicacy. For centuries, the Moslem Turks forbade the eating of pork. To this day in some areas of Greece, a pig is only slaughtered on special occasions and the roasting of pork and the making of sausages is an event. This family recipe for sausages *loukanika* was brought to America by my mother, Kereakulla Zakas Karadimou of Kalamara, near Kalamata.

1 pound casings (special order from butcher)	1 teaspoon cracked pepper
	2 tablespoons fresh orange peel
Leg of fresh pork or pork butt (2 pounds minimum)	1 teaspoon thyme
	1 tablespoon savory (thrombi)
2 teaspoons salt	1 clove garlic

Put casing to soak in salted cold water overnight. Rinse under running water. If casing is frozen, only rinsing is necessary. Attach each casing to faucet and let water run through it gently as it does through a hose. Cover with water and boil 5 minutes.

Prepare meat for stuffing. Cut pork and fat into little pieces with sharp knife or put through coarse grinder. Remove white pulp from orange peel. Add remaining ingredients and mix well.

Tie one end of casing with string. Tie the other end around a wide mouth funnel and stuff. Tie again where stuffing ends. Save any unused casing by freezing, and keep sausage refrigerated or frozen until cooked.

To cook sausage: Fry or broil 15 minutes until browned and well done.

SUCKLING PIG

ΓΟΥΡΟΥΝΟΠΟΥΛΟ ΨΗΤΟ   (gourounopoulo psito)

A suckling animal, whether pig, lamb or kid, is the traditional meat for barbecuing for holidays and family gatherings. A barbecue picnic in Greece is very much the same as anywhere else. It is a gathering of the clan and friends, with much beer drinking, card playing among the old men, gossiping among the women, business discussions by the younger men, flirting adolescents and children running and playing, all waiting for the roast on the spit to finish cooking. The delicious odor from a suckling pig, kid, or lamb turning on a spit over charcoal fire can be duplicated in your own barbecue or oven with no more effort than it takes to prepare a turkey.

Suckling pig, kid or lamb
2 tablespoons salt
½ teaspoon pepper
3 lemons, juice only

1 orange
1 apple, cranberries, black olives or
  cherries

Order suckling animal from butcher two weeks in advance.

Scrub skin with stiff brush and cold water, and rinse cavity with cold water. Pat dry, rub with salt and lemon juice. If desired, stuff with any kind of dressing. Sew cavity with white thread. Tie front legs together facing forward. Tie hind legs together and bring forward also. Cover ears with aluminum foil. With sharp knife make 6 small 1"-long slashes all over top of animal to enable fat to escape. Place orange in mouth. Bake at 350° F. for 4 hours or longer, allowing 25 minutes per pound, or barbecue on a spit over burning coals. (For a Greek flavor, add pine boughs to the fire. You will then have *Arnakia Palikare*, "Soldier's Lamb.") Baste while roasting.

To decorate animal: replace orange with red apple. Use olives or cherries for eyes and make a necklace of cranberries. Garnish serving platter with slices of pineapple, red apple and chopped parsley.

Note: If the suckling animal is too large for your home oven, then you must ask a restaurant to cook it for you.

BAKED HARE MACEDONIA

ΛΑΓΟΣ ΚΡΑΣΣΑΤΟ   (lagos krassato)

On the northern border of Greece in Macedonia and Thrace, the women of the village of Kavalla, Naoussa and Kastoria prepare hare simmered in the strong red wine made in the peninsula of Chalkidiki.

1 rabbit or hare (or game bird such as woodcock, quail, wild duck or partridge)	½ cup mushrooms or walnuts
	3 onions, chopped coarsely
water to cover	2 cups red dry wine
1 tablespoon vinegar	¼ cup honey
¼ cup oil	2 tablespoons mixed pickling spices:
2 tablespoons butter	peppercorns, chili, pepper, bay
1 teaspoon salt	leaf, clove, garlic, thyme
⅛ teaspoon pepper	1 teaspoon parsley
	1 tablespoon cornstarch

Marinate rabbit in cold water to cover with vinegar, for 1 hour. Drain. Rinse with cold water. If using wild duck, discard liver and sear insides with hot poker.

Melt butter and oil together and add a little to a baking pan. Place rabbit or hare in baking pan and rub salt and pepper inside and out. Place chopped vegetables around it. Baste top with some oil. Bake in preheated oven at 450° F. for 30 minutes.

Bring wine, honey and spices to a boil and pour over rabbit. Reduce heat to 350° and continue baking 1½ hours or longer. Transfer to a serving dish.

Add cornstarch to 1 cup cold water and add to sauce in pan. Return to oven and stir until it thickens. Ladle sauce over rabbit.

RABBIT

ΛΑΓΟΣ, ΚΟΥΝΕΛΛΙ   (lagos, kounelli)

The rabbit is of Mediterranean origin and recipes for it must be at least three thousand years old. Many ancient vases and kylix have been found with decorations of long-legged rabbits in running positions. It is a versatile meat and can be substituted in any chicken or beef recipe. Prepare rabbit by marinating in cold water to cover with 1 tablespoon of vinegar and 1 tablespoon salt. Rinse with cold water and use whole or disjointed in any of the following recipes.

GREEK OVEN RABBIT

See Greek Oven Chicken (page 120).

HELLENIC RABBIT STEW

See Hellenic Pot Roast (page 131).

SKEWERED RABBIT

See Skewered Lamb Souvlakia (page 136).

RABBIT STIFATHO

See Beef Stew Kalamara (page 129).

STOLEN RABBIT

See Stolen Chickens (page 121).

RABBIT TAVERNA STYLE

See Chicken Taverna (page 118).

THE BYZANTINE
PASTRY CALLED
PITTA

Greek pastries are made from a paper-thin dough called *filo,* sometimes spelled "fillo" or "phyllo," and pronounced fee/low. *Filo* looks and feels like baked sheets of paper, crackling and crumbling at a touch. The dough is made from flour and stretched either by hand or machine until it becomes thin as tissue paper. It is used as a crust in pie and tart recipes. The number of layers that go into a recipe will vary, depending on the cook, how thin the dough is and what kind of pie or tart is being made. For pies, the sheets are laid flat in a square or rectangular pan; for tarts, they are rolled around a filling. *Filo,* a Greek word for leaf, is very descriptive of these pastries. As many as ten to twenty sheets or leaves are used for the top and bottom crusts.

Making good thin *filo* is one of the pastry arts of the world. Though ancient Greeks knew the secret of making this flaky pastry, whether they originated one of the world's greatest recipes is lost in antiquity. The Indians, Persians, Syrians, Yugoslavs and Turks all claim it as their own, as do the Germanic people who call their *filo,* strudel.

Commercially prepared *filo* is available frozen in the United States, making it easy to prepare exotic pastries like *baklava* and cheese *trigonas,* at a moment's notice.

FILO DOUGH

ΦΤΛΛΟ ΖΥΜΑΡΙ   (feelow zymari)

Practice will improve your ability to make *filo;* it's messy but fun and not too difficult.

2 eggs
½ teaspoon salt
1 cup warm water

3 tablespoons oil
4 cups flour

Beat eggs, salt and liquids together. Add flour and knead until smooth. Rub hands with oil occasionally while kneading. Let dough rest in a plastic bag at least an hour or longer, even overnight, before stretching it.

Divide dough into small pieces the size of a small orange. Cover remaining dough. Dust a cloth covered table lightly with flour. Roll dough flat and round using a long rolling pin made from a broomstick handle or a dowel ½″ thick by 4′. Continue stretching the dough thinner on the table by pulling it with your palms, fingers together. Do not worry about a few holes that appear.

If a friend is near to hold the other end, transfer dough to a 4′ dowel or a broom handle and let gravity help stretch it, using your palms to help it fall.

Pillow Method for Stretching *Filo:* Use pillows to help support dough as you stretch it. After flattening the dough with a rolling pin, transfer it to a pillow, which will help support the dough and give way as you slide your palms, face up, under the thinning layer. As you stretch it the dough will fall down the sides of the pillow. This method allows you to sit down while stretching it.

After stretching as thinly as possible, trim the thicker edges, return trimmings to remaining dough to be rekneaded and allow sheet to stiffen 15 minutes. Start stretching another ball of dough on another table or pillow and repeat procedure.

When the sheets have stiffened slightly, cut into desired size and use immediately; or store by laying the *filos* on top of each other with no waxed paper between them. Fold and keep in airtight plastic bags. Will keep in refrigerator for 3 days or freezer until needed. Bring to room temperature before using.

COMMERCIAL FILO

Filo is sold in 1-pound and ½-pound packages and is available in frozen foods sections of any good gourmet grocery shop. See page 147. To prepare it, simply remove it from its carton but not out of its plastic bag, at least 2 hours or more ahead of time, until it is at room temperature and has completely defrosted.

PASTRY ENTREES

CHEESE PIE

ΤΥΡΟΠΗΤΑ   (tiropitta)

Follow instructions for Spinach Pie Spanakopitta (page 149), omitting spinach.

CRETAN CHEESE PIE BOUGASTA

See Hellenic Custard Pie (page 156). Add ½ pound of crumbled Feta cheese to cooled filling.

THREE-CORNERED CHEESE TARTS

ΤΡΙΓΟΝΑ ΤΥΡΟΠΗΤΕΣ   (trigona tiropittes)

When you visit a Greek home or restaurant you will invariably be served a crispy hot pastry tart called *trigona* which is filled with fragrant Feta cheese. The name means three-corners and indicates the shape of this delicious tart. Once you have mastered the art of folding the *filo* you will make this recipe as frequently as the Greeks.

½ pound *filo*, cut into strips 2" x 18". (See page 149). For appetizers, cut into 1" x 12"; for entrees, using meat, fowl, vegetable or seafood fillings, cut into strips 4" x 18".
½ pound sweet butter or 1 cup oil

FILLING:
1 pound Feta, hoop, or cottage cheese
¼ teaspoon salt
3 eggs, beaten
(for other suggested fillings, see page 34)

If using commercial *filo,* set it out to defrost to room temperature at least 2 hours in advance. Do not remove from box or cut open plastic bag or leave it exposed to air.

Crumble cheese into a bowl, using fork to break it up. Add salt and eggs and mix in. If using hoop or cottage cheese, add more salt to taste. Set aside.

Heat butter or oil in a small pot. Brush a large shallow baking pan generously with some hot butter. Keep butter in pot in order to reheat it when you see that it is cool and does not flow easily. Straighten the *filo,* smoothing it with palms. Do not separate the sheets. With a sharp knife or scissors, cut off a straight strip 2″ wide x 12″ or longer. (Cover remaining *filo* with plastic to keep it from drying out while working.) Separate the layers from the strip of *filo* one thin layer at a time. If it is difficult to separate, then use 2 or 3 layers. If *filo* tears, lay it over the other strip and continue to fold. No need to throw any of it away; it is all edible.

To Fold:
1. Spread a layer of filo horizontally on table or counter. Brush with melted butter.
2. Put a teaspoonful of filling in the center about 1½″ in from left end.
3. Pick up top left hand corner and bring it over 2″ to the right to meet the bottom edge and form a triangle. (If cheese oozes out, let it.)
4. Fold over at the straight edge in the center, from left to right.
5. Pick up the left hand bottom corner and bring it over 2″ to the top edge.
6. Fold over in the center, from left to right. If you practice with a paper napkin marking the points as you go along the method of folding will become very clear to you. Continue until all the strip of *filo* is used.

Lay each tart on oiled pan with tucked edge underneath. Brush tops with melted butter. Bake 45 minutes at 350° F.

SPINACH PIE SPANAKOPITTA

ΣΠΑΝΑΚΟΠΗΤΑ   (spanakopitta)

This pie is served on all festive occasions. The Feta cheese makes this *pitta* rich and fragrant although other cheeses may be substituted.

1 pound *filo* (about 12 to 15 sheets)
  (page 148)
FILLING:
2 packages (10 ounces each) frozen
  spinach or 1 pound fresh
1 pound cheese: Feta, hoop, or
  cottage

¼ teaspoon salt
6 eggs, well beaten
½ cup oil
¼ pound butter or margarine

If using frozen *filo*, defrost 2 hours ahead of time.

Filling: Thaw out frozen spinach. If using fresh, steam for 5 minutes until wilted. Crumble cheese, using fork to break Feta cheese up. Add more salt if using hoop or cottage cheese as substitute. Mix in eggs. Set aside.

Heat oil and butter in a small pot. Unwrap *filo* and smooth creases out. Plan to use half of the *filo* sheets for the bottom layers and the other half for the top. (Keep covered while using, *filo* dries out quickly.) Oil pan generously, bottom and sides, using pastry brush.

Lay first sheet of *filo* in square or rectangular cake pan, letting excess lap over edges. Sprinkle with warm oil. Lay a second layer and sprinkle with a little more oil. Continue until half of the *filo* is used. Spread all the spinach mixture evenly over the *filo*, including the corners. Cover with remaining *filo*, oiling between sheets. Do not throw any *filo* away; include it in; it is all edible. Roll and tuck all the *filo* around the inside edges of the pan. Do not trim with scissors or knife as one would for pie crust. Brush top and edges with remaining oil. Bake at 350° F. for 50 minutes. Serve hot, cut into square pieces like a cake. Reheat when necessary; never serve cold.

CRETAN CHICKEN PIE

КОТОПНТА   (kotopitta)

FILLING:
4 cups chicken, cooked
5 scallions, chopped
1 teaspoon salt
pepper to taste
3 tablespoons cornstarch

2 cups milk
1 tablespoon butter
2 eggs beaten

½ pound *filo* (page 148)
½ pound melted butter or 1 cup oil

Chop chicken and scallions. If chicken is raw, cook in 1 cup of water for 15 minutes until tender. Dilute cornstarch in ½ cup cold milk. Bring remaining milk to a boil, add cornstarch mixture, salt and butter and cook until thick. Remove from fire. Add eggs, chicken and scallions. Cool. Use as a filling in Three-Cornered Tarts (page 148) or as a filling for pie (page 149).

GREEK FREIGHTER MEAT PIE

ΚΡΕΑΤΟΠΗΤΑ   (kreatopitta)

Whether you are traveling on a luxurious liner, a Greek freighter on which passengers dine with the captain or on a new Greek airship, you will be offered a slice of this superb meat pie.

FILLING:

2 tablespoons butter, oil or margarine	½ cup chopped parsley
1 onion, chopped	2 teaspoons salt
2 cups cooked meat, chopped: beef, lamb, veal or pork	pepper to taste
	1 cup Feta, hoop or cottage cheese
OR 1 pound ground or chopped meat, raw	1 egg
	½ cup pine nuts or walnuts, chopped
1 cup rice or diced potatoes	
1 teaspoon spearmint flakes	½ pound filo (page 148)
1 teaspoon marjoram	¼ cup oil and 2 tablespoons butter or margarine

Heat oil and fry onions until soft. If using raw meat and potatoes, brown for 5 minutes and add 1 cup of hot water or 2 cups if using rice, herbs and seasonings. Cover and cook 20 minutes until meat is cooked and potatoes or rice are soft. Remove from heat. Mix in cheese, egg and nuts.

Mix with all ingredients. Melt butter and oil in a small pot. Oil a square or rectangular baking pan. Lay half of the sheets of *filo*, oiling lightly between each sheet. Spread meat filling. Lay remaining *filo* sheets oiling lightly between each one and bake at 350° F. for 1 hour.

ATLANTIS SEAFOOD PITTA

ΘΑΛΑΣΣΙΝΟΠΗΤΑ   (thalassinopitta)

This recipe is a specialty of the seaports of Greece where the bounty of the sea allows extravagance.

FILLING:
2 cups or more chopped scallops, or
   any shellfish: mussels, clams, crab,
   lobster and shrimp
1 tablespoon butter
2 tablespoons flour or cornstarch
1 cup milk
2 eggs, beaten

2 scallions, chopped
1 teaspoon salt
pepper to taste
pinch of nutmeg (optional)

½ pound filo (page 148)
¼ cup melted butter or oil

Cook for 5 minutes, in its own liquor, any of the seafood listed. Melt butter and dilute flour or cornstarch in cold milk. Add liquor from seafood and cook until thick. Add beaten eggs and cook over low heat until thick, stirring all the while. Add scallions, seasonings and chopped seafood. Allow to cool slightly. Use as filling in Three-Cornered Tarts (page 148) or in a pie (page 149).

DESSERT FILO PASTRIES

BAKLAVA

ΜΠΑΚΛΑΒΑΣ   (baklahvas)

Baklava is the aristocrat of pastry desserts. It is of Byzantine origin, made in all countries of the Near East, and each one claims it for its own. This fabulous pastry is recognized internationally by its layers of nut filling and the many sheets of *filo*, from twenty to forty of them. It is usually bathed in syrup flavored with rose or brandy.

1 pound filo (page 148)

FILLING:
3 cups or more chopped nuts; walnuts, pecans, almonds, pistachios
   or any combination desired
¼ cup sugar
½ teaspoon cinnamon
1 lemon, grated rind only
½ pound melted sweet butter or
   clarified salted butter (see page
   178)
whole cloves or cassia buds

TOPPING: Simple Syrup (page 178)
3 cups sugar
2 cups water
⅛ teaspoon cream of tartar
juice of 1 lemon
2 teaspoons rose or brandy flavoring
   or ¼ cup honey

Defrost frozen *filo* to room temperature. Mix ingredients for filling in a bowl and set aside. Melt butter and clarify. Keep it in pan to reheat if it cools and doesn't flow easily while you are working with *filo*. Use pastry brush to oil generously the bottom and sides of a large rectangular baking pan. Cut *filo* an inch larger than your pan. Use scissors. Place sheet of *filo* in pan and sprinkle lightly with warm butter. Place another sheet of *filo* on top of the first sheet, and sprinkle lightly with butter again. Continue until you have spread 6 or more sheets. Spread half of the filling, including the corners. Cover with 6 or more sheets of *filo* sprinkling with butter between. Add remaining filling. Cover with remaining sheets, oiling between each one. Roll edges and tuck inside of pan. Do not trim as one would do for a pie. Oil the top with remaining butter. Before baking, cut through the top layers only, into the traditional diamond shapes. Use a small sharp knife with a ruler to guide you.

To Make Diamond-Shaped Pieces

Make vertical cuts, 1″ apart. Turn pan horizontally and make cuts at an angle, 1″ apart. Stick a whole clove in the center of each diamond. Besides adding flavor, it keeps the layers together. Bake at 350° F. for 1 hour. Check it during the last 20 minutes to see if it is browning evenly. Begin boiling the syrup 20 minutes before taking baklava out of the oven. Pour hot syrup over hot baklava immediately after removing it from oven. Use ladle or large spoon to distribute syrup evenly over all of it. Set aside to cool, at room temperature, not in the refrigerator. Keep in pan overnight or at least 4 hours before cutting and serving.

HONEY NUT ROLLS, BOUREKAKIA

ΜΠΟΤΡΕΚΑΚΙΑ   (bourehkakia)

These flaky pastries, full of nuts and sweet with honey syrup, are now called by a name of Turkish origin, *bourekakia*. The Greeks have been making them for such a long time that the Crusaders in the 13th century who remained in Constantinople (now Istanbul) recorded their delight with this new pastry in their letters.

FILLING:
2 cups or more chopped nuts: walnuts, almonds, pecans or pistachios
¼ cup sugar or 1 cup orange marmalade
½ teaspoon cinnamon
rind of one orange, grated
½ pound *filo* (page 148)

½ pound melted sweet butter or 1 cup oil (to clarify salted butter see page 178)

TOPPING:
Honey Syrup (page 178)
2 cups sugar
½ teaspoon cream of tartar
1 cup water
1 cup honey

Defrost *filo* to room temperature at least 2 hours before using. Mix filling in a bowl and set aside. Melt butter in a small pan, and return to heat when it cools and doesn't flow easily while you are working with *filo.*

Smooth 3 sheets of *filo* flat on a cutting board. With a pastry brush, dribble warm butter between sheets. Sprinkle ⅔ cup of nut filling over top, spreading to corners. Lay another 3 sheets of *filo* over filling, buttering between them. Fold edges over on each side to keep nuts from rolling out. Starting with the end nearest to you, roll away from you as tightly as you can. Cut into 1" slices.

Place each roll in oiled pan, next to each other, snugly, nuts facing upwards. Continue using all the *filo* and filling. When all the slices are in the pan, dribble a teaspoon of warm butter on top of each slice. It will disappear into the layers of nutmeats.

Bake at 350° F. for 45 minutes. Begin making syrup 20 minutes before the pastry is ready to be taken out of the oven. Pour hot syrup over rolls immediately upon removal from oven. Use a spoon to ladle it over each one. Set aside to absorb syrup for 4 hours. Do not refrigerate.

CORINTHIAN APPLE PITTA

ΚΟΡΙΝΘΙΑΚΗ ΜΗΛΟΠΗΤΑ   (meelopitta)

This Greek version of an apple pie is a delightful variation of a classic recipe. The tangy apples that go into this pie are the small juicy crab-apple variety, not those beautiful large red eating apples which are served at the end of a Greek meal.

1 pound *filo* (page 148)

FILLING:
8 apples, cored, peeled, chopped, or
  2 cups canned apples, drained
½ cup sugar
½ teaspoon each cinnamon and allspice
1 tablespoon cornstarch

¼ cup currants or raisins
½ cup chopped walnuts
¼ cup cherries, fresh or canned,
  drained (optional)
½ cup melted butter or oil

TOPPING:
1 cup powdered sugar

Defrost frozen *filo* to room temperature 2–4 hours. Mix filling in a bowl tossing ingredients with a spoon. Set aside.

Lay 5 sheets of *filo* flat, one on top of each other, with a little melted butter between the sheets. Spread 1 cup of filling along one end. Roll *filo* over the apple filling so you will have a long filled tube. Fold side edges over ½ inch so filling won't fall out. Continue rolling.

Place in a buttered baking pan or cookie sheet. Brush tops generously with melted butter. Bake at 350° F. for 1 hour. Sift powdered sugar over tops and sides as soon as it is taken out of the oven and while still hot. When cool, cut into 2″ pieces and serve.

CRETAN TARTS SKALTSOUNIA

ΣΚΑΛΤΣΟΥΝΙΑ   (skaltsounia)

Throughout Crete you will find these flaky pastry tarts filled with cheese and custard, flavored with the honey of Sphakia. Some Cretan women make them from pastry dough shaping them into three-cornered *trigona* tarts and others roll them into little logs.

PASTRY DOUGH:
2 cups flour
1 teaspoon baking powder
⅛ teaspoon salt
½ cup cold margarine or shortening
1 egg

FILLING:
1 pound cheese: Feta, hoop or
  cottage cheese
1 8-ounce package of cream cheese
1 egg yolk (save white for pastry
  seal)

¼ teaspoon cinnamon
½ pound *filo* or pastry dough recipe
  (see below)
¼ pound melted sweet butter or
  margarine, if using *filo*
1 cup oil for frying if using pastry
  dough

TOPPING:
1 cup honey
½ cup hot water

Sift flour, baking powder and salt into a bowl. Cut in margarine or shortening until blended as meal. Add egg and make a ball. Cover and let rest while making the filling.

Blend or beat ingredients for filling until smooth.

Sprinkle board lightly with flour and roll out dough as thinly as possible. Cut into 3″ or 4″ rounds with cookie cutter and place a tablespoon of filling in the center. Fold and seal edges with white of egg. Fry in hot oil for 5 minutes on each side, or bake 20 minutes in 400° F. oven.

Heat honey and water and dribble over tart. If using *filo* instead of pastry dough, follow directions given for Three-Cornered Tarts (page 148).

HELLENIC CUSTARD PIE

ΓΑΛΑΚΤΟΜΠΟΤΡΕΚΟ, ΜΠΟΥΓΑΤΣΑ   (galactoboureko, bougatsa)

Thick rich sheep's or goats' milk is used to make this rich custard *pitta* pie. It is a sweet, delicate pie, exquisite with its crisp crust of *filo* leaves. In Crete and northern Greece, particularly in Yannina, it's still called by its Turkish name, *bougatsa.*

FILLING:
1 quart of milk
½ cup sugar
1 tablespoon butter
⅓ cup farina, regular
4 large eggs, well beaten
1 teaspoon vanilla
½ pound *filo* (page 148)

½ cup melted butter or oil

TOPPING:
Simple Syrup (page 177)
1½ cups sugar
⅛ teaspoon cream of tartar
1 cup water
1 tablespoon lemon juice

Heat milk and sugar in a deep pot. Add butter and farina slowly. Cook 10 minutes stirring constantly. Remove pot from heat and cool. Add eggs and flavoring, mixing in quickly. Set aside.

Melt butter in a small pot and oil a rectangular or square baking pan with some of it. Lay 6 sheets of *filo,* sprinkling a little warm butter between each sheet. Pour custard over *filo.* Cover with remaining sheets of *filo,* sprinkling with warm butter between each sheet as before. Cut partially through the top layers only, making squares. Bake at 350° F. for 45 minutes.

While *pitta*-pie is baking, prepare syrup by boiling vigorously for 10 minutes. Pour hot syrup over hot *pitta*-pie as soon as it comes out of the oven. Allow to cool before cutting.

Note: To make *bougatsa,* use confectioners sugar instead of syrup as a topping. Sift 1 cup confectioners sugar and sprinkle heavily with cinnamon over the top of the pastry as soon as it comes out of the oven.

THE SWEETS OF GREECE

ΓΛΥΚΙΣΜΑΤΑ   (glykismata)

Many of these recipes for cakes, cookies, puddings, candies and preserves are thousands of years old. The Greeks and Egyptians made confections with honey, fruits, wines, nuts, eggs and flour. Here you will find spices and flavorings used in new ways. There are cereals, which you may have considered baby food, made into exotic puddings; cakes and cookies which have rose-flavored syrups or honey to sweeten or preserve them; little fried cakes, once considered such delicacies that they were given as prizes to heroes; fruits, flowers and vegetables being candied into desserts.

The art of cake baking began about the 5th century B.C. when the Greeks discovered the secret of making yeast. They also refined flour to make the various sweet breads and cakes light and soft. A slave or attendant usually sat before the portable clay oven in which cakes and breads were baked to watch the fire and keep it from going out or burning too brightly.

These cakes often included honey, nuts, cheese, fruits and sesame seeds and were molded in the shapes of animals, flowers, mushrooms, women's breasts, whatever the occasion called for. Sometimes they were given as prizes in festivals or games or were made for religious holidays just as the Christmas and Easter cakes are today. Certain days of the year were dedicated to the different gods who were honored with sweet cakes. The tradition continues today in modern Greece where each day of the year is consecrated to a different Christian saint and is celebrated with sweets and feasts as a name day by all those who are named after each particular saint. Birthdays are not considered as important.

One of the more delightful experiences in Greece today is the coffee and sweets break. Every pastry shop provides a few tables and chairs outside on the sidewalk for its patrons to sit down and watch the traffic go by with a selection of pastry called *glyko tou tapsiou* ΓΛΥΚΟ ΤΟΥ ΤΑΠΣΙΟΥ which translates as "a sweet (usually a piece of cake or pitta) from a large pan."

CAKES

ALMOND COFFEE CAKE

ΑΜΥΓΔΑΛΟ ΓΛΥΚΙΣΜΑ   (amgdalo glykisma)

The generous amount of nuts which go into every Greek cake or pastry indicates how fruitful the trees are in Greece. In the United States, a baker is an excellent source of chopped nuts by the pound.

4 eggs, separated
1 cup sugar
1 teaspoon vanilla
½ cup melted sweet butter or oil
½ teaspoon cream of tartar
2 cups cake flour
3 teaspoons baking powder
2 cups ground and chopped almonds
   (10 ounces)

TOPPING:
Honey syrup (page 178)
1½ cups sugar
1 cup water
1 cup honey
(Optional topping: 2 cups powdered
   sugar)

Blend yolks, sugar and vanilla in blender or mixer, adding warmed butter or oil until thick. In another bowl, beat egg whites with cream of tartar until stiff. Fold the yolk mixture into the whites. Sift flour and baking powder and fold in. Add nuts last. Pour into greased tube cake pan, bread pan or fluted mould. Bake in a pre-heated oven at 350° F. for 40 minutes.

Make syrup by boiling sugar and water for 10 minutes. Remove pot from fire and add honey. Pour over cake as soon as it is taken out of the oven.

Optional topping: Remove cake from pan to a dish which has been sprinkled with ½ cup powdered sugar. Sift remaining powdered sugar over hot cake.

BYZANTINE SPICE CAKE

ΤΟΥΡΤΑ ΒΥΖΑΝΤΙΝΟ (tourta Vizantino)

This recipe comes from the island of Sifnos, in the Cyclades, where the art of cookery has been developed to a high degree. It is not only famous for its spiced honey cakes as this one, but also renowned for the chefs it has produced who practice Siphniac cooking throughout the world.

½ pound butter or 1 cup oil
1½ cups sugar
3 eggs
½ cup yogurt or sour cream
2¼ cups cake flour
3 teaspoons baking powder
½ teaspoon each: cinnamon, ground cloves, nutmeg, mace
¼ teaspoon soda
¼ cup orange juice

TOPPING:
Honey Syrup (page 178)
1½ cup sugar
1 cup water
1 cup honey

ALTERNATE TOPPING:
Sugar icing
1½ cups powdered sugar
5 tablespoons water
1 teaspoon vanilla

Beat butter until creamy. Add sugar and beat 3 minutes more. Add eggs, and ½ of the yogurt. Sift flour, baking powder and spices and add. Add remaining yogurt. Mix soda into orange juice and add. Bake in a greased square pan in preheated oven at 350° F. for 45 minutes.

While cake is cooking, make syrup. Pour hot syrup over cake immediately after it's brought from the oven. Or, if icing is preferred, mix until smooth and dribble on in a design when cake is cool.

COPENHAGEN PITTA

ΓΛΥΚΟΠΗΤΑ ΚΟΠΕΝΓΧΑΓΗ (glykopitta Kopenhaghi)

This rich cake dessert which bears the name of the capital city of Denmark has a cookie crust on the bottom, an angel food cake with nuts for the center, *filo* sheets for the top crust and a bath of syrup over the whole pastry after it is baked. It is a gourmet pastry, expensive to make. The royal baker created this pastry in 1863 to honor the Dane, King George I, upon his coronation as king of Greece. The cake was barely out of the royal oven when the women of Athens had the recipe and were making it for their own heads of state.

BOTTOM CRUST:
1 cup of sweet butter (page 178) or oil
1 cup confectioners sugar
2 egg yolks
1 teaspoon vanilla
2 cups flour

FILLING:
6 eggs, separated
1 cup sugar
½ teaspoon each: cinnamon and nutmeg
1 ounce brandy or whiskey
1 teaspoon baking powder
1 cup finely ground crumbs of rusk, vanilla cookies or graham crackers

2 cups walnuts or almonds chopped finely

TOP CRUST:
½ pound *filo* (10 sheets)
¼ pound sweet butter melted or ½ cup oil

TOPPING:
Simple Syrup (page 177)
2 cups sugar
¼ teaspoon cream of tartar
1 cup water
1 teaspoon lemon juice
1 ounce of whiskey
½ cup honey

Bottom crust: cream butter and sugar. Add egg yolks, vanilla and sifted flour. Beat 10 minutes until smooth. Spread dough into a buttered pan, 10" x 14" or longer. Put aside to chill in refrigerator while making filling.

Filling: Beat egg yolks until thick. Add sugar, spices, brandy and beat in. In a separate bowl beat all egg whites until stiff and add baking powder. Fold yolks into egg whites. Add crumbs and nuts. Pour into pan over the bottom crust.

Top Crust: Lay *filo* on top of filling one sheet at a time. Dribble melted butter between each sheet. Cut through *filo* partially, making four vertical lines. Bake in preheated oven for 1 hour at 350° F.

Combine ingredients for syrup and boil vigorously for 10 minutes. Cover pot last 4 or 5 minutes. Remove syrup from heat. Add ½ cup honey. Pour hot syrup over cake as soon as it is taken from the oven. Set aside to absorb syrup and cool for 4 hours before cutting into squares or diamond-shaped pieces (page 152). Do not refrigerate.

ATHENIAN CHEESE CAKE

ΑΘΗΝΑΙΚΗ ΤΥΡΟΠΗΤΑ   (Athenaiki tyropitta)

Thousands of years ago, the respected Greek poet and gourmet, Archestratus, wrote, "Forget all other desserts, there is only one: the Athenian cheese cake with Attica honey from Hymettus." The original recipe is lost but this one is so old it may be it. The famous Hymettus honey is still available.

FILLING:
4 eggs, separated
½ cup honey or sugar
1 lemon, juice and rind
⅓ cup flour
1 pound pot cheese, either small curd
   cottage, hoop, mezithra or cream
1 cup sour cream or yogurt

CRUST:
1 cup crumbs from zwieback rusks,
   cookies or graham crackers
¼ cup ground walnuts or almonds
2 tablespoons oil or butter

In a large bowl, beat egg whites until stiff (with a sprinkle of salt). In a blender, blend yolks, honey, lemon juice, rind, flour and cheese for a few seconds. Fold batter into egg whites using spatula. Fold in sour cream.

In a separate bowl mix crumbs and nuts together. Grease the bottom and sides of a large cake pan or spring-form cake pan. Spread crumbs over bottom and sides. Pour mixture in cake pan and bake at 325° F. for 45 minutes. Chill in cake pan 6 hours before cutting and serving.

KARAGHIOZ CHOCOLATE CAKE

ΚΕΪΚ ΜΕ ΣΟΚΟΛΑΤΑ   (keik meh sokolata)

This delicious dark chocolate cake with its candy sesame tahini frosting is named after Karaghioz, a shadow puppet, who for centuries was the beloved clown folk hero and philosopher comic of the Greek people. Of Turkish origin, Karaghioz, a shadow puppet, seen only in profile, was the main character in the puppet plays which were the only form of theater in Greece during the centuries of Turkish occupation. The Turkish government, having banned Karaghioz for over a hundred years, has belatedly recognized that he is a true folk hero and is trying to revive him in Turkey, but in Greece and in the United States, Karaghioz continues to delight both new and old generations in comic strips and plays.

¾ cup dark breakfast cocoa
½ cup boiling water
⅔ cup butter, oil or shortening
2 cups sugar
2 eggs

1 teaspoon vanilla
2½ cups cake flour
3 teaspoons baking powder
½ teaspoon baking soda
1 cup sour cream

Melt cocoa in hot water. Set aside to cool.

Beat shortening until fluffy. Add sugar, and continue beating 2 minutes more. Add eggs and vanilla. Sift flour, baking powder and soda and add half of it. Beat in sour cream and remaining flour. Add cocoa mixture last.

Pour into buttered cake pan and bake in preheated oven at 350° F. for 40 minutes. Allow to cool before frosting with Halvah Frosting.

HALVAH FROSTING

ΓΛΥΚΟ ΑΠΟ ΤΑΧΗΝΙ   (glyko apo tahini)

½ cup sesame *tahini*   2 cups confectioners sugar
1 teaspoon vanilla   4 tablespoons boiling water

Beat *tahini* until smooth. Add vanilla, sugar and water, beating constantly until smooth. Spread on cake.

KATAIFI ROLLS

ΚΑΤΑΪΦΙ ΜΠΟΥΡΕΚΑΚΙΑ   (kataifi bourekakia)

Fresh or frozen *kataifi* dough, which resembles shredded coconut, must be bought. Special cooking equipment is needed to make the thread-like shredded dough. The dough or batter is poured through a perforated press onto a hot revolving griddle and strands of thin noodles form, which are then made into sweet pastries or cakes. *Kataifi* dough must be treated like *filo;* it dries out quickly.

FILLING: 1 pound *kataifi* dough
3 cups ground nuts: walnuts, almonds
  or pistachios   TOPPING:
½ cup honey   Honey Syrup (page 178)
1 teaspoon cinnamon   2 cups sugar
½ pound sweet butter or margarine,   1 cup water
  melted   1 cup honey

Mix filling in a bowl and set aside. Melt butter in a small pot. Place *kataifi* dough between damp towels to keep it moist while working with it. If it is frozen, defrost to room temperature.

Take a handful of dough and pat it gently between your palms to make a 3″ x 4″ piece. Put 1 teaspoon of filling at one end. Fold edges over and roll into an oblong roll. Place rolls in greased baking pan, 1″ apart. Brush tops with warm butter. Bake in preheated oven at 350° F. for 30 minutes.

Prepare syrup and pour over hot rolls as soon as they are removed from oven. Let rolls absorb syrup for 2 hours before serving.

SHREDDED WHEAT CAKE KATAIFI

ΨΕΤΤΙΚΟ ΚΑΤΑΪΦΙ   (pseftiko kataifi)

The common shredded wheat cereal becomes an exotic dessert with a name that sounds like something out of a sultan's harem. The thread-like *kataifi* dough which makes this sweet dessert so unusual is difficult to obtain so many Greek women in the United States have evolved this mock *kataifi* cake.

8 large shredded wheat squares
½ cup melted butter or oil

FILLING:
1 cup walnuts or almonds, chopped
1 teaspoon cinnamon
½ cup cream

TOPPING:
Simple Syrup (page 177)
2 cups sugar
1 cup water
¼ teaspoon cream of tartar
1 teaspoon vanilla or rose flavoring

Dip each biscuit in boiling water for a quick second. Use a slotted spoon. Place biscuits in a dish, cover and chill in refrigerator for 1 hour. Mix filling.

Spread a little melted butter on the bottom of a square baking pan. Slice biscuits in half lengthwise and arrange half of them in pan. Dribble half of the melted butter over them. Spread filling. Cover with a layer of the remaining biscuits. Pour remaining butter over them and add cream. Bake in preheated oven at 350° F. for 20 minutes.

Prepare syrup and pour over hot cake immediately. Cool 2 hours before cutting.

OLYMPIAD SUGAR CAKE

PABANI   (ravani)

In the ancient Pan-Hellenic games which were held in Olympia between the years 776 B.C. and A.D. 393, the athletes who won were crowned with wild parsley and awarded spicy sweet cakes. The stadium where the foot races, boxing and wrestling matches were held and the hippodromes where the chariot races took place are still impressive, though now silent ruins, but the sweet cakes which the athletes loved continue to be baked.

½ pound sweet butter or margarine
¾ cup sugar
6 eggs, well beaten
1 teaspoon vanilla
1 cup farina, regular not instant
1 cup cake flour
2 teaspoons baking powder

TOPPING:
Simple Syrup (page 177)
2 cups sugar
1 cup water
¼ teaspoon cream of tartar
⅛ teaspoon cinnamon
¼ cup rum, whiskey, cognac or
   brandy (optional)

Beat butter until fluffy. Add sugar, eggs and vanilla. Add farina, mixing in well. Sift flour with baking powder and add.

Pour batter into buttered square cake pan and place in pre-heated oven at 425° F. for 5 minutes. Reduce heat to 350° F. and bake 30 minutes longer.

While cake is baking, prepare syrup. Add liquor last or when serving. Pour over hot cake as soon as it is out of the oven. Cool. Transfer cake to cake plate.

Minutes before serving, heat the liquor for 2 minutes over low heat. Pour alcohol slowly over the top of cake and ignite with match. Enter room with flaming cake like an Olympiad torch-bearer.

SPONGE CAKE PANTESPANI

ΠΑΝΤΕΣΠΑΝΙ   (pantespani)

This is a sponge cake, known throughout Greece as *pantespani.* It is very light in texture and is sometimes served with powdered sugar, smothered with fresh fruit slices or in a bath of honey syrup. It can be a jelly roll, a rum cake or a nut cake. Different regions of Greece will have their special ways of serving this cake, but the basic recipe is the same.

8 large eggs, separated (to make 1
   cup egg whites)
½ teaspoon cream of tartar
1 cup sugar

1 teaspoon vanilla
1½ cups cake flour
2 teaspoons baking powder

Remove eggs from refrigerator 2 hours ahead. Whites should be at room temperature. Beat egg yolks, sugar and vanilla until thick and creamy. Sift flour and baking powder and add egg yolks, mixing in well. Beat egg whites with cream of tartar until stiff. Fold batter into egg whites, using a spatula.

Pour batter into greased tube pan and bake in a preheated oven at 350° F. for 45 minutes. Serve plain, or with fresh fruit and whipped cream topping.

WALNUT SUGAR CAKE

PABANI ME KAPTΔIA   (ravani meh karidia)

Follow recipe for Olympiad Sugar Cake (page 163) and add to the list of ingredients the following:

1 teaspoon orange peel, grated
1 teaspoon cinnamon

1 cup chopped walnuts, almonds or pecans

WALNUT WINE CAKE MESSINIA

KAPTΔOΠHTA   (karidopitta)

When my mother talked about the products of Messinia she had a tendency to exaggerate. I am sure the walnuts were not as large as plums, though she insisted they were. The children had to shake the trees, pick up the walnuts, and crack them for this elegant walnut cake.

6 eggs, separated
1 cup sugar
¼ teaspoon cinnamon
½ teaspoon orange peel, grated
⅛ teaspoon cream of tartar
1 cup ground zwieback crumbs or
   cake flour
2 teaspoons baking powder
⅛ teaspoon salt
1 cup ground walnuts

TOPPING:
1 cup confectioners sugar or
   Honey Syrup

HONEY SYRUP:
1 cup honey
½ cup water
1 teaspoon orange zest
½ cup port wine

Beat egg yolks until thick. Add sugar, cinnamon, and orange peel. In another bowl, beat egg whites with cream of tartar until stiff. Fold yolk mixture into egg whites gently. Sift flour, baking powder and salt. Fold into egg whites. Add nuts last.

Bake in a greased cake pan or tube pan in a preheated oven at 350° F. for 40 minutes. Sift ¼ cup confectioners sugar onto a cake plate and place hot cake on it. Sift remaining sugar over cake.

Alternate topping, Honey Syrup: In a medium sized pot bring

honey, water, wine and orange peel to a boil and pour over hot cake before removing from baking pan. Transfer to cake plate when cool.

ALMOND WINE CAKE

ΑΜΙΓΔΑΛΟΠΙΤΤΑ   (amigthalopitta)

Follow recipe for Walnut Cake Messinia, above, substituting 1 cup ground almonds for walnuts.

YOGURT CAKE METEORA

ΓΑΟΤΡΤΗ ΓΛΤΚΙΣΜΑ   (yaourti glykisma)

Near the majestic region of Meteora where gigantic rock pillars rise eighteen hundred feet into the sky, the women of Trikala use yogurt made from goat's milk to enrich their cakes and breads.

4 eggs, separated   1 cup yogurt or sour cream
1 cup sugar
½ cup melted butter or oil   HONEY SYRUP:
2 ounces whiskey (optional)   1 cup honey
2 cups cake flour   ½ cup boiling water
3 teaspoons baking powder
pinch of salt   TOPPING:
¼ teaspoon soda   ½ cup sliced almonds, toasted

Beat yolks until thick. Add sugar and melted butter, continue beating. Add whiskey. Sift flour with baking powder and add to yolk mixture. Mix baking soda in yogurt and add. Beat egg whites with pinch of salt until stiff. Fold into batter.

Bake in a buttered square or tube cake pan in a preheated oven at 375° F. for 45 minutes. Bring honey and water to a boil and pour over hot cake as soon as it comes out of the oven. Sprinkle with almonds. Allow to cool 2 hours before serving.

FRIED CAKES

GREEK CRULLERS DIPLES

ΔΙΠΛΕΣ   (diples)

These fried crisp crullers are so thin and flaky that they crumble at a bite. The Greek cook will shape the dough into a figure eight or make a complicated rosette as it is dropped into the hot oil. Often they are sold at ΠΑΝΗΓΥΡΙΑ (*paneghyria*), the country fairs, where the people come for miles to exhibit their best crafts, wearing the colorful costumes of their region.

3 eggs
2 tablespoons orange juice
¼ cup oil
2¼ cups flour or farina
½ teaspoon baking powder
1 quart of oil for frying

TOPPING:
2 cups honey
1 cup water
½ cup ground nuts
cinnamon

OPTIONAL TOPPING:
1 cup powdered sugar

Beat eggs until thick, adding juice and oil as you beat in blender or mixer. Sift flour and baking powder and add. Finish by kneading. Let dough rest about 1 hour.

Divide dough into 4 balls. Roll one ball at a time, as thin as possible, on a lightly floured board. Using a pastry wheel, cut strips 3″ x 1″. Shape strips into knots, pretzels, figure 8's, or rosettes and drop each one in hot oil. Do not crowd. Use a slotted spoon to pick up each cruller. Fry on both sides. Transfer to tray lined with paper towel.

When all crullers are fried, arrange on a large tray. Dilute honey with water and dribble a spoonful over each one. Sprinkle with nuts and cinnamon, or sift powdered sugar over them. Serve the same day as these do not keep well.

HONEY TOKENS

ΛΟΥΚΟΥΜΑΔΕΣ   (loukoumathes)

The Greek cook usually has flour, water, and honey in her cupboard. From these simple ingredients she makes feathery light puffed fried cakes called *loukoumathes* which are so delightful that at one time they were given as prizes to the winners of the night festivals in the games. They were called *charisioi,* meaning little gifts or tokens. According to Callimachus, the ancient Greek poet who mentioned these in *The Vigil,* the athletes were "delighted to get them."

1 package dry yeast
¼ cup warm water
2 cups flour
1 teaspoon sugar
a few grains of salt
1 cup warm water

1 quart of oil for frying

TOPPING:
2 cups honey
1 cup water
cinnamon

Dissolve yeast in warm water. Put dry ingredients in a bowl, add warm water and yeast mixture. Mix well with spoon. Soft dough will form and batter should plop from a spoon. Set aside in a warm place to rise 2 to 3 hours.

Heat oil in a large frying pan to 375° F. Drop a teaspoon of batter into hot oil, using two teaspoons, one to assist you to push the dough off the other. Fry 4 minutes and turn each one over until they are light brown on all sides. Use slotted spoon to remove from oil. Transfer to a long-handled wire basket and shake off excess oil.

Heat honey and water and dip each token into it quickly. Stack on a large platter. Taste one, and if you prefer, sprinkle with cinnamon. Serve hot and immediately.

COOKIES

ALMOND MACAROONS

ΑΜΗΓΔΑΛΩΤΑ   (amigthalota)

Every family in Paros and Hydra tries to have a Jordan almond tree tucked in its garden. It's delicious nuts are used in many ways and this simple recipe has become a classic cookie, throughout the world, even in areas where the Asiatic almond tree doesn't grow.

3 egg whites
pinch of salt
1¼ cups confectioners sugar

1 or more cups ground almonds
3 tablespoons flour

Remove eggs from refrigerator 2 hours ahead. Whites should be at room temperature. Beat egg whites with a pinch of salt until stiff. Beat in sifted sugar. Fold in flour and almonds. Drop by spoonfuls on greased cookie sheet and bake at 300° F. for 25 minutes.

Variations: For Coconut Macaroons substitute for almonds 1 or more cups dry or flaked coconut.

Date and Nut Macaroons: Add 1 teaspoon vanilla, ¼ cup chopped dates and substitute chopped walnuts and coconut for almonds.

SWEET KOULOURAKIA

ΚΟΥΛΟΤΡΑΚΙΑ   (koulourakia)

These rolls look and taste like cookies. They are the traditional Greek sweet bread, sometimes shaped in a hairpin twist, a wreath, or coiled into a snake, a design dating from the Minoans when pagan Greeks worshipped the snake for its healing power.

1 cup butter or oil	1 teaspoon vanilla
(see page 178)	5 cups flour
1 cup sugar	3 teaspoons baking powder
3 eggs (save 1 egg white for topping)	¼ cup sesame seeds
¼ cup milk	

Allow butter to soften at room temperature. Beat until light and fluffy. Add sugar, eggs, milk, and vanilla beating all the while.

Sift flour, baking powder, and salt into mixture and combine. Knead until well blended.

Shape each cookie. Place on oiled baking sheet, 2″ apart, and glaze tops with beaten egg white. Sprinkle with sesame seeds. Bake in a preheated oven at 350° F. for 25 minutes.

To shape sweet koulourakia

Break off a small piece of dough. Roll between palms of hands or on cutting board to make a rope 4″ long. Braid or coil it, or twist it to make a hairpin, a wreath, a figure "8" or a letter "S."

KOULOURAKIA EPIRUS

ΚΟΥΛΟΥΡΑΚΙΑ ΗΠΕΙΡΟΥ   (koulourakia Epirus)

To the recipe for Sweet Koulourakia, above, add the following
ingredients before adding flour:

½ teaspoon each: cinnamon, anise,   4 grains of mastic (optional)
    nutmeg, orange peel   ½ cup ground nuts, almonds or wal-
2 tablespoons whiskey   nuts

Bake as directed.

VENETIAN HONEY COOKIES

ΦΟΙΝΗΚΙΑ, ΜΕΛΟΜΑΚΑΡΟΝΑ   (fenekia, melomakarona)

These marvelous honey cookies fragrant with spice were brought
to Greece by Venetian bakers during the time Venice ruled certain islands of Grece from the 14th to 17th centuries. The women
of these islands, particularly those of Kefallinia, Zakynthos, Corfu,
and Ithaka which are part of the Ionian Islands, pride themselves
on making the best *fenekia* or *melomakarona* in all of Greece.

1 egg yolk   ¼ teaspoon soda
¼ cup orange juice   ½ teaspoon each: clove and grated
1 ounce whiskey   orange rind
½ cup sugar   1 teaspoon cinnamon
1¼ cups butter or oil
⅛ teaspoon salt   SYRUP:
3½ cups flour, or a mixture of 1½   2 cups honey
    cups farina (regular) and 1½ cups   1 cup boiling water
    flour   ½ cup ground nuts: walnuts or
2 teaspoons baking powder   almonds

Melt butter. Allow to cool slightly. In a bowl or blender, put
egg, juice, soda, whiskey, and sugar and mix or blend together.
Add butter or oil and continue blending until thick as mayonnaise.

In a bowl, sift flour with baking powder and spices. Add orange
peel. Mix in batter, and finish by kneading smooth. Dough will be
stiff. Place a tablespoon of dough in your hand and squeeze
slightly to form an oblong egg shape. If a filled cookie is desired,
add a small amount of nuts in the center before pressing it.

Place on an ungreased cookie sheet and press top slightly
with a fork making a crisscross design, or press with a cookie or

butter mold. Bake in a preheated oven for 20 minutes at 350° F.

Bring honey and water to a boil and allow to simmer. Dip cookies for a few seconds in syrup and place on a cookie sheet to absorb syrup. Sprinkle with nuts and allow to cool. These cookies keep very well and taste better after a day.

GREEK WEDDING COOKIES

ΚΟΥΡΑΜΠΙΕΔΕΣ   (kourambiethes)

These exquisite cookies, always blanketed with powdered confectioners sugar like fresh snowfall, appear at all christenings, namedays, holidays, weddings and any other festive occasion. The texture is smooth as ice cream and the cookie melts in one's mouth. They improve with age but it is difficult to keep them away from eager hands. Next to *baklava,* this is the most popular Greek dessert.

1 pound sweet butter or clarified salt
   butter (page 178)
1 egg yolk
¼ cup confectioners sugar
¼ cup orange juice
1 ounce brandy, whiskey, or ouzo
   (optional)

3¾ cups flour
½ cup cornstarch
¼ cup ground almonds (optional)
whole cloves or cassia buds for
   garnish (optional)
1 pound box confectioners sugar for
   topping

Allow sweet butter to soften to room temperature. (If using salted butter, follow directions for clarifying on page 178). Beat with electric mixer for 10 minutes until white and creamy. Add sugar, egg yolk, orange juice and brandy, beating all the while until thick as mayonnaise. Sift flour and cornstarch into the bowl and continue mixing. Finish by kneading for 5 minutes. Add nuts last.

Pinch off a small piece of dough. (If dough is too soft to work with, do not add more flour. Refrigerate for 1 or 2 hours.) Shape dough in crescents for Turkish style, or into small balls, but do not press down or make them flat. This cookie does not rise during baking. (Greek baker's shortcut: Roll dough into a round log and cut diagonally into ½" thick slices.)

Place on ungreased cookie sheet, ½" apart. Stick a whole clove or cassia bud in the center of each one. Bake in preheated oven at 350° F. for 25 minutes.

While cookies are baking: Sift 1 cup confectioners sugar on a clean shallow pan, or waxed paper spread on the counter. Cover the bottom thickly. Using a spatula, transfer hot cookies on to sugar gently, the moment you take them out of the oven. Do not pile them on top of each other, but place them side by side as close as possible. Sift all the remaining sugar on top and sides through a strainer. Cool 4 hours before serving or transferring to a serving dish. These cookies are better the next day and keep well.

SHORT CUT BLENDER METHOD:

Put ingredients in blender in order listed: egg yolk, juice, sugar, brandy. Blend 1 second. Continue blending and add melted, slightly cooled butter. Sift flour and cornstarch into a bowl. Add mixture from blender and mix. Finish by kneading. Shape and bake as directed above.

MONASTERY COOKIES

ΚΑΡΥΔΑΤΑ   (karithata)

Throughout Greece you hear the clanging of the monastery bells calling the monks to prayer. If you visit these peaceful retreats, often tucked away in rather remote places, you will be welcomed and shown a simple hospitality of wine and sweets, cookies or rose jam. Whatever it may be, you can be assured that the monks have made it themselves from the products of their land.

½ pound butter, or 1 cup oil
½ cup sugar or honey
1 egg, separated
2¼ cups flour
½ cup confectioners sugar

1 cup chopped nuts: walnuts, almonds, pistachios or sesame seeds
½ cup tart preserve: apricot, quince, raspberry or rose (optional)

Beat butter until fluffy. Add sugar or honey, and beat in. Add the yolk of an egg. Sift flour with confectioners sugar and add. In a separate bowl beat egg white with a fork slightly.

Spoon out a small amount of dough and roll into a ball. (If dough is too soft, refrigerate for 1 hour. Do not add more flour.) Dip in egg white and then roll in chopped nuts or sesame seeds. Place on greased cookie sheet. Poke a hole in the middle for preserves, or press slightly to flatten.

Bake in a preheated oven at 400° F. for 12 minutes. While still warm, fill holes with preserves or jam.

SESAME SUNDAY COOKIES

ΚΟΥΛΟΥΡΑΚΙΑ   (koulourakia)

Each Greek cook has her own knack for making *Koulourakia*, a name given to any cookie or roll covered with sesame seeds. This recipe is for the sweet kind usually reserved for guests.

1¼ cups butter or oil
½ cup sugar, or ¾ for a sweeter
  cookie
2 eggs
1 teaspoon vanilla

½ teaspoon anise, seeds or oil
4½ cups flour
5 teaspoons baking powder
½ cup cream or milk
½ cup sesame seeds

Cream butter or oil until light and fluffy. Add sugar and continue beating. Add eggs, saving one yolk for topping and beat in with flavorings. Sift flour with baking powder and mix in half of it. Add milk, beat, and then add remaining flour. Continue beating. Knead to finish blending.

Break off a piece of dough and roll into a long rope. Form a wreath or a hairpin twist, and lay it on a greased baking pan. Continue until all dough is gone. In a small bowl, mix a teaspoon of milk or water with egg yolk and rub on top of cookies, using fingertips. Sprinkle with sesame seeds. Bake in a preheated oven at 350° F. for 30 minutes.

SWEET KOULOURAKIA

(page 169).

KOULOURAKIA EPIRUS

(page 170).

PUDDINGS

ATHENIAN CARAMEL CREAM

ΚΡΕΜΑ ΚΑΡΑΜΕΛΑ   (krema karamela)

This custard is a dessert served throughout Greece and the Mediterranean region, including Spain, France, and Italy. When made
with rich goat's or sheep's milk it becomes so thick it cuts like
a cake.

1 quart milk   pinch of salt
½ cup sugar   1 cup brown sugar
2 whole eggs and 4 egg yolks

Bring milk and sugar to a boil. Remove from heat. Beat eggs
with a pinch of salt and add milk. Heat brown sugar slowly in a
small frying pan for 5 minutes.

Coat bottom and sides of individual custard molds with melted
sugar. Pour custard into molds and set them in a pan in the oven.
Pour 2 cups boiling water into the bottom of the pan. Bake at
300° F. for 1 hour. Unmold by turning upside down on to a plate.
Serve chilled.

CRACKED WHEAT PUDDING

ΠΟΤΤΙΓΓΑ ΑΠΟ ΣΙΤΑΡΙ   (poutigka apo sitari)

Goat's milk was specified in the original recipe for this ancient
Greek dish. Cracked wheat also makes a delicious *pilafi* (page
61).

1 quart milk   2 tablespoons pine nuts or walnuts
1 cup soaked cracked wheat   2 eggs
¼ cup sugar   ½ cup honey
2 tablespoons butter   cinnamon
¼ cup raisins or currants

Bring milk to a boil. Add wheat, sugar, butter and raisins. Cook
20 minutes, stirring often. Beat eggs and add to pudding stirring
in quickly. Cook 2 minutes longer. Pour into individual bowls.

Heat honey and pour over pudding. Sprinkle with cinnamon
and nuts and serve warm or chilled.

GRAPE PUDDING DIONYSUS

ΜΟΤΣΤΑΛΕΒΡΙΑ   (moustalevria)

At one time this popular and unusual grape pudding was made only when fresh grapes and must were available with the vintage harvest. Today, with frozen juices and instant farina at one's fingertips, it's no trick at all to make a recipe that was prized for its exotic ingredients and rarity.

2 tablespoons sesame seeds
4 cups grape juice or wine
¼ cup honey or sugar
½ cup instant farina (cream of wheat, semolina)

¼ cup chopped walnuts
cinnamon
(Optional: Yogurt or whipped cream topping)

Toast sesame seeds in 325° F. oven for 10 minutes. Heat grape juice and honey to boiling and add farina. Cook 5 to 7 minutes.

Pour into individual glasses and sprinkle with nuts, cinnamon and sesame seeds. Chill. Serve with a dab of yogurt or whipped cream topping.

GREEK RICE PUDDING

ΡΙΖΟΓΑΛΟΝ   (rizogalon)

This is the famous creamy rice pudding that every Greek housewife makes for family and guests. Although the traditional Grecian flavor is lemon, vanilla seems to mate better with milk.

½ cup rice, long grain
1 cup water
1 quart milk
¾ cup sugar
pinch of salt

1 teaspoon vanilla
¼ cup currants or raisins
2 eggs, separated
cinnamon

Boil rice in water for 5 minutes. Bring milk, sugar, and vanilla to a boil. Add rice and raisins and reduce fire. Stir with spoon to circulate rice once or twice. Simmer 45 minutes.

Remove pot from heat. Beat egg yolks and add 1 cup rice pudding. Mix the rest in. Beat egg whites until thick and peaks form. Mix into pudding.

Pour into individual bowls. Sprinkle with cinnamon. Serve warm or chilled.

ORIENTAL HALVAH

ΧΑΛΒΑΣ   (halvas)

This recipe originated in the tents of the Persians and was later refined by the Greeks. Here, Farina becomes an exotic cake filled with nuts, honey and spices of the East. It is cooked in a saucepot, then poured into a cake pan to cool, and served in slices, like cake.

SYRUP:
  2 cups sugar
  1 cup water
  1 cup honey
  1 tablespoon rose flavoring
½ cup butter or oil

1 cup farina, regular (cream of
  wheat, semolina)
1 teaspoon cinnamon
½ cup blanched almonds, halved or
  whole
maraschino cherries for garnish

Dissolve sugar in water and bring to a boil. Boil vigorously for 10 minutes, covering pot for the last 5 minutes. Remove pot from fire. Add honey and flavoring.

Meanwhile, fry almonds in a tablespoon of butter for 3 minutes to brown. Remove almonds and set aside.

Melt remaining butter until it bubbles. Add farina slowly and fry over medium heat stirring constantly until it turns to a golden brown, about 15 minutes. Add almonds (save a few to decorate top).

Pour hot syrup into farina slowly, stirring constantly. Simmer 5 minutes. Pour into buttered pan. Sprinkle with cinnamon and decorate with almonds and cherries. Cool. When ready to serve, cut into diamond-shape pieces.

VILLAGE FARINA CUSTARD

ΠΟΥΤΙΓΓΑ   (poutika)

Farina is the main ingredient in this custard. This cereal, usually a breakfast and baby food, is treated in an exotic manner in Greece and throughout the Near East. Fresh fruit or preserves often accompany it to accent the fine texture of the custard.

1 quart milk
½ cup farina, regular (cream of
  wheat, semolina)
½ cup sugar
1 teaspoon vanilla
2 tablespoons butter or margarine
2 eggs, well beaten

SYRUP:
  1 cup honey or sugar
  1 tablespoon lemon juice
  ½ cup water
¼ cup almond or pistachio nuts
cinnamon
fresh fruit slices or preserves

Bring milk to a boil. Add farina, sugar and vanilla and cook 15 minutes stirring often. Remove from fire. Mix in butter. Beat eggs and mix some farina mixture into it. Add to remaining farina.

Pour into buttered baking dish. Decorate top with nuts. Bake at 350° F. for 20 minutes.

Prepare syrup by boiling honey, lemon juice, and water for 5 minutes. Pour over baked custard. Sprinkle generously with cinnamon. Set aside to cool and absorb syrup for 4 hours. Cut into squares like cake. Serve plain or with slices of fresh fruit or fruit preserves.

SYRUPS

Most Greek pastries and cakes are bathed in hot syrup as soon as they are taken out of the oven. You would think the pastry would become soggy after being bathed in hot syrup but this does not happen: the syrup is absorbed immediately. These desserts remain moist and fresh without refrigeration for a long time.

SIMPLE SUGAR SYRUP

ΣΙΡΟΠΙ ΑΠΟ ΖΑΧΑΡΙ   (siropi apo zahari)

3 cups sugar
2 cups water
¼ teaspoon cream of tartar
rind of one lemon, grated

juice of one lemon
flavoring of any *one:* rose, whiskey, brandy, rum, ouzo (optional)

Dissolve sugar in water, stirring gently, in a deep saucepot. Add remaining ingredients and boil vigorously for 10 minutes or to 215° F. on a candy thermometer. Cover pan the last 5 minutes of cooking to wash down sugar crystals from the side of the pot and prevent the syrup from graining.

Pour over hot pastry immediately or store in clean jar with cover. Reheat to boiling point before pouring over pastry.

HONEY SYRUP

ΣΙΡΟΠΙ ΜΕ ΜΕΛΙ   (siropi meh meli)

The fame of the flavorful honey from Hymettus and Kythera islands has spread from country to country.

2 cups honey   **2 cups sugar**
1 cup water   **1 tablespoon lemon juice**

Put all ingredients in a deep saucepot. Stir until sugar is dissolved. Bring to a boil slowly. Watch it carefully because it boils
over quickly. Reduce heat. Simmer 15 minutes. Cover the last
5 minutes.

Pour hot over pastries as soon as they are taken out of the
oven or cool and store in a clean jar with cover. Reheat before
pouring over pastries.

CLARIFIED BUTTER OR MARGARINE

ΒΟΥΤΥΡΟ/ΦΥΤΙΝΙ   (voutiro/fytini)

Although the Ancient Greeks knew about butter, they did not
prefer it over olive oil and considered it a food which barbarians
used because they couldn't get olive oil. Even today, oil is still
used for most phases of cooking, but where butter is used, it is
clarified of salt and milk solids first by melting; then allowed to
harden again and used immediately or stored in jars. Clarified
butter produces a better flavor and texture in cakes and cookies.
Try this Greek cooking secret in all your recipes.

½ pound butter = ⅝ cup butter oil   **1 pound butter = 1⅞ cups butter oil**
(scant)

Melt butter in medium-size pot on low heat until it foams, about
10 minutes. Watch it carefully, avoid browning or burning. Remove from heat and let stand 2 minutes while milk solids settle
to bottom and salt crystals settle on top.

Using a tablespoon, skim off the salt crystals floating on top
and discard. Even if butter is sweet there will be some crystals.
(Taste these crystals and you'll know why you wouldn't want to
put them in your pastry.)

Slowly pour the oil into a small bowl, being careful not to disturb the unwanted milk curds which are white and have sunk to the bottom. Use a teaspoon to skim the last of the oil. Store clarified butter oil in jar in refrigerator or use as directed in recipes. See Greek Wedding Cookies (page 171).

THE FRUITS OF GREECE

ΦΡΕΣΚΑ ΦΡΟΥΤΑ ΕΛΛΗΝΙΚΑ
(freska fruta ellenehka)

Chilled fruits were enjoyed by the ancient Greeks long before refrigeration. In those days it was a long run to nature's refrigerator; slave runners had to bring ice and snow from the nearest mountain top. Naturally only the wealthiest Greeks and aristocrats could afford to enjoy this luxury, so the next time you are stuck with the problem of dessert and have some fruit in the kitchen, put it on ice and call it Fruit, Mount Olympus, or dip it in honey and call it Fruit, Alexander the Great. Any familiar fruit will do because the fruits of the Mediterranean are known and enjoyed everywhere.

Among the well-known fruits are: apples, ΜΗΛΑ (milla) the best of which come from Florina; marvelous peaches and nectarines, ΡΟΔΑΚΙΝΟ (rodakino) and apricots, ΒΕΡΙΚΟΚΑ (verikoka), from Naoussa in Macedonia; and big yellow peaches called ΓΑΡΜΑΔΕΣ (yarmades) from Argos where yellow fleshed melons, ΠΕΠΟΝΙΑ (peponia) also grow, equaled only by the melons from Methana. Grapes, ΣΤΑΦΥΛΙΑ (stafilia) from the province of Achaea are more delicious when dried into currants. Figs, ΣΥΚΑ (syka) are best when they come from Kalamata and Skyros, an island of the Sporades which produces a sweet green variety. Prunes, ΛΑΜΑΣΚΗΝΑ (thamaskina) also are grown in Skopelos, another island in the Northern Sporades, their season being in August, when they are dried in home ovens, and the fat juicy kind eaten fresh are called ΚΟΡΟΜΗΛΑ (koromila). Oranges, ΠΟΡΤΟΚΑΛΙΑ (portokalia) particularly blood oranges from Messolongi have a special taste as do the mandarins, ΜΑΝΔΑΡΙΝΙΑ (mandarinia) from Rhodes, and lemons ΛΕΜΟΝΙ (lemoni) from Patras.

Other fruits of the temperate climate category are cherries, ΚΕΡΑΣΙΑ (kerasia); strawberries, ΦΡΑΟΥΛΕΣ (fraoules); pears, ΑΧΛΑΔΙΑ (ahladia); and watermelons, ΚΑΡΠΟΥΖΙ (karpouzi) from Cos.

The sub-tropical fruits consist of those whose taste you know very well and others you may not have tried: bananas, ΜΠΑΝΑΝΑ (banana) from Messara in Crete; pomegranate, ΡΟΙΔΙ (roydy); loquot ΜΟΥΣΜΟΥΛΑ (mousmoula) which is a small fruit like an apricot but shaped like a tiny pear: prickly pear οαοτυο, ΦΡΑΓΚΟΣΥΚΑ (fragosyka) delicious to eat fresh, resembling a peach studded with cloves, treacherous to touch because of the fine thorns; wild strawberries, ΚΟΥΜΑΡΑ (koumara), a round red berry with yellow sweet pulp grown on a small tree, the arbutus unedo: mulberries, ΜΟΥΡΑ (moura) a purple berry, delicious in jams or in a sauce for baked fish; carob or St. John's bread, ΧΑΡΟΥΠΙΑ (haroupia) looking like black leather tongues from high buttoned shoes but sweet as chocolate; lotus fruit, ΛΩΤΟΣ (lotos) a large and mealy fruit from which the ancient Greeks believed a wine could be made that could cause forgetfulness.

The grapes of Greece are praised in song and poetry. The black sweet Corinthian grapes, when dried become Zante currants, (also called Greek currants), which make up most of the world's supply. The word itself, currant, comes from the city's name, Corinth. These same Zante grapes grown also in Kefallinia gives their wines a distinctive flavor characteristic only to that island in the Ionian Sea. The muscat grape, grown in Cyprus, Samos and Monomevasia, is the Alexandria variety that is turned into muscatel and malmsey wine, immortalized by Lord Byron.

The fig is the earliest fruit known to the Greeks and, in ancient times, Attica figs were in such great demand that special laws were made to regulate their exportation. The Messinia variety, from Kalamata is a gourmet treat. You can recognize these figs at a glance; they are strung on reeds like a necklace. Fresh figs do not transport easily or cheaply, so whenever you see them, do not waste the opportunity to enjoy the taste of a fruit that is as old as the Greek civilization.

PRESERVES

SERVING OF PRESERVES

ΤΡΟΠΟΣ ΣΕΡΒΙΡΙΣΜΑΤΟΣ ΓΛΥΚΟΥ
(tropos servirizmatos glykou)

With the words "ΚΑΛΟΣ ΟΡΙΣΑΤΕ" (kalos oresate), good wel-
come, the Greek hostess greets her guests. Conserves and something sweet are offered to the callers after they are comfortably
seated. This custom of offering something sweet by hosts to their
guests began centuries ago with the Persians when they wanted
to demonstrate hospitality and promise that the food was not
going to be poisoned.

After the initial greeting, the Greek hostess will excuse herself
and hurry to return with a tray on which there will be a napkin,
probably embroidered, a glass of cold clear water, a jam jar
and a teaspoon face down, resting on top of each glass of water
and a small glass of liqueur, wine or cognac. The jam is not in a
dab on the dish with a clean spoon by its side, as is the custom
in the west. The hostess waits, with tray in hands, while the guest
takes the spoon, napkin in one hand and helps himself to one
spoonful of preserve. He returns the spoon to its dish and sips
the water. He then picks up the glass of wine and proposes a
toast to the hostess and her family's health with the proper
phrase, "ΣΤΗΝ ΥΓΕΙΑ ΣΑΣ" (estin eyea sas), "To your health."
If a tray is offered on which there are placed two or more varieties
of preserves in small jam jars, tiny saucers and spoons will be
served alongside. The guest picks up the small dish and spoon
and serves himself one spoonful of one kind. He does not eat
from the bowl nor take more than one spoonful. The hostess ex-
presses her thanks for his gracing her house with his visit, and
returns with cups of Turkish coffee, cookies, cakes, and sweets to
join her guests for the serious business of gossiping and nibbling.

Often the formality of serving glica, as these sweets are called,
falls upon the young daughters of the household to show what

good homemakers they will make. This custom still prevails throughout Greece; it has almost disappeared in the United States.

The kinds of preserves, jams and jellies used are quite unusual and deliciously different. They are eaten as candy and a little bit suffices. Typical *glica* are: wild cherry, *visino,* made from tart sour cherries In a thick sweet syrup, with a color of deep burgundy red; orange marmalade, *portokalli,* made with thicker slices of rind than those found in the English variety of bitter marmalade; or tiny sour oranges in green syrup, *narantzi;* quince jam, *kydoni peltes,* a thick pulpy mixture with an apple flavor, on the tart side; rose petal jam, *triantafillo glyco,* thick, delicate and slightly chewy; strawberry-flavored grapes, *fraoula; anthos* made of lemon blossoms; tiny eggplants called *melanzanakia* in a sweet syrup or *ipovryhion*—a spoonful of white mastic jam served in a glass of water. These sweets, known as *glyco tou koutali,* which translates into "spoon sweets," are imported into the United States but a reasonable substitution can be made in the kitchen.

FIG CONSERVE

ΣΥΚΟ ΓΛΥΚΟ   (syko glyko)

4 cups sugar
1½ cups water
juice of 1 lemon
¼ teaspoon cream of tartar

¼ teaspoon anise seed
1½ pounds dried figs or apricots
½ cup walnuts

In a deep saucepot stir all ingredients except figs and walnuts until sugar is dissolved. Bring to a boil. Add figs. Boil on medium heat until figs are tender, approximately 30 minutes. Cover pot the last 10 minutes. Remove from fire. Add walnuts and cool. Pour into clean jar.

ORANGE MARMALADE

ΠΟΡΤΟΚΑΛΛΙ ΓΛΥΚΟ   (portokalli glyko)

The bitter marmalade of England is a transplanted Greek delicacy which dates back to the time when only bitter citrons were used for this recipe because the lemon, orange, kumquat, tangerine and mandarin were still unknown fruits. From the time of Theophrastus, the citron has been called "the golden apple of Hesperides."

6 or more oranges, preferably thick-
   skinned navels or any *one* of the
   following: lemon, grapefruit, citron,
   tangerine, lime, kumquat, mandarin or sour orange (*narantzi*)
⅛ teaspoon baking soda

4 cups sugar
1 cup corn syrup
½ teaspoon cream of tartar
2 cups water
3 drops green food dye (optional)

Peel citrus. (Leave whole if using kumquats or whole sour oranges, *narantzi*.) Trim off white pulp; it's bitter. Cut rind into thin strips or make strips ½" wide and roll into tight balls. With heavy thread and a large darning needle sew each one, making a necklace. Tie ends.

Place rinds or whole oranges in a large deep pot and cover with water. Add baking soda. Bring to a boil, reduce heat to simmer and cook 1 hour. Drain. Add fresh water and boil 1 hour as before. Drain a second time and repeat, boiling in fresh water for a third hour. This procedure eliminates bitterness in rind. Remove rolled citrus from string. Allow whole citrus to dry off on a paper towel.

Prepare syrup by boiling remaining ingredients until thick, or to 220° F. on a candy thermometer. Add citrus to syrup and simmer together 10 minutes. Remove from heat and allow to set 6 hours, in the pan in which it was boiled. Return pot to heat and bring to a boil. Add color if using whole oranges, if desired. Reduce heat and simmer 10 minutes. Syrup should be thick and the orange peel beautifully candied in syrup.

FRAGRANT BLOSSOM JELLY

ΑΝΘΑΚΙ   (anthaki)

If you have ever become intoxicated from the exquisite odor of blossoms of orange trees or from lemon, honeysuckle, or jasmine in bloom and longed to hold that moment of summer forever, then you must try this recipe. Your house will smell divine.

1 to 2 cups minimum of fragrant
   blossoms: orange, lemon, honeysuckle or jasmine. (Do *not* use
   plumeria or frangipani or any
   euphorbia.)

4 cups sugar
2 cups water
½ cup corn syrup
¼ teaspoon cream of tartar
juice of one lemon

For orange and lemon trees

Gently shake limb and drop petals into a wide bag or cake pan, which you are holding underneath. Pull only the petals off; leave stems on tree to bear fruit. Spread petals on dish and pick out any hard green stems.

Pack blossoms into measuring cup. Try to have a minimum of 1 to 2 cups. Place in bowl and cover with sugar. Set aside for 6 hours or overnight, tossing with fork occasionally.

Bring water to a boil in a large pot. Add petals and remaining ingredients. Stir gently until sugar melts. Reduce heat and simmer on medium heat for 45 minutes or to 220° F. on candy thermometer. Cover pot the last 10 minutes of cooking time. Strain into clean jars and seal. ((To prevent jar from breaking when hot syrup enters, place a spoon in it before pouring.) When cool, tighten lid.

GRAPE PRESERVES

ΣΤΑΦΤΑΙ ΓΛΤΚΟ   (stafili glyko)

1 pound grapes, seedless variety
2 cups sugar
¼ teaspoon cream of tartar

1 tablespoon lemon juice
1 teaspoon cornstarch
1 cup water

Clean grapes, removing all stems. Add sugar and cornstarch. Set aside for an hour.

In a large deep pot, bring water to a boil. Add all ingredients and cook on medium heat until syrup is thick or to 220° F. on candy thermometer. Cover pot last 10 minutes. When slightly cooled, pour into jar.

QUINCE PRESERVE

ΚΤΔΩΝΙ ΠΕΛΤΕΣ   (kydoni peltes)

Some Biblical scholars maintain that the apple which Eve gave Adam was really a quince. If true, he deserved a stomach-ache because quince must be cooked before it is eaten. Some Greek cooks use quince as a vegetable and add to it stews or stuff it with rice filling. Quince is full of pectin and is an excellent fruit candied or preserved.

| 4 cups quince, chopped or grated | 1 cup water |
| 4 cups sugar | juice of 1 lemon |

Peel and cut or grate quinces in small pieces into a large deep pot. Cover with sugar, water and lemon juice. Bring to a boil. Reduce heat to medium and cook 1 hour. Stir occasionally to avoid sticking. Remove from heat and when cooled, store in clean jar.

For candied quince, continue simmering slowly over very low heat until liquid is reduced to a thick glaze. Pour into a shallow baking pan. Dry paste into candy by leaving it in a 200° F. oven for 2 hours. When ready, cut into squares and roll in powdered sugar. Store in plastic bags.

ROSE PETAL JAM MOUNT ATHOS

ΤΡΙΑΝΤΑΦΥΛΟ ΓΛΥΚΟ   (triantafilo glyko)

The next time you receive a bouquet of red roses, don't just use them for a centerpiece; cook them. Or, if your rose garden is blanketed with snow, capture a summer memory by making some of this preserve. This exquisite jam is served frequently throughout Greece and is easy to make.

2 dozen roses, red preferably, or 4 cups rose petals (wild, garden, or florist variety)	½ cup corn syrup
	juice of one lemon
	¼ teaspoon cream of tartar
4 cups sugar	2 drops red food dye (optional)
2 cups water	

Pull off petals. Snip off white base, using only top parts of petals. Put in a bowl and cover with sugar. Set aside for 4 hours or overnight, tossing occasionally with fork to mix sugar and petals.

Bring water to a boil in a large pot. Add sugared petals and remaining ingredients and stir gently until sugar melts. Add red dye if desired. Reduce heat and simmer on medium heat for 45 minutes until jam thickens or to 220° F. on candy thermometer. Cover pot the last 10 minutes of cooking time. The steam will wash the sugar crystals down the sides of the pot and prevent the preserve from graining when cooled. Pour into clean small jam jars and seal lightly. (To prevent jar from breaking when hot syrup enters, place a spoon in it before pouring.) When cool, tighten lid.

WILD CHERRY PRESERVES

ΒΙΣΙΝΟ ΓΛΥΚΟ   (visino glyko)

Originally, only the tiny wild sour cherries that grow profusely in Chios, birthplace of Homer, were used for this distinctively flavored tart preserve. It can be duplicated with domestic sour cherries, fresh, canned or frozen. If you insist upon the original, you can buy the imported wild cherry preserve canned in Greece in most Greek shops. Ask for *visino kerasi.*

1 pound of pitted tart red cherries   **¼ teaspoon cream of tartar**
  (canned in water)   **1 tablespoon lemon juice**
1 cup sugar   **1 teaspoon cornstarch**

Strain cherries, draining juice into deep saucepot. Add remaining ingredients to juice and stir until sugar dissolves. Bring to a boil. Add cherries and continue boiling vigorously until syrup thickens, about 10 minutes. Cover pot the last 3 minutes. Watch jelly carefully to avoid burning.

Remove from fire, set pan immediately in cool water, otherwise the heat of the pan will continue to cook the syrup. Let stand until cool enough to pour into jar.

CONFECTIONS

ΖΑΧΑΡΩΤΑ-ΓΛΥΚΙΣΜΑΤΑ-ΚΑΡΑΜΕΛΛΕΣ
(zaharota-glykismata-karamelles)

Sugar was not introduced to Greece until well into the 15th century, although the Crusaders had brought it earlier to Europe from Arabia, but sweets were nothing new. The Greeks had been making *glykismata* (sweet things), from fruits, dates, figs, nuts and spices for thousands of years with honey which could be cooked to the various stages of hardness, just like sugar. They were happy to add the new Arabic words for sugar, *zahari,* and *zaharota,* meaning hard candies.

The Venetians, who were occupying the Greek islands and some of the coastal cities of Greece at the same time the Turks were lords of the mainland, between the 1200s and 1600s, were the first to begin using sugar for candies. The Greeks refined their own classic recipes to include this miraculous new sweetener and discovered they had an affinity for the art of candy making. Today every western country (including their dentists) is indebted to the Greek candymakers who introduced the brittles, the nougats, the caramels and the hard candies.

GRAPE NUT ROLL

ΣΟΥΤΖΟΥΚΙ   (soutzouki)

Candied nuts and grape juice, *soutzouki,* is an ancient candy recipe still being used in the villages of Greece. The traditional recipe is quite involved, calling for the stringing of walnuts like beads on linen thread, boiling many pounds of grapes into a thick syrup and coating the nuts by pouring the thick syrup over them just as if you were making candles until a purple necklace is formed. You can make this recipe in a simpler way without having to stamp on the grapes with bare feet.

1 can (6 oz.) frozen grape juice,
  undiluted
½ cup sugar or honey
1 small box pectin jell

citric acid, size of a pea
  or juice of 1 lemon
½ cup whole walnuts
3 tablespoons cornstarch
¼ cup cold water

In a large deep pot bring juice and honey or sugar to a vigorous boil. Add pectin and boil 5 minutes. Dissolve citric acid first in a tablespoon of hot syrup, then add to the rest of the syrup, mixing it in. Add nuts. Dissolve cornstarch in cold water and mix into syrup, stirring quickly. Cook 1 minute more.

Ladle thick mixture on to heavy waxed paper. Make a long thick roll. Pick up two sides of paper and press together to make a fat sausage of candy. Let set at room temperature. Store in plastic bag. Slice as needed.

HALVAH FUDGE

ΧΑΛΒΑ   (halvah)

Sesame tahini goes into this candy recipe to make a delicious variation of fudge.

2 cups brown sugar
⅔ cup milk

⅔ cup sesame Tahini
1 teaspoon vanilla

Cook sugar and milk in a sauce pot over medium heat to just under the soft-ball stage, to 230° F. Remove from fire and add tahini and vanilla but do not mix in immediately. Let it cool about 2 minutes. Beat with paddle or spoon for a few seconds and pour quickly into a buttered pan.

MARZIPAN

ΓΛΥΚΥΣΜΑΤΑ ΑΠΟ ΑΜΥΓΔΑΛΑ   (glikismata apo amigdalo)

Every Greek candymaker and baker makes these attractive fruits and flowers from almond paste made from ground almonds. It is one of the easiest candies to make although, at one time, only the wealthy could afford to eat marzipan delicacies.

1 cup almond paste (available in
   stores or through a baker)
or 1 pound of almonds, blanched,
   skinned and blended or pounded to
   a paste

2 egg whites
3 cups powdered sugar
½ teaspoon vanilla
cornstarch
food coloring, cotton swabs

Knead paste for a few minutes, adding egg whites and kneading a total of 5 minutes. Add sugar, 1 cup at a time, kneading after each addition. Add flavoring last. Marzipan should feel like pie dough.

Dust cutting board lightly with cornstarch and roll dough out ½″ thick. Cut with fancy shaped cookie cutters, the tinier the better. Use cotton swabs, dip in color and tint designs on fruit, etc. To blanche, drop almonds into boiling water. Let stand 3 minutes. Transfer to cold water and rub skins off. Drain and blend or pound to paste.

SYROS ISLAND NOUGAT

ΝΟΤΓΑΤΑ   (nougata)

When you buy a box of nougat that comes from the Syros Island, you are tasting a candy that is as old as its pre-Hellenic Cycladic art. The Venetian lords and ladies introduced sugar to these islands, it was much too precious a commodity for commoners, in the 13th century. This recipe was refined to include the new sweetening agent, and today it is one of the delicacies for which Syros is famous.

1 cup roasted pistachios and almonds
2 cups sugar
1 cup corn syrup
1 cup honey
½ teaspoon cream of tartar
3 egg whites

¼ teaspoon salt
1 teaspoon vanilla
¼ cup oil for pan
cornstarch or sweet rice flour or thin
   rice wafers to line pan

Roast nuts on shallow pan in preheated oven at 350° F. for 10 minutes.

Combine sugar, corn syrup, water, and cream of tartar in a deep sauce pot. Stir gently over medium heat until sugar dissolves and bring to a boil. After it comes to a boil, cover pot for 5 minutes, then wash down sides of pot with a clean brush to remove sugar crystals. Continue cooking on medium-high heat to 272° F. on a jelly thermometer. Remove from heat.

In a separate pot heat honey to a boil.

Whip egg whites and salt until stiff and dry using a heavy electric mixer and large bowl. Add a small amount of honey at first in a thin stream, very slowly. Beat in vanilla and continue adding remaining honey and then syrup. Beat until batch thickens and the beater slows down. Add nuts and blend in.

Oil a long shallow pan. Sift a thick layer of cornstarch or sweet rice flour over it or lay rice wafers over bottom. Pour out the nougat. Dust top with more rice flour or thin rice wafers and let stand overnight to set. Cut into rectangular pieces about ¾" by 1" and wrap individually in heavy waxed paper.

SESAME HONEY STICKS PASTELLE

ΠΑΣΤΕΛΛΙ, ΜΤΛΛΟΙ   (pastelle, melloi)

This candy recipe can be traced back into ancient Greek history to a poet named Philyllius, 600 B.C., who obviously had a sweet tooth when he described this sweet which he called *mellol*. It Is still sold everywhere in Greece and is available in the United States in many health food stores.

1 cup sesame seeds   **1 cup honey**

Spread sesame seeds on a pan and toast in preheated oven at 350° F. for 5 minutes. Bring honey to a boil. Add seeds and continue cooking on medium heat to 280° F. (light crack reading). Watch it carefully, it burns quickly.

Pour into buttered pan, and flatten with spatula to ½" thickness. Score into 2" pieces while hot. Allow to cool. Store in pastic bag.

TURKISH DELIGHT

ΛΟΤΚΟΤΜΙ   (loukoumi)

The words, Turkish Delight, may be used to describe the sultan's favorite belly dancer, but more likely the reference is made to the very popular sticky candy gumdrops which were brought to Greece by the Turks. The traditional shape of these jellies Is square and they are studded with chopped pistachios and almonds and covered with powdered sugar. The most common flavors are rose, mastic, orange, lemon, and strawberry.

2 cups sugar
2 tablespoons cornstarch
1 cup water
½ teaspoon cream of tartar
1 tablespoon flavoring: rose, or
   mastic, strawberry, orange, or
   lemon

Food coloring: red, yellow, green or
   orange (depending upon the
   flavoring used)
½ cup toasted nuts, pistachios or
   almonds, chopped
confectioners sugar for dusting

Dissolve sugar and cornstarch in water. Add cream of tartar. Boil to 220° F. Cover pot the last 5 minutes. Add flavor and food color. Add nuts.

Pour into oiled shallow pan. When cool, cut into squares and roll each piece in sifted powdered sugar. Store in plastic bag.

THE NUTS OF
GREECE

ΞΤΡΟΙ ΚΑΡΠΟΙ
(ksiroi karpoi)

Greek recipes reflect the abundance of the nut trees of Greece. Many of them call for pounds of nuts, such as almonds ΑΜΥΓ-ΔΑΛΑ (amigdala), chestnuts ΚΑΣΤΑΝΑ (kastana), pine nuts or *pignolias* ΚΟΥΚΟΥΝΑΡΙΑ (koukounaria), walnuts ΚΑΡΥΔΙΑ (karidia), pistachio ΦΥΣΤΙΚΙΑ (fistikia), hazelnuts ΛΕΠΤΟ-ΚΑΡΥΔΙΑ (leptokaridia), and filberts ΦΟΥΝΤΟΥΚΙΑ (foundoukia).

Of all the nuts the almond is the most prized. The Jordan variety is used in cakes, candies and in the most famous of all pastries, baklava. For centuries It has been used as the symbol of fertility and good fortune and ancient custom still obliges the host to distribute almonds at weddings and christenings.

Chestnut trees grow in many places but there is a chestnut forest in the town of Tsangaradha, outside of Volos in Pelion, that is an experience to drive through. When in season street vendors sell roasted chestnuts everywhere.

Pine nuts or pignolias are the seeds of pine cones from the stone pine, found in the Mediterranean regions, and in California in the United States. Skiathos has a magnificent grove of stone pine trees. Many Greek recipes for stuffings, pilafis or stews, as well as cakes and puddings, are all the more delicious because of them.

Hazelnuts and filberts are roasted and eaten fresh or lend their special flavor to many cake and pastry recipes.

Pistachios, grown in Aeghina in the Argo Saronikos Islands off the shores of Attica, are the peanuts of Greece, and are nibbled on at all hours of the day.

BOILED CHESTNUTS

ΚΑΣΤΑΝΑ ΒΡΑΣΤΑ   (vrasta kastana)

Cover chestnuts with water. Bring to a boil and simmer one hour. Allow chestnuts to cool in the water before removing and peeling. Use in Chestnut Dressing Peleponnesus (page 124) or purée in blender with some simple syrup (page 177) and serve as topping over ice cream.

SALTED SEEDS PASATEMPO

ΠΑΣΑΤΕΜΠΟ   (pasatempo)

Spread pumpkin, squash, or melon seeds on shallow pan. Salt slightly. Bake at 375° F. for 20 minutes. Serve as nuts, eating kernel inside shell.

STREET VENDOR'S ROASTED CHESTNUTS

ΚΑΣΤΑΝΑ ΨΗΤΑ   (kastana psita)

Slit 1 pound of chestnuts with a small sharp knife so they will not explode while baking. Put in a shallow pan. Add 1 cup or more water. Bake at 400° F. for 45 minutes. Peel while hot.

ROASTED NUTS

ΨΗΤΑ ΚΑΡΤΔΙΑ   (psita karidia)

Put any kind of shelled nuts such as almonds, walnuts, pistachios, hazelnuts, or filberts in 375° F. oven for 10 minutes. Use in any recipe required.

BLANCHED ALMONDS

ΑΜΥΓΔΑΛΑ   (amigdala)

Plunge whole almonds with skins into boiling water for 2 minutes. Remove skins and peel by rubbing them off with fingers.

BEVERAGES

ΡΟΦΗΜΑΤΑ   (rofemata)

Charming outdoor cafes in every village or city beckon you to sit down and have a drink. The selection is excellent whether you like liquids hot, cold, plain or alcoholic.

You cannot escape from Greece without tasting its alcoholic beverages, especially the anise-flavored liqueur, ouzo, turned milky in water and the water glass filled with resinated wine called retsina or its unresinated counterpart aretsinoto. The beer, a light lager, is good and strong which should come as no surprise if one remembers that the ancient Greeks knew how to make good beer they called ΒΡΤΤΟΝ (vryton) from barley and rye. According to Sophocles, "the Tracians made good beer" and Aristotle said observantly, "the peculiar thing about beer drunks; they would fall backwards and lie flat, where wine drunks would fall in all directions." The wines and brandies of Greece have a distinct flavor due to the various kinds of grapes and their praises have been sung in poetry and song. Many of the prescriptions of Hippocrates, the Greek physician whose code of ethics hangs on every physician's wall, are still served as soothing hot beverages, tisanes or teas.

Sodas made from velvety ice-cream and fruit flavored syrups cool instantly when you've been under the hot Mediterranean sun. Lemonade stands are everywhere and especially good is the one bottled in Agria in Pelion, while in Cyprus you can drink a *tsintsibira,* ginger beer.

The Greek never scorn the best of all beverages, pure cold clear water and it is a sign of hospitality when offered. He appreciates the mineral waters from the health spas of Loutraki, Platystomon, Kallithea, Sariza and Nigrita which he believes have curative properties.

There is the ubiquitous black Turkish coffee, always served in tiny demitasse cups, being sipped at any time of the day and at all hours of the night. Coffee originated in the sixteenth century in Kaffa, Ethiopia, and was introduced to Greece by the Moslem Turks who, forbidden to drink wines and alcoholic beverages, were able to indulge in this stimulating drink as much as they wished without breaking religious laws. Soon the coffeehouse, the *kafeneon,* spread throughout the Middle East, including Greece. It became a meeting place for men, where they spent a few moments or hours of escape from the world of women. There they could sit for hours, sipping coffee, *kahfe,* fingering their *komboloi,* worry beads of Baltic amber, exchanging news, discussing politics and gossip or playing *barbuti,* a fast game of dice. Today, only in larger cities of modern Greece are women entering the once forbidden world of the *kafeneon.* In the smaller cities and villages, it is still the men's club where no self-respecting woman enters. But once a year, on the 11th of January, in the villages of Serrai, Eastern Macedonia, the women take over for the day, sitting in the coffeehouses while the men stay home and perform the household tasks.

HOT BEVERAGES

GREEK OR TURKISH COFFEE

ΕΛΛΗΝΙΚΟΣ ΚΑΦΕΣ   (ellenehkos kahfes)

Greek or Turkish coffee is a powdered coffee, not instant. In the United States, it is available in cans labeled Turkish Coffee or Powdered Demitasse Coffee, but the ultimate gourmet will purchase a brass Turkish coffee grinder (approximately twelve dollars) and grind the coffee beans himself. Instant coffee cannot be used as a substitute, it dissolves in water and Turkish coffee doesn't. The grounds settle to the bottom of the cup. You may sip this thick liquid or eat it. It is always served black and burning hot with a head of frothy foam floating on top in a demitasse cup; no spoon is served with it. It is customary to tell your hostess or waiter what degree of sweetness you prefer: ΠΙΚΡΟ (pikro) bitter; or ΣΚΕΤΟΣ (sketos) without sugar; ΜΕΤΡΙΟ (metrio) medium for ½ teaspoon sugar and ΓΛΥΚΟ (glyko) sweet, meaning 2 teaspoons sugar and ΒΑΡΥ ΓΛΥΚΟ (variglyco) for heavy-sweet, meaning strong in coffee and sugar, the latter being a favorite with men in the coffeehouses. Milk or cream is never served with it. The coffee is very strong and is boiled three times in a special coffeepot called a ΜΠΡΙΚΙ (bricky) to get it that way. Often, it is brewed over an alcohol burner at the table.

The most accomplished hostess can make her coffee with a head of high foam, and making Turkish coffee is one of the first skills taught the daughter of the household. It is she who does the honors of making it and serving it to the guests as well. Often, it is brewed over an alcohol burner at the table.

Many customs have grown around the drinking of Turkish coffee. One custom revolves around courtship. In arranged marriages, a custom still maintained in isolated villages of Greece, the girl did not have the privilege of choosing her husband, but she could reject offers providing she did it subtly, without anyone losing face. If a courting young man had been successful enough in his suit to be allowed into her parents' home and was sitting there with his relatives, waiting to be served coffee, a girl could indicate her dislike of him by serving his coffee with no foam or head (Kaimaik) on it. He and his relatives did not need words to be told his suit wasn't welcomed. Later, a wife could indicate her displeasure in the same manner; her husband would quickly get the point.

The Greeks have always loved oracles, and fortune telling by reading the coffee grounds became another custom. To tell fortunes the procedure is as follows: After drinking the coffee, turn the cup over quickly upside down on the saucer. Wait 1 minute. Lift the cup and examine the pattern of the grounds in the cup. The future can be clearly read. If the grounds are separated by wide spaces, it indicates a long voyage; smaller spaces, a short trip. A large blob means money, small blobs mean trouble. For a more detailed look into the future you need a Greek gypsy to advise you.

SERVES 1
1 demitasse cup water
1 teaspoon sugar (*metrio*)
1 heaping teaspoon Turkish coffee

SERVES 4
4 demitasse cups water
4 teaspoons sugar
4 heaping teaspoons coffee

Use a coffee *bricky* or a small sauce pot. Bring water and sugar to a rolling boil. Remove pot from fire and stir in coffee. Return *bricky* to fire. Coffee will boil to the top immediately, so be ready to take pot off the fire for a few seconds until coffee simmers away from the brim. Do not take your hand off the handle. Return pot to fire for the second time and allow it to boil to top again. Take coffee off fire once more, until coffee simmers down. Return to fire for the last time and allow to boil for the third time.

Pour immediately into demitasse cup filling it ¼" from the top. If making 4 cups or more, skim off a teaspoon of foam (*kaimaik*) into each cup before filling with coffee. If making a second batch of coffee, do not throw away the remains of the first pot. Just add more water and more coffee each time.

MOUNTAIN TEA

ΤΣΑΙ ΤΟΥ ΒΟΥΝΟΥ   (tsai tou vounou)

Though one associates tea with the Chinese, the Greeks have brewed various kinds of sweet smelling leaves for many centuries. Hippocrates, the Greek physician, used tisanes or *tsies* as prescriptions for curing colds, fevers and stomach ailments. Many of his recipes are still in use today. One such tea is made from camomile leaves with various herbs added to make it more flavorful. This is what you would get if you ordered tea in the villages of Greece. It is quite pleasant when laced with honey and lemon, but if you are one of those people who needs to have your tea, carry your own tea bag and ask for boiled water: ΤΟ ΝΕΡΟ ΝΑ ΒΡΑΖΗ (toe nehro nah vrahzi).

4 cups boiling water
½ teaspoon dried camomile leaves
    or sage leaves (faskomila)

2 teaspoons honey or to taste
1 slice of lemon
dash of cinnamon

Bring water to a boil. Add leaves. Let seep 2 to 5 minutes. Strain. Add honey, lemon and cinnamon.

GREEK EGG NOG

ΚΟΥΡΚΟ   (kourko)

1 egg, well beaten
3 teaspoons sugar
½ teaspoon vanilla

1 glass hot milk
dash of nutmeg or cinnamon

Beat egg, sugar and vanilla until thick. Add hot milk. Sprinkle with spice.

GREEK HOT CHOCOLATE

ΚΑΚΑΟ   (kakao)

2 teaspoons breakfast cocoa ½ teaspoon vanilla
1 tablespoons sugar   1 pint of hot milk
¼ cup boiling water   dash of cinnamon

Dissolve cocoa and sugar in hot water. Mix in vanilla and hot milk. Sprinkle with cinnamon.

GREEK HOT MALTED MILK

ΣΑΛΕΠΙ   (salepi)

1 tablespoon malt powder (*salepi*) 1 pint milk hot or cold
3 teaspoons sugar   dash of cinnamon

Heat milk first, if desired, and beat all ingredients together until thick and foamy.

COLD BEVERAGES

ALMOND DRINK SUMADA

ΣΟΥΜΑΔΑ   (soumada)

1 teaspoon almond flavoring or 3 teaspoons sugar
 almond syrup (*sumada*)   1 cup milk or soda water

Mix in blender or shaker with ice and blend. Garnish with a sprig of ivy.

ALMOND TAMARIND MILKSHAKE

ΤΑΜΑΡΙΝΤΙ ΚΑΙ ΣΟΥΜΑΔΑ ΜΕ ΓΑΛΑ (tamarinti kai soumada meh gala)

A tamarind is a sweet fruit about the size of a cherry with a prune-like taste, which is eaten fresh, preserved or made into a syrup. A delicious Mediterranean milkshake can be made from tamarind syrup.

1 tablespoon tamarind syrup (or   sugar to taste
   prune syrup)   1 cup milk
1 teaspoon almond flavoring

Blend all ingredients in blender with ice for a few seconds.

FRUIT PUNCH DELPHI

ΗΥΜΟΙ ΑΡΟ ΦΡΟΥΤΤΑ   (himoi apo froutta)

1 can pineapple, including syrup   1 large can frozen lemonade
1 can peaches, including syrup   1 teaspoon vanilla
1 large can frozen orange juice   1 quart water

Blend ingredients in a blender until smooth. Add 1 cup punch base to 1 quart of water. Serve cold. *Variation:* Add 4 cups punch base to 3 bottles of ginger ale. Float scoops of orange sherbet on top. Serve in a punch bowl or in a pitcher.

SUBMARINE

ΥΠΟΒΡΥΧΙΟ   (ipovryhio)

You will hear waiters in Greece shouting their orders to the kitchen for a submarine drink, but the drink they bring to you is no drink at all. It is a tall glass of water with a spoonful of sweet mastic taffy submerged in it. The mastic candy does not dissolve in the glass of water but remains clinging to the spoon. The proper way to eat it is to nibble it off the spoon, then sip the water.

1 tablespoon mastic syrup (page 217)   10 ounces cold ice water

Spoon mastic from jar with long soda spoon. Place spoon in glass of water.

YOGURT MILKSHAKE

ΓΙΑΥΡΤΗ ΚΟΥΡΚΟ   (yaourti kourko)

This is a delicious tart drink, refreshing on a hot day.

½ cup cold yogurt   ½ cup or more mashed fruit (fresh
½ cup cold milk   or canned, drained): strawberries,
1 tablespoon sugar   peaches, apricots, pineapple,
                                            boysenberries, mandarins

Blend all ingredients in blender or beat by hand until thick and smooth.

ZAPPEION FRUIT DRINKS AND SODAS

ΠΟΤΑ ΑΡΟ ΦΡΟΥΤΑ ΚΑΙ ΣΟΔΑ   (pota apo frouta keh soda)

The Greeks sing a gay song about the Zappeion gardens, a delightful place to visit. It is the sunniest corner of Athens in winter and the coolest place in summer. There are cafes and pastry shops and an open air cinema during the summer. These fruit drinks are very refreshing to sip while watching the rest of the people stroll through the gardens.

Mix: **ice or ice cream**
2 tablespoons of any fruit juice   **sugar to taste**
10 ounces of soda water

Use cherry syrup for ΒΥΣΣΙΝΑΔΑ (visinatha); Almond syrup for ΣΟΥΜΑΔΑ (oumada); Lemon juice and sugar for ΛΕΜΟΝΑΔΑ ΧΥΜΟΣ (lemonatha himos); Orange juice and sugar for ΠΟΡΤΟ-ΚΑΛΛΑΔΑ (portokalatha), or pomegranate juice and sugar for ΓΡΑΝΙΤΑ (granita).

THE WINES OF GREECE

ΤΑ ΚΡΑΣΙΑ ΤΗΣ ΕΛΛΑΔΟΣ   (ta krasia tis ellados)

Dionysus, sometimes known by his Roman name, Bacchus, was the Ancient Greek god of wine, and worshipped as the protector of the vineyards. Wine festivals were celebrated with special customs and rituals at each phase of the growing grapevine. The mythical king of Athens, Amphictyon, supposedly was the first to mix wine with water thereby setting the precedent for the Greek respect towards the power of alcohol. The favored formula was half wine, half water. Wine was always mixed with water at meal-times. The phrase "watered wine" dates from this time. The practice is still followed today when wine is given to children and women. Today in Greece, as in Ancient times, wine is considered an addition to the zest of living and drunkenness is not approved in men, and absolutely unheard of for women. A mellowness is the desired effect and loss of self-control is not excused. Plato expressed the Greek attitude when he said, "Wine causes most drinkers who have no sense to think that they have."

Greece has many excellent wines but the most famous are retsina, mavrodaphne and muscatel. Various regions produce different kinds and the character of each wine differs depending upon the variety of grapes used. Each wine has particular qualities to recommend it. A Greek dinner may be accompanied most appropriately with only one kind of wine with all the courses throughout the complete dinner.

The most famous wine of Greece is retsina. It is the one which it is said tastes like turpentine. This is because of the resin used to give it a subtle aroma and flavor. Retsina has been found in wrecked ships at the bottom of the Aegean and Mediterranean

Seas, sealed in ancient amphora, thousand of years old. The ancient Greeks used pitch from the pine-covered slopes of Mount Olympus to line these pots, to prevent the jars from sweating and spoiling the wine. The practice of storing wine in this manner, gave a distinct resin flavor to the wine, which in time became so popular that to this day, even though it is no longer stored in terra cotta containers, the wine is still flavored with pitch by simply putting a pine cone filled with resin into the vat.

It is a light wine, better when served chilled, that comes in golden, red or rose hue. It is proper to serve it any time of the day, in a wine glass or a water glass, taverna style. It is not expensive to buy but the quality, as in all wines, can vary. The resin strength may also vary from strong to mild. Wines from Greece are imported into the United States, but California also produces excellent retsina wines.

Mavrodaphne wine is Greece's other most distinctive wine with its sweet flavor and deep rich maroon color which comes from the sweet black grapes grown in Attica around Megara and Patras. The train on its way to Corinth always stops at Megara for a few minutes for passengers to disembark and taste a bit of its famous wine. This wine is best chilled or poured over cracked ice as a cocktail. While it is not considered a wine to use in cooking, I have found that a half cup in the filling for Stuffed Grape Leaves (page 89) or the sauce in Baked Fish Plaki (page 102) makes a delicious recipe a great one.

Commanderie St. John from Cyprus is an exquisite dessert wine, sweet heavy and aged, surprisingly inexpensive as most of the Greek wines are. It's a grape wine originally made during the Crusades (A.D. 1204 to 1246) by the Knights Hospitaller of the Order of St. John of Jersualem from the vines of the Commanderie of Kolossi Castle in Cyprus. They brought the European method of making wine, introducing the barrel and wood stop which allowed the wine to age. Previously, Greek wine could not be allowed to age longer than three years.

Some wines from Greece and the area in which they are produced are listed below. A few of them are being imported into the United States and may be available through liquor distributors.

White Wines

ARCADIA	Peloponnesus
ACHAIA	Peloponnesus
APHRODITE	Cyprus
BOUQUET	Kea
CHATEAU DECELIE	King's vineyards
CORONA	Thessaloniki
DEMESTICHA	Achaia
GOLD OF ATTICA	Attica
HYMETTOS	Resinated wine of Achaia, Attica
KAMPA	A popular dry wine, Attica, Sounion
KING AND MINOS	Golden wine from Crete, dry
NEMEA	White or red wine from Patras, dry
PALLINI	Attica
ROBOLA	Samos and Kefallinia
ST. HELENA	A light flavorful wine, Peloponnesus
RETSINA	White, red or rose made in all Greece
RHODOS	Island of Rhodes
THEOTOKI	Corfu
VISSANTO	Santorini
ZITSA	A champagne from Epirus
MANTINIA PHELERI	Peleponnesus

Red Wines

BROUSSKO	A sweet port from Crete and a dry kind on draught, made in Arakhova near Delphi
CASTEL DANIELIS	Red dry burgundy
CHEVALIER di RHODI	Rhodes
CLARET	Cyprus
KAMINIA	Lemnos
BOUQUET	Tinos, Kea
KISSAMOS	Crete
NAOUSSA	Red dry wine, Macedonia
NEMEA	Rich and strong from Peloponnesus
MUSCADINE	Crete

MT. AMBELOS	Cyprus
OTHELLO	Cyprus
PENDELI	A dry wine
RED	Kaminia, Lemnos
RHODOS	Rhodes
SANTA MAURA	A rough red wine from Levkas, Ionian Islands
MUSCATO	Island of Samos
NICKTERI	A dark red wine from Santorini and Paros
VERATEA	Zante

Rose Wines

KOKINELLI	Resinated, made in all provinces
RODITYS	Made in all provinces
ROBOLA	Ionnina, Kefallinia, Corfu
VERDEA	Strofadia Islands, Zakynthos

Dessert Wines

BLACK WINE	Kea
BROUSSIKO	A sweet port from Crete
COMMANDERIE ST. JOHN	Cyprus
MAVRODAPHNE	Achaia, Patras
MALMSEY, MONEMVASIA	Malvasia, Crete and Cyclades
MOSCHATO, MALVAZIA	Rhodes
MISTELLI, KOKIANO	Samos
VINO SANTO	Santorini
ROUPA (Moselle)	Corfu
VERMOUTH CINZANO	Locally produced
VALDJI	Locally produced

LIQUEURS AND OTHER SPIRITS

RAKI-OUZO-MASTICHA-TSIPOURO-TSIKOUDIA
ΡΑΚΙ-ΟΤΖΟ-ΜΑΣΤΙΧΑ-ΤΣΙΠΙΟΤΡΟ-ΤΣΙΚΟΤΔΙΑ

These related liqueurs are flavored either with anise seed or mastic. They are all strong alcoholic drinks with a base of plum or grape. Tsipouro and tsikoudia are brandies, made from the left over grape mash after the juice has been squeezed from the grapes. Tsikoudia is the local firewater of Crete and tsipouro is made by most villagers throughout Greece.

The difference between raki, ouzo and masticha is slight; they all turn milky when combined with water. Often they are made at home. Ouzo and Cognac are made from the mash of grapes, what's left after the wine press, throughout Greece but the city of Plomari on Lesbos has a large industry in its production. Naxos concentrates on making a sweet lemon liqueur, Kitra, and Masticha is made only on Chios where the mastic resin is harvested. All the taverns in Greece serve these alcoholic beverages, and it is the mark of a foreigner to drink any of them fast. Their potency is recognized by the manner in which they should be sipped.

In the United States, these liqueurs may be purchased under the brand names of Metaxa or Cambas. Metaxa makes one of the great classic brandies of the world in 92 proof and 96 proof.

SPECIAL
TRADITIONAL AND
RELIGIOUS FOODS

Η ΘΡΗΣΚΕΥΤΙΚΕΣ ΣΥΝΤΑΓΕΣ
(e threskeitikes syntages)

Special foods are served on religious holidays and occasions. These ancient recipes with religious significance have been handed down for thousands of years. Some of the customs such as the serving of *kolliva* to honor the dead, or the cracking of eggs to celebrate Easter are older than Christianity and have been incorporated into the Greek Orthodox rituals.

CHURCH BREAD

ΠΡΟΣΦΟΡΟΝ   (prosforon)

Although the Greek Patriarch and the Pope of Rome are now talking to each other again after one thousand years of silence, there is still a minor disagreement over this recipe. Bread has always played an important part in the church and has important symbolic meaning in the divine liturgy; the authority for its use is found in the Greek bible, ΚΑΙΝΗ ΔΙΑΘΗΚΗ *JOHN 6:48,* "I am the BREAD OF LIFE." The Greek *prosforon,* bread of offering, is leavened whereas the Latin or Roman bread of offering is unleavened, a custom which began long after the Christian church was formed. Because of it, the Greek church calls its Roman catholic brethren *azymites* meaning those who eat unleavened bread in the eucharist.

The bread is distributed in church to the Greek Orthodox parishioners after each Mass. Usually the Priest stands at the altar steps at the end of the services and greets each member of his congregation as he offers his hand to be kissed, after which he gives the communicant a small piece of the Prosfora. The parishioner leaves, walking down the center aisle munching his tiny piece of delicious bread while greeting friends. It is part of a social ritual as well as a religious one. The Prosforon is baked and contributed by a pious woman who is given the honor of making it. It is not baked in everyone's home. The religious seal is in the possession of the priest who gives it to the chosen woman to use only for this special bread. The Byzantine Greek letters of the seal IC XC NIKA mean Isous Hristos Nika, Jesus Christ Conquers.

1 cake of yeast or 1 package dry yeast	6 cups flour (save ½ for the board)
¼ cup warm water	1 teaspoon salt
2 cups warm water	Religious seal, *sfragetha*

Dissolve yeast in ¼ cup warm water. Let stand 5 minutes. Measure flour and salt into a large bowl leaving some in the measuring cup to flour hands and board. Make a hole in center. Pour yeast and remaining water into hole. Use spoon to mix flour and water, then finish by kneading for 10 minutes. The dough will be sticky. Put in a large bowl, cover and let it rise for 1 hour.

Sprinkle board with flour and place dough on board. Knead for 20 minutes. Add ½ cup more of flour to hands if needed. Dough should be firm and smooth. Form dough into 1 round loaf. Make an impression with the seal. Let rise in a warm place. Bake in preheated 350° F. oven for 50 minutes in floured pan.

EASTER EGGS

ΠΑΣΧΑΛΙΝΑ ΑΥΓΑ   (pascalina avgha)

The Greek Church follows the Julian calendar in determining the date of Easter. Red eggs are dyed for the Easter Sunday church service, and after the service the priest distributes one egg to each parishioner as he passes the altar steps to receive the blessing. The Easter egg is dyed a deep red, never any other color, to symbolize the blood of Christ. The Easter greeting of "ΧΡΙΣΤΟΣ

ΑΝΕΣΤΕΙ" *"Christus Aneste!"* (Christ is Risen!), and the reply "ΑΛΤΘΩΣ ΑΝΕΣΤΕΙ" *"Alethos Aneste!"* (Truly, He is Risen!), is repeated all day long and all week long as the general form of greeting. The custom of cracking eggs is a charming one. Egg challenging is done all day, outside church, at home, between relatives and friends, by young and old. The pointed end of the egg is used and one holds his egg still while the other strikes. If both eggs remain uncracked, the defender has his turn to attack. The person whose egg is uncracked is the winner. It is only a game.

1 dozen or more white eggs, at room temperature	1 teaspoon paste, food color or powder, brilliant scarlet
1 tablespoon salt	water to cover
¼ cup vinegar	1 tablespoon oil to polish

Wipe eggs clean with a damp cloth. If eggs are cold, place them in a bowl of warm water for 20 minutes so they won't crack when placed in boiling water. Bring water and salt to a slow boil. Mix paste in vinegar and add to water. Stir well to dissolve. Place eggs gently one by one in boiling water. Simmer 40 minutes. Dry and polish with an oiled cloth.

GREEK EASTER SOUP

ΜΑΓΕΙΡΙΤΣΑ   (mayeritsa)

Midnight service at Greek Easter is the most dramatic of all the rituals in the Greek Orthodox Church. Just before the clock strikes twelve midnight, all the lights are turned off and silence prevails in the crowded church. The congregation waits—each one holding an unlighted candle. As the clock strikes twelve, it is Easter and the Priest lights a candle from the perpetual light in the inner sanctum of the altar. One by one, each candle flickers alive as the flame is passed around, while the choir and congregation sing an ancient Byzantine chant, *"Christus Aneste"* (Christ is Risen). The whole church becomes bright with candle glow.

Immediately upon returning home, the family breaks the fast by eating the traditional symbolic soup made of lamb's lungs and heart called *mayeritsa.* This soup is made only at Easter time, both in Greece and in the United States. If you are touring Greece at this particular time of the year, take the opportunity to try it.

2 pounds lamb lung, liver, heart, feet	1 teaspoon spearmint leaves
2 quarts water	1 tablespoon fresh fennel
2 teaspoons salt	1 tablespoon dill
pepper to taste	1 cup rice
4 stalks celery, chopped	Egg Lemon Sauce (page 67)
1 bunch scallions, chopped	5 eggs
1 sprig parsley, chopped	juice of three lemons

Wash lamb organs in cold running water. Put meat into a pot with water and salt. Bring to a boil, remove frothy scum which forms on top, and cook 30 minutes. Remove meat from pot. Strain broth. Chop meat, discarding membranes and cartilage.

In a large kettle, heat oil and fry scallions, celery and other herbs for 10 minutes. Add strained broth and meat. Bring to a boil, reduce to medium and cook 1 hour. Add rice and continue cooking 45 minutes, until rice and meat are tender. Remove from heat.

Beat eggs until thick. Add lemon juice, then slowly add 2 cups hot broth. Pour this sauce over soup. Mix in very quickly and serve immediately. Serve at Easter midnight supper or through-out Easter week.

WEDDING KOUFETA

ΚΟΥΦΕΤΑ   (koufeta)

Candy-coated almonds called *koufeta* are the time honored symbols of fertility and good wishes at Greek Orthodox weddings. These candies are wrapped attractively in pretty cloth or put in tiny white or silver boxes, put on a silver tray, and presented to each person attending the wedding at church and later at the reception where congratulations are offered for a happy and blessed life. It is also the custom to throw these *koufeta* like rice at the bride and groom as they leave the church. In the hands of well-wishers these hard candies can become lethal weapons. Unmarried maidens take the *koufeta* home to put under their pillows in the hopes they will dream of their future husband. The custom of giving *koufeta* at weddings is an ancient one. It was recorded in 177 B.C. that a patrician Roman family used honeyed almonds at the marriage of their only child as a token of rejoicing.

Jordan almonds, white only, (available at candy shops) 72 per pound (allow 6 per bouquet)	5 sprigs of artificial lily of the valley flowers
white net, cut into 6" squares; one yard of 72" width makes 72 squares	12" lengths of 5/16" width, white satin ribbon (3 bows per yard)

Place 5 or 6 almonds in the center of the square piece of net. Bring corners together. Tie a ribbon around it. Tuck a flower in center. Arrange and serve on a silver tray. Present one to each guest as a wedding favor.

KOLLIVA—WHEAT FOR MEMORIAL SERVICES

ΚΟΛΛΤΒΑ (kolliva)

Among the rites of the Greek Orthodox Church there is a special memorial servioo for departed souls, called *Mnemosimon*. After the Maee ie read, a dish of boiled sweetened wheat kernels and fruits called *kolliva,* which is prepared by members of the family, is distributed in remembrance of the dead. The *kolliva* is blessed by the priest and then eaten at the church by friends, relatives and anyone who accepts it. The boiled wheat germ symbolizes resurrection, and is traditionally offered forty days after death and one year after death. It is quite delicious but it is prepared In the following manner only to remember the dead; it is not served at any other time.

In Ancient Pagan time, dating back to Minoan Crete and into the prohistory of Greece, the custom of bringing food to remember the dead was known as *panspermia. Kolliva,* the sweetened wheat, was called *pankarpia* and was made the same as it is today, with a mixture of fruits and nuts, including the seeds of the pomegranate which Persephone was supposed to have eaten during her stay in Hades. The ancient Greeks brought this special food to their temples to honor the dead on All Soul's Day, called the *CHYTROI.* The Greek Orthodox Church has continued this five thousand-year-old custom by including it in their religious rituals.

10 cups whole wheat kernels
2 cups sesame seed
½ cup anise seed
2 cups chopped walnuts
3 cups golden currants
pomegranate seeds from 1 or 2 poms
grated rind of 2 oranges
3 cups sugar
4 teaspoons cinnamon
2 cups graham cracker or zwieback crumbs

4 cups confectioners sugar
¼ cup silver dragees (silver candy balls)
2 cups candied Jordan almonds, white only
1 cup blanched whole almonds
100 small bags
large tray
small silver scoop
paper doilies
waxed paper

Inspect wheat for sticks, stones, etc. Pour into large kettle. Cover with cold water. Fill to the top. Allow to stand overnight. Drain. Cover with fresh water. Bring to a boil and simmer for 4 hours until wheat splits in two. Stir often to prevent sticking. Drain. Spread on clean towel to absorb excess moisture.

Spread sesame and anise seeds on shallow pan and bake at 325° F. for 10 minutes.

Mix in a large bowl: wheat, sesame seeds, anise seeds, walnuts, currants, pomegranate seeds, rind, sugar and cinnamon. Toss until well mixed.

Line a large tray with aluminum foil. Put the wheat on it, shaping it with the palms of your hands into a mound so there will be a slight rise in the center. Fill the whole tray with the *kolliva*. Cover wheat with a layer of graham cracker crumbs, patting and pressing down, using a square piece of waxed paper. The crackers will absorb the moisture.

Sift confectioners sugar over the whole top at least ¼" thick. Press down with folded waxed paper to form a smooth compact top. Make a Greek cross in the center using tiny silver candy balls to make the outline. On the right side, form the letters *IC XC NIKA* ("Jesus Conquers"). Fill these letters with white Jordan candy almonds. On the other side, form the initials of the deceased with blanched almonds. Use the rest of the almonds to decorate a border.

Use a silver scoop to distribute the *kolliva* by putting some directly into the proferred palms or into little bags.

GREEK SPICES, HERBS AND FLAVORINGS

ΜΠΑΧΑΡΙΚΑ ΚΑΙ ΑΡΩΜΑΤΙΚΑ
(baharika kai aromatika)

Most of the herbs and flavorings used in Greek recipes are those which originated in the Mediterranean or in Western Asia and have long since found their way to Europe and the United States: bay leaves, basil, chervil, celery and fennel leaves, garlic, oregano, parsley, mint, marjoram, rosemary, sage, summer savory, saffron, and thyme. Occasionally a traditional spice will be used in an exotic manner. Cinnamon will be put into meat or fish stews. Spearmint, the chewing gum flavoring, is tucked into meatballs. Originally cloves, cinnamon, cassia, pepper, mace and nutmeg were used only in medicines, body salves and perfumes, but soon Greek cooks began to enhance food with these exotic flavors. For many centuries the spices of the East were carried over the caravan route to the Spice Bazaar in Constantinople, now Istanbul, coming by sailing ships from Arabia, India and the islands of Molucca, Malaya and Ceylon and by camels and Mongolian horses from China and Persia. Mastic from Chios, and mahaleb from Persia, now Iran, are important in Greek cooking also. You will enjoy experimenting with traditional herbs and spices to flavor your favorite recipes in the Greek way.

ANISE SEED

ΓΛΥΚΑΝΙΣΟ (glykaniso)

The licorice flavor of anise which come from the seeds of a feathery light green plant of the parsley family, is one of the spices added to holiday sweet breads, cakes, pastries, and even the well-known ouzo of Greece. It is put into tomato sauces and meatballs.

BASIL

ΒΑΣΙΛΙΚΟΣ   (vasilikos)

In the springtime, a Greek housewife always plants a few seeds of basil, the herb of royalty, in a pot outside her kitchen door to have fresh basil for soups, stews and salads or to give a sprig to a friend to protect her from the evil eye. In order to exorcise the evil eye, the ancient Greek chant: ΩΣ ΜΗ ΒΑΣΚΑΝΘΩ ΤΡΙΣ ΕΠΤΥΣΑ (os mi vaskantho tres eptysa) ("I spat three times that I might not be bewitched.") is spoken while waving basil leaves.

BAY LEAF (LAUREL)

ΔΑΦΝΗ   (daphne)

The leaves of the sweet bay tree or laurel add a distinct flavor to meat, fish and stew. At one time, laurel wreaths were placed on the heads of victorious Olympic athletes.

CASSIA

ΑΚΑΚΙΑ   (akakia)

Cassia is so similar to cinnamon in flavor that it takes an expert to tell them apart. In ancient times, both spices were so valuable they were always included along with ivory, camels, slaves and gold as gifts for conquerors. Today, the Greek cook uses the buds to decorate cookies and the powder when a subtle flavor is desired.

CINNAMON

ΚΑΝΕΛΛΑ   (kanella)

Cinnamon and its oil was used medicinally and to perfume the body. At one time it was one of the spices used in sacrificial rites and in potions for lovers.

CITRON (*Citrus medica*)

ΚΙΤΡΟΝ   (kitron)

From the time of Theophrastus, 375–287 B.C., the citron was known as the "golden apple of the Hesperides." Its juice was used in food and medicine. Not only was it considered a preventative against snake bite, Phoenias of Eresus also advised drinking citron juice before meals to shrink one's stomach and thus lose weight. This last advice, using lemon juice, is still given today. It is still used as a sweet preserve.

CLOVE

ΓΑΡΥΦΑΛΛΟ   (garifallo)

The clove has been important to Greece since the Arabs brought it by caravan through Alexandria to Greek cities. It was prized for its oil which was used as medicine, mouth deodorant and perfume. Many Greek women still make sachets for their clothes closets with clove, or chew the buds.

CORIANDER

ΚΟΛΙΑΝΤΡΟ   (koliantro)

The aromatic seeds are used to spice cheese, meat and pastries. The Cypriots put this spice in their sausages.

CUMIN

ΚΙΜΙΝΟ   (kimino)

Cumin was introduced to Greece from Ethiopia and is a spice used to flavor meat by those Greeks who come from Smyrna, now Izmir. The Cypriots like to flavor their cheese with it also.

DILL

ΑΝΙΘΟΣ   (anithos)

Dill seeds are similar to fresh fennel. It is one of the flavorings used in soup.

FENNEL

ΜΑΡΑΘΟ   (maratho)

Fennel is a feathery green plant which grows wild in the Mediterranean. The leaves add a sweet licorice flavor to soups, particularly, the Easter soup, *mayeritsa*, stews and vegetables. Its seeds
go into cakes and cookies and its stalks and base are boiled as a
green vegetable.

GINGER (*Zingiber officinale*)

ΖΙΓΓΙΒΕΡΟ   (zigivero)

The ancient Greeks believed ginger was a product of South
Arabia because it came by way of the Red Sea. It is a spice that
was always difficult to get so recipes including it are few.

GARLIC

ΣΚΟΡΔΟ   (skordo)

Only a few recipes call for this herb, and the Greek cook uses it
sparingly. Hippocrates classified it as a sudorific drug, bad for
the eyes, and to be used for medicinal purposes only. Many
Greek peasants use mashed garlic as a poultice for chest colds
which they swear is effective.

LEMON

ΛΕΜΟΝΙ   (lemoni)

Lemon was introduced to Greece in the thirteenth century after
the Crusaders found it growing in Palestine. It replaced the citron
and today lemon is the most important fruit flavoring in Greek
cooking. It is the secret ingredient in the syrup in Greek desserts,
and in the Egg and Lemon Sauce. Mated with oregano, lemon is
used to flavor fish, meat and fowl. (After fish has been fried, a
piece of lemon rind is burned to deodorize the house.)

MAHALEB

ΜΑΧΛΕΠΙ   (mahlepi)

This Persian spice grows on a small tree similar to a flowering cherry (*Prunus cerasus Mahaleb*). The seeds are used in cakes and holiday breads; its flavor is subtle but distinct. The Greeks who came from Cyprus and Asia Minor introduced it to the Greek *kuzina* (cuisine).

MARJORAM

ΜΑΤΖΟΥΡΑΝΑ   (matzourana)

Marjoram is another herb that was once considered a perfume. Today, it is used as frequently as basil or oregano to flavor a stew or fish.

MASTIC

ΜΑΣΤΙΧΑ   (mastiha)

This unusual Greek flavoring, amber-colored resin drops tapped from the lentisk bush, grows only on the island of Chios in Greece. The mastic plantations begin at Aghios Minas, and during the months of August and September workers can be seen busily tapping the bushes. At one time, during the Turkish domination, it was a punishable offense for a harvester to keep any of this resin. All of it went to the Empress Mother and to the seraglio in Istanbul. The resin makes a delicious chewing gum; in fact, the word masticate comes from this flavoring agent. It is also used in cakes, cookies, drinks, liqueurs and candies.

MINT

ΔΙΟΣΜΟΣ   (diosmos)

The mint used in most Greek cooking is the spearmint, an herb that flavors candy in the United States. In Greece, it is an important flavor with lamb, beef and vegetables. Mastic gum is now being flavored with this spearmint but that is a new development. It is grown extensively in Greece and is the same herb as runt, that was eaten with the pascal lamb, mentioned in the scriptures.

MUSTARD SEED

ΜΟΤΣΤΑΡΔΑ (ΣΙΝΑΠΙ)   moustarda (sinapi)

Mustard seed was called silphium by the ancient Greeks, and sprinkled over vegetables, meat and fish as pepper. It has been cultivated over two thousand years and was used medicinally by Hippocrates.

NUTMEG

ΜΟΣΧΟΚΑΡΤΔΟ   (moshokarido)

The Greeks call this the sweet-smelling nut and it is ground into a powder for desserts, drinks, cakes and cookies.

OREGANO, RIGANI

ΟΡΙΓΑΝΟ   (origano)

The Greek mountains and meadows abound with this wonderful herb. In the preChristian era of pagan rites, oregano was sprinkled on the sacrificial animals which were offered to the gods. The Greek continues today in the same tradition. Without the flavor of oregano on his pork, lamb, fowl, kid or beef, he would not consider the meat properly prepared.

ORANGE, TANGERINE

ΠΟΡΤΟΚΑΛΙ   (portokalli)

The popular orange in Greece is called *Portocalli* after the place of its origin, Portugal, where the thick-skinned navel orange was discovered. The rind and juice are used to flavor sausages, stews, desserts, candies, cakes and beverages.

PARSLEY

ΜΑΙΝΤΑΝΟΣ   (maintanos)

The Greek cook is generous with parsley. Both the dense-leaved parsley and the open-growing variety, described by Theophrastus in the fourth century B.C. and introduced to America in the seventeenth century, are native to the Mediterranean, growing there since time immemorial. Like the laurel, parsley was once used as a garland for Olympic heroes.

PEPPER

ΠΙΠΕΡΙ   (piperi)

Pepper was one of the first spices to be introduced into Greece from the Indian Archipelago. Because it was so expensive, myrtle berries, now called Jamaican pepper, were used in its place. Even Hippocrates used it only for his prescriptions and Theophrastus writes of it as an antidote to hemlock poison.

ROSE

ΤΡΙΑΝΤΑΦΥΛΛΟ   (triantafillo)

The use of the rose as a flavoring is as ancient as man's desire for attractive food. The strong yet delicate flavoring of roses was put into everything from drinking and bathing water, and finger bowls, to meat, fowl, desserts, and other foods. Today, it is used primarily to flavor desserts, syrups and candies.

ROSEMARY

ΔΕΝΔΡΟΛΙΒΑΝΟ   (dendrolivano)

This herb comes from a sweet-smelling bush with tiny, needle-like leaves which are used to flavor meat, fish and sauces. It is a strong herb and should be used sparingly.

SAGE

ΦΑΣΧΟΜΗΛΙΑ   (faskomilia)

The sweet-smelling sage encompasses a group of related herbs which are used to flavor poultry, pork and stuffings. A tea is made from the dried leaves of one variety grown on the mountainsides.

SALT

ΑΛΑΤΙ

Salt evaporated from the sea was the first kind the early Greeks knew and used. The Greek phrase, "Trespass not against the salt between us," meant there was a bond, a covenant of salt and incense. The caravan trade of the Sahara was the salt trade. Greeks prefer liberal amounts of salt on their food and if you are eating in a Greek restaurant or home, test your food before salting it. The quantities in this cookbook call for a medium amount of salt.

SAVORY

ΘΡΤΜΒΗ   (thrumbi)

Savory is a green herb similar to sage, and is delicious sprinkled over poultry or pork.

SESAME

ΣΗΣΑΜΙ   (sesame)

Sesame seeds, grown on the island of Kos, have a nutlike flavor and are used as topping for breads and sweet cookies. When pressed, the seeds emit an oil of very fine quality. A paste called *tahini* is also made from the seeds, similar in consistency to peanut butter. The popular candy called Halvah is made with this paste.

THYME

ΘΥΜΑΡΙ   (thmari)

Thyme was once considered food for the poor and the slaves; the rich used it only in cosmetics. Now the dried leaves lend their pungent flavor to fish and fowl, and most importantly, to lamb. After a rainstorm, snails are collected and fed thyme for a week to give them a sweet taste.

VINEGAR

ΞΥΔΙ   (ksidi)

The writers of Attica, three thousand years ago, referred to this seasoning with delight; it was used liberally in cooking and over salad greens. Any dish heavily seasoned with vinegar was called Laconian style because the Laconians were notorious for their generosity with it. The vinegar used by Greeks is naturally a wine vinegar.

SUGGESTIONS FOR A GREEK PARTY

Classical Greece provides an exciting and original theme for a party. A wealth of ideas, simple to execute, can be brought into play whether you are a wealthy hostess, a school teacher on a budget, a harassed fund-raising chairman, or simply an original party giver. Color schemes, arrangements, decor and entertainment as well as costuming can be joined harmoniously and successfully.

The choice of colors lending themselves to a Greek theme are varied: the blue of the Mediterranean, the browns of the arid mountains, the gold of the Byzantine and Greek icons, or the blue and white of the flag. Perhaps even one of the striking combinations found in Greek pottery: the black and white with purple and terra cotta which dates back to the sixth century, or a white background with accents of metallic gold, red yellow and light blue. Important accent colors in Greek culture are royal purple and turquoise; purple worn by royalty and turquoise worn to ward off the evil eye.

Use flowers and fruit to decorate walls, tables, and people. Present a garland of flowers or ivy to guests as they enter the room. A crown of ivy promotes favor from the Gods on Mount Olympus and wards off the effects of drinking; a crown or wreath of parsley is for the guest of honor. Use vases of roses, lilies, carnations, narcissus, violets or flowering branches of trees and bushes such as pine, mock orange, acacia or apple. Grapes, lemons, oranges and pomegranates are in keeping with the Greek spirit, and olive tree branches make delicate arrangements and are the symbol of the goddess Athena. Hanging a pine or laurel wreath and ivy, always plentiful, is most appropriate. Ivy was the symbol of the wine god, Dionysus, and was displayed when drinking would be unrestrained and there would be no water mixed in the wine. The remnants of this symbol remain as a pattern on goblets and stemware.

The Greek key, a design found in every aspect of Greek life, be it clothing, art or architecture, is easy to copy or sketch on cloth or paper. Braid with this design is also available. The design it-self can be used on anything connected with the party, including place mats, programs, tablecloths, wall friezes, menus, etc.

For any lettering, such as invitations, menus or programs, writ-ing English capital letters in the Greek style will give the illusion of being written in Greek while still being readable.

Reproductions of ancient Greek pottery, dishes and dinner-ware are available in many import shops. For statuary, the place to go is a garden shop which may have suitable reproductions to use in a garden or a large room.

For table service, use bronze, silver or gold platters and cups or pottery and woven baskets. Forget knives, forks and spoons, ancient Greeks did not use them, but remember the finger bowls.

To reproduce the *triculina* of the first century, A.D. Attica, small dining tables with three legs should be placed next to couches. Cushions may be arranged to simulate couches for guests to recline on while dining. To reproduce the dining rooms of Homer's time, about 900 B.C., or that of the ancient Spartans, 500 B.C., or even Alexander the Great's Macedonian chamber, 300 B.C., all you need are arrangements of long tables and benches.

Play records of Greek music now available at any music store and try to find music which features the boujouki, an instru-ment with a long neck and eight metal strings, tuned like a guitar. It is an instrument of the taverns and peasants and generally not considered a classical instrument and came to Greece only re-cently by way of Turkey. This bit of anachronism would be tol-erated at any Greek party because music of classical Greece, were it available, would be quite dull by today's standards. Au-thentic costuming is very simple to achieve. The ancient Greeks, both men and women, wore chitons which were basically tubular garments of wool, linen or silk, either plain or pleated, fastened with pins at the shoulders. Lengths vary from short to long, with or without a belt; styles changed then as now and hemlines bounced up and down. A man could wear a cloak (himation) or a Thes-salian cloak, a chlamys, by fastening it with a broach at the right shoulder leaving the right arm free. The peplos, a woman's gar-ment, could be worn with the right side unsewn, just like the hip-showing Spartan women did.

The menu would be simple to determine and you need not confine your selection to the Dining in Ancient Greece chapter. See menu for large group (page 228).

MENUS

ΚΑΤΑΛΟΓΟΣ ΦΑΓΗΤΩΝ   (katalogos fayeton)

Average Greek meals taken at home will consist of: a simple breakfast at 8, 9 or 10 o'clock; luncheon at 2 or 3 o'clock which will be the big meal of the day, eaten before the afternoon nap and *mezethes* nibbled from 5 to 9 P.M. Dinner at home will be simple and served about 9 P.M. or 10 P.M.

Dining out presents a different eating plan. Dinner will begin at 10 P.M. or later. Midnight is a normal time to go to a restaurant for dinner in any large city of Greece.

Breakfast planning requires little more than coffee and *koulouria* and perhaps cheese. Luncheon should consist of liberal portions of one important main dish. Only the households maintaining European traditions will serve a seven course meal. Dinner again will be simple. *Mezethes,* the snack meal that is eaten between meals at all hours, can consist of a great variety of foods served in small portions.

GREEK RESTAURANT BREAKFAST MENU

ΕΛΑΦΡΟ ΠΡΟΓΕΤΜΑ   (elafro proyevma)

Coffee	French Coffee	Tea	Milk
ΚΑΦΕ	(with milk)	ΤΣΑΙ	ΦΡΕΣΚΟ ΓΑΛΑ
(kahfe)	ΓΑΛΛΙΚΟ ΚΑΦΕ	(tsai)	(fresko ghala)
	(ghaliko kahfe)		
	Sweet Rolls	Toast	
	ΚΟΤΛΟΤΡΑΚΙΑ	ΦΡΙΓΑΝΙΑ	
	(koulourakia)	(friganyia)	

Fruit in Season
ΦΡΕΣΚΑ ΦΡΟΥΤΑ ΕΠΟΧΗΣ
(freska froutta epohis)

Fruit Juices
ΧΤΜΟΤΣ ΤΩΝ ΦΡΟΤΤΩΝ
(himos ton froutton)

Preserves
ΜΑΡΜΕΛΑΔΑ
(marmelahtah)

Eggs

Scrambled	Fried	Boiled	Poached
ΟΜΕΛΑΤΑ	ΑΤΓΑ ΤΗΓΑΝΙΤΑ	ΑΤΓΑ ΒΡΑΣΤΑ	ΑΤΓΑ ΠΟΣΕ
(omeleta)	(avgha tiganita)	(avgha vrasta)	(avgha poseh)

Ham	Bacon	Sausages	Cheese
ΖΑΜΠΟΝ	ΜΒΕΚΟΝ	ΜΙΚΡΑ ΛΟΤΚΑΝΙΚΑ	ΤΤΡΙ
(zambon)	(bakon)	(mikra loukaneka)	(teree)

Butter
ΦΡΕΣΚΟ ΒΟΤΤΤΡΟ
(fresko voutiro)

AFTERNOON CALL

ΑΠΟΓΕΤΜΑΤΙΝΗ ΕΠΙΣΚΕΨΙΣ   (apoyemtine epekepsis)

The Greek custom of the afternoon call which corresponds to afternoon tea is described in detail on page 182.

Serve in order listed
Jellied fruit or preserve
Cold water

Any *one* of the following liquors: Ouzo, Brandy, Mavrodaphne or Retsina wine

Any *one* of the following desserts: Greek Wedding Cookie (page 171). Baklava, or Honey Nut Roll (page 153). (See Pastries, Desserts)

Demitasse of Turkish Coffee (page 196)

FAMILY DINNER

ΟΙΚΟΓΕΝΕΙΑΚΟΝ ΔΕΙΠΝΟΝ   (oikoyeneakon deipnon)

Appetizers (any one)
Olives   Feta Cheese   Yogurt   Bean Purée

Salad (any one)
Tomato Salad Santorini (page 73)
Greek Tossed Salad (page 72)
Lettuce Salad With Feta Cheese (page 73)

Main Dish or Casserole (any one)
Greek Roast Beef or Lamb with Potatoes or Pilaf (page 138)
Stuffed Vegetables, Tomatoes and Pepper (page 97)
Spaghetti with Brown Butter (page 62)
Baked Fish Salonika (page 101)
Beef Stew Kalamara (page 129)

Breads
Greek Bread and Butter

Desserts (any one)
Sponge Cake Pantespani (page 164)
Honey Tokens (page 167)
Greek Rice Pudding (page 175)

Beverages
Wine or Beer   Fruit Juices   Milk

INFORMAL OR SIMPLE DINNER

ΑΠΛΟ ΔΕΙΠΝΟΝ   (aplo deipnon)

Cocktails
Ouzo or Mavrodaphne on ice

Appetizers
Greek olives   Feta Cheese   Skewered Meat   Bean Salad
Baby Beets Meze   Sardines   Yogurt

Soup
Little Meat Barrels Soup (page 57)

Entree
Roast Beef Greek Style (page 128)
Baked Fish Salonika (page 101)

Salad
Tomato Salad Santorini (page 73)
Vegetables Greek Style (page 71)

Dessert
Olympiad Sugar Cake (page 163)   Fresh Fruit (page 180)

Beverages
Coffee   Retslna Wine

GREEK WEDDING CUSTOMS

Ο ΓΑΜΟΣ   (o gamos)

In some parts of Greece, the dowry system, a 3000-year-old custom inherited from the ancient Greeks, still survives, and a girl without a dowry has a difficult time finding a husband indeed. There is some misinterpretation concerning the dowry; it should be understood that the requirement of a dowry is not to buy a husband, but rather it is a statement of the wlfe's status and independence and is not given as a personal gift to the husband to squander. If it is in the form of property it may even be in her name for her protection. The wedding ceremony including the feast and all its costs, is often borne by the groom or his parents. A Greek wedding party is likely to be given in one of three ways: a feast which lasts far Into the night or for many days, common in the villages where everyone is a friend, relative, or acquaintance; an afternoon or evening buffet prepared by the family and offered in a rented banquet room or in the home of the bride; a formal banquet given late in the evening, served and catered in the home, hotel, restaurant or private club, with a few Greek delicacies prepared by others if the chef is a foreigner and doesn't know how to bake *baklava, trigona* and *kourambiethes.*

FORMAL BUFFET OR WEDDING BUFFET

ΕΠΙΣΗΜΟΣ ΜΠΟΥΦΕΣ   (epismos boufes)

Liquors
Retsina or Zitsa Wine   Metaxa and Ouzo

Appetizers
Olives   Feta Cheese   Toursi (page 74)   Tarama (page 103)
Cheese Tart Trigona (page 148)   Stuffed Grape Leaves (page 89)
Keftedes (page 132)   Stuffed Eggplants   Sardines

Meat
Roast Suckling Pig, Lamb or Goat (page 143)
Greek Roast Lamb (page 137)
Greek Oven Chicken (page 120)

Vegetables
Artichokes, Greek Style (page 78)
Greek Lettuce Salad (page 72)

Farinaceous
Rice Pilafi (page 58)   Meat and Macaroni Pastitso (page 62)

Breads
Koulourakia (page 41)   Crescent Rolls (page 42)
Greek Bread (page 40)

Sweets
Jordan Almond Wedding Koufeta (page 210)
Greek Wedding Cookies (page 171)
Baklava (page 152)   Custard Pie (page 156)
Rose Jam (page 186)   Chocolates
Venetian Honey Cookies (page 170)

BUFFET

ΜΠΟΥΦΕ ΔΙΑ ΠΟΛΛΑ ΑΤΟΜΑ   (boufe dia polla atoma)

This menu was served to five hundred people at the annual
fund raising party held at a museum. These recipes were chosen
because they included foods which would remain delicious when
they became cool.

Appetizers
Feta Cheese   Black Calamata Olives

Stuffed Grape Leaves (page 89)

Salad
Greek Lettuce Salad (page 72)

Meats, hot:
Greek Meat Balls With Mint (page 132)

Meats, cold:
Greek Roast Lamb (page 137)
Baked Ham

Farinaceous
Rice Pilaf (page 58)

Breads
Crescent Rolls (page 42)
Butter

Desserts
Baklava (page 152)
Greek Wedding Cookies (prepared as described in short-cut method—page 171)

Beverages
Retsina   Mavrodaphne   Other wines and liquors
Shopping list for Buffet:

Salad: 24 heads of lettuce, 2 dozen scallions, 2 dozen bunches of radishes; 12 celery stalks, 12 bunches of parsley

Finger food: 25 pounds Feta cheese; 10 pounds olives

Roast Lamb: 12 legs of lamb, 4 whole cloves of garlic, jar dried spearmint

Greek Meat Balls: 50 pounds ground chuck beef, mint, 25 pounds onions, 4 boxes bread crumbs, 3 quarts tomato sauce, 5 lbs. flour

Salad Dressing: 1 quart vinegar, 1 large jar oregano, box of salt, 1 gallon olive oil, 1 can dry mustard, garlic cloves

Stuffed Grape Leaves: 12 jars vine leaves, 2 quarts tomato sauce, 5 pounds rice, 5 pounds onions

Hams: 8 whole hams, 1 pint prepared mustard, box whole cloves, 3-pound can honey

EQUIVALENT MEASUREMENTS AND WEIGHTS

EQUIVALENT MEASUREMENTS AND WEIGHTS FOR UNITED STATES, ENGLAND, GREECE

ΜΕΤΑΤΡΟΠΗ ΜΕΤΡΩΝ ΚΑΙ ΣΤΑΘΜΩΝ

These comparative figures are approximate

Dry or Solid Measure

	American	English	Metric-Modern Greek	Old Greek oka no longer used
Rice	1 teaspoon	1/16 ounce	5 grams	
Salt	1 tablespoon	1/2 ounce	15 grams	
Sugar, Granulated	1/2 cup	4 ounces	120 grams	50 drammia
			0.133 kilogram	
Butter, Fats	1 cup	8 ounces = 1/2 pound	240 grams	ena tetarto
Dried Fruit	2 cups	16 ounces = 1 pound	500 grams	1/2 oka = 200 drammia
Jams	3 cups	1 pound 6 1/2 ounces		
Meats				
Spices	1 teaspoon	1/12 ounce	2 1/2 grams	
Bread Crumbs, Fresh	1 cup	1 1/2 ounces	45 grams	
Brown Sugar	1/2 cup	2 2/3 ounces	80 grams	
Grated Cheese	1 cup	4 ounces	100 grams	
	2 cups	8 ounces = 1/2 pound	250 grams	
Flour, Unsifted	1 tablespoon	1/2 ounce	15 grams	
	1/4 cup	1 ounce	30 grams	
	1 cup	4 ounces	120 grams	ena tetarto (1/4 kilo)
	2 cups	8 ounces = 1/2 pound	240 grams	meso kilo (1/2 kilo)
	4 cups	1 pound = 16 ounces	500 grams	ena kilo
	8 1/2 cups	2 pounds 3 ounces	1 kilogram	1 oka = 400 drammia
		2 pounds 13 ounces	1.420 kilograms	

Liquid Measure

American

3 teaspoons = 1 tablespoon
2 tablespoons = ⅛ cup
8 tablespoons = ½ cup = ¼ pint = 4 ounces
1 cup = ½ pint
2 cups = 1 pint
4 cups = 1 quart
2 quarts = ½ gallon

American	English	Metric-Modern Greek	Old Greek
1 teaspoon	⅙ ounce	5 milliliters	1 dessert spoon
1 tablespoon	½ ounce	15 milliliters	
1 ounce	1 English tablespoon	30 milliliters	1 soup spoon
	⅕ English pint	⅒ liter	
8 ounces	⅖ English pint	¼ liter	
16 ounces		½ liter	
20 ounces	English pint		
32 ounces			½ oka
34 ounces	1¾ pints	1 liter	
64 ounces			1 oka
68 ounces		2 liters	

INDEX